INDIAN
SCHOOL DAYS

INDIAN
SCHOOL DAYS

BASIL H. JOHNSTON

University of Oklahoma Press: Norman

By Basil H. Johnson

Ojibway Heritage (Toronto, 1976)
Moose Meat and Wild Rice (Toronto, 1978)
Ojibway Ceremonies (Toronto, 1983)
Indian School Days (Toronto, 1988)

Library of Congress Catalog Card Number: 89–40217

ISBN: 978-0-8061-2610-4

The paper in this book meets the guidelines for permanence and durability of the Committee on Production Guidelines of Book Longevity of the Council on Library Resources, Inc.

Published by the University of Oklahoma Press, Norman, Publishing Division of the University, by arrangement with Key Porter Books Limited, Ontario, Canada. Copyright © 1988 by Basil H. Johnston. First printing of the University of Oklahoma Press edition, 1989. Manufactured in the U.S.A.

Contents

The area around St. Peter Claver's, or Garnier, Indian Residential School in the town of Spanish, northern Ontario.

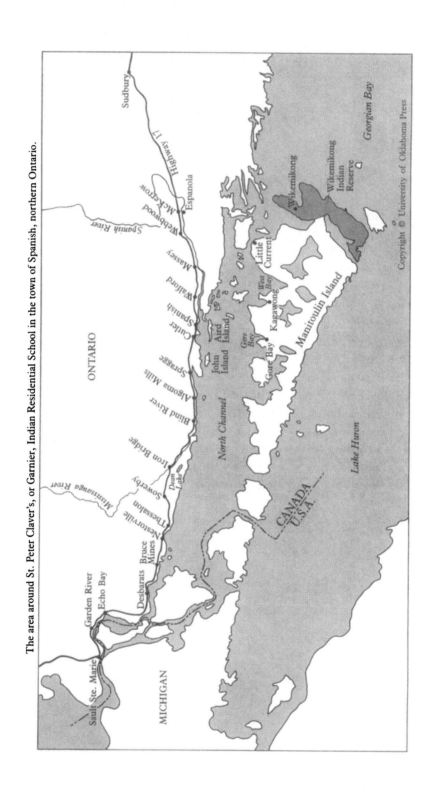

Introduction

Spanish! In its most common application the word refers to a citizen of Spain, and his or her language, and evokes romantic images of senoritas and dons, matadors and conquistadors, flamenco dancers and Don Quixote, castles and courts of inquisition.

Spanish! But the word has another application less romantic than the first. It is the name of a small village, a pinpoint on the map, in northern Ontario about 130 km west of Sudbury on Highway 17 and 200 km or so from Sault Ste. Marie.

Once, according to the old-timers, Spanish was a bustling village, thriving on timber and lumber and destined for growth and prosperity. But the village's prospects declined as those of Blind River and Espanola improved, so that in the 1930s and 1940s Spanish was struggling to keep from becoming a ghost town like Spragge. What kept the village from extinction in the 1930s were "the school" and the Depression; the residents had nowhere to go. And what kept the village from complete abandonment during the 1940s was the war and "the school." All the able-bodied men had gone to Europe and other places more exotic than Spanish; the women, the very old, and the very young were there, rooted, with nowhere else to go.

The people of Spanish had nowhere to go and little to do. The monotony of their existence was broken once in a while by the arrival of the Swiss Bell Ringers, the showing of a film, the holding of a church bazaar, a Christmas concert, a funeral or two. Once the Canadian Armed Forces gave a demonstration of efficiency and strength to tempt more recruits from the area. A large crowd assembled to watch Bren-gun carriers crawl and claw over the tracks and rocks; overhead Avro Ansons flew, with bombardiers throwing out sacks that looked like small bundles of flour but were supposed to represent bombs and bombing. During the course of this demonstration the commanding officer invited able-bodied young men to ride these wretched little vehicles that squeaked and rattled and reeked of oil. All the boys from "the school" volunteered for a free ride. "Me, sir! . . . Me, sir," but were refused with, "You're too small! Some of you might be ready in a couple of years." Eventually the officer espied a fine-looking candidate in the Spanish crowd. "There! You! You, back there! . . . Yes! You! You're a fine specimen. Why aren't you in the army? Would you like to ride in this latest-model armoured vehicle?" The candidate shook his head. "No, sir!" But the officer insisted. "The Canadian Army has extended you an invitation . . . sir! The Canadian Army is not accustomed to having its invitations turned down . . . sir!"

Two soldiers wearing black arm-bands with the letters MP on them in white hustled the fine-looking young man into the carrier, which promptly set off at top speed, roaring and rattling, bouncing and careening and crawling in and out of the ditch that separated the railway and the highway. The Avro Ansons returned, and a flour bomb was tossed out just as the Bren-gun carrier climbed out of the ditch. The "bomb" fell on the carrier and exploded in a cloud of white powder; the carrier keeled over amid a torrent of curses and a grinding of gears. The soldiers leaped out of the carrier, but the fine-looking young man rolled on the ground, holding his left arm, and moaning and cursing the "bas----s." His arm was broken.

The demonstration ended then and there. Although the officer tried to sound and appear collected as he invited the fine-looking young men of Spanish to come to the Lake Huron Hotel to "sign up," the conviviality of the occasion cooled off and the men and women drifted back sullenly to their homes and their lives, to resume chopping wood, weeding their gardens, scrubbing the floors, hauling water for their laundry, scraping their knuckles raw once or twice weekly on the scrubbing board, preparing their salt pork and baloney in hundreds of combinations for their broods or doing whatever they had been doing before the interruption.

There was little to relieve the monotony of working, eating, and sleeping; the town had no library, no theatre, no dance hall. But there was a railway station, which served as a meeting place and provided a pastime, however brief. The train stopped twice a day, once at 10:30 A.M. on its way to Sault Ste. Marie and again at 7:30 P.M. on its return to Sudbury, stopping to take on or discharge passengers and to fill its enormous boiler with water, hundreds of gallons. There, every evening, as regular as the train itself, dozens of villagers came to the station to watch the engine, to welcome a visitor or to bid farewell to some lucky friend who was bound for a life more rewarding than Spanish could ever offer. Perhaps, if they themselves could not leave, the young people could do so vicariously.

Were it not for "the school," Spanish might have been as dull as Walford. But Spanish had "the school," and the good people of the village forsook the train to watch baseball, softball, football and hockey games, or to attend *The Pirates of Penzance* and other dramas put on by the boys.

Despite the depressed times and the scanty population, there were no less than five stores struggling for existence by extending credit generously, all within half a mile of one another: St. Denis's, Sonny Bishop's, and Johnny Joncas's shops on the north side of Highway 17, sharing the strip with Gignac's Smoke and Billiard Shop, a BA service station and the Lake Huron Hotel. On the south side of the highway and the railway, on a road parallel to both, were the general stores of Dugas and of Moses Solomon. Sandwiched between the highway and the railway was the CPR railway station.

There were a few residents on the north side of the highway, eking out a living on the outcrops of the Laurentian Shield in hillbilly style. But most of the inhabitants lived on the south side — Solomons, Dugas, Sauves, Joncases, McGraths, Muncasters, Beauchamps, Pilons, Carriers, des Couteaux, Hamiltons, McLeods, Kellys, Greniers, Boulrices, Smiths, a May, a Brebant, a Frost, a Pollock, Gignacs (some on the north side, too), Lorties, Vances and a Foltz, who lived near Brennan Harbour. Spanish was a mixture of French, English, Irish, Scottish, half-breeds, full breeds and one Syrian, all living more or less peacefully with one another. The lucky ones worked for the CPR, Hydro, the Department of Highways and "the schools"; a few unlucky ones struggled to make ends meet by fattening a pig in the back yard and keeping a few chickens that ranged free to fend and forage for themselves.

Some families boasted multiple branches, but most did not. From this fact could be deduced the depths of the roots of Spanish. Gignacs,

Vances, Joncases and perhaps one or two others could claim some length of heritage; the rest had come, got stuck, and now longed for some miracle to uproot them.

To the east, five miles away, was Walford, where were grown inimitable potatoes. Seven miles from Walford was Massey; it had a real high school (or "continuation school"). Downstream and across the Spanish River was Sagamok, an Indian Reserve, accessible only by boat or dog paddle, whose band members survived from one season to the next by hunting, fishing, trapping and, if they were lucky, cutting pulpwood for the KVP (Kalamazoo Vegetable Parchment of Kalamazoo, Michigan). Next was Webwood, whose outdoor rink was enclosed by a high wall to prevent pucks from flying out and the west wind from blowing snow onto the ice. Another nine miles down the line was Espanola, headquarters for the KVP, the chief employer in the district, as well as the chief pollutant of the air and the rivers.

Immediately west of Spanish, five miles distant, was Cutler, another Indian Reserve. As it was in Sagamok, the present there was grim, and the future scarcely better. The trappers were away all winter tending their trap lines; in the summer they cut pulpwood for the McFadden Lumber Company of Blind River to pay off Moses Solomon, Art St. Denis or Sonny Bishop, who had extended them credit. A few lucky ones worked as miners in Sudbury, or on the boats in the summer. But of course, though it had a chief and council, Cutler's affairs and prospects were governed by an "Indian agent" who ruled with autocratic hand and ill-informed dedication.

Spragge had once been the next village, but by the 1940s it was just a name, a ghost town that even the ghosts had deserted. Next to Spragge was Algoma Mills, where trains and buses seldom stopped. Beyond Algoma Mills was Blind River, situated at the mouth of the Mississauga River, which carried in its current timber and pulpwood from the interior to the McFadden Lumber Company mill. To Blind River went the unwell and the wounded and the pregnant, to be repaired or attended to by either Dr. Hamill or Dr. Pigeon at St. Joseph's Hospital. Besides the hospital, there were other important institutions there: a district high school, a district office of the Department of Lands and Forests, a district office of the Department of Highways, a detachment of provincials (Ontario Provincial Police), and docks and wharves to oblige a fishing industry, all of which lent importance to Blind River.

Less than five minutes' drive westward from Blind River was the Mississauga Indian Reserve, but being located near a large town was of no special advantage to the Mississauga Indians except that such closeness represented a considerable saving in bus and taxi fares. But this proximity also had its disadvantages. Bootleggers offered powerful inducements in the form of wines of various brand names — Four Aces, 777, Catawba, Zing — to Mississauga types, some of whom could not resist such friendly offerings. On their way back home the Mississaugas had to run or walk a gauntlet of "provincials" who set ambushes as diligently as Custer might have longed to do. On more than one occasion the game wardens did a snow job on trappers and their families by the rigid enforcement of game regulations while closing their eyes and ears to American tourists who frequently exceeded their game limits. In no instance did an Indian agent installed in Sault Ste. Marie come to the aid of the Indians. Instead he discharged his duties as if his mandate were to keep his "wards" under strict check and control. Farther on there were Dean Lake, Iron Bridge, Sowerby, Thessalon, Nestorville, Bruce Mines, Desbarats, Bar River and Echo Bay, where dwelt as honest a shop-keeper as one would like to do business with. Next was Garden River Indian Reserve, with many residents who were trilingual. At the end of the line was Sault Ste. Marie.

Spanish, the village; Spanish, the river; Espanola, the town. Espaniel or Spaniel, the family. Where did the name come from? Was there a Spanish presence? Apparently there was.

According to one widely circulated story, a party of enterprising Ojibway warriors undertook an expedition around 1750 deep into the heart of Spanish-occupied territories. On their arrival in the far south and on beholding ravishing senoritas for the first time, the warriors were instantly turned on; lust and love displaced malevolence and aggression. They took possession of a winsome senorita whom they brought north, in full view of the envious and admiring eyes of the Choctaw, Muskogee, Cherokee, Yuchi, Shawnee, Susquehanna and Six Nations, through whose homelands they passed. Not a tomahawk was raised against them on their long return homeward. On arrival in Rainbow Country the senorita was married off to a chief and gave birth to a large family whose descendants still bear the name Espaniol; the senorita also named the village, the town and a river after her homeland. So the story goes.

There is only one thing wrong with this account. Our ancestors, better disposed for love than war, would not have gone all the way to Florida or Louisiana for only one damsel; they would have spirited away and returned with a whole entourage of senoritas as helpmates to their women and as playmates for themselves. And, liberal-minded though the tribal women were, it would have been difficult for them to welcome other women, no matter how comely, who knew nothing of post–Stone Age technology but had to be trained from scratch.

Whatever the truth, a town, a village, a river and a family got the names Spanish, Espanola and Espaniol.

The word or the name "Spanish" might seem to be no more filled with menace than any other word; but it inspired dread from the very first time that we Indian boys heard it. From the tone in which statements like, "You should be in Spanish!" or "You're going to Spanish! Mark my words!" were delivered, we knew that "Spanish" was a place of woe for miscreants, just as hell and purgatory were for sinners. What the difference was we were unable to guess, but if we were to avoid dispatch to Spanish, we'd be wise to listen to Liza Jones and comply instantly with her command to "Gowaun home!"; and to obey old Susan Taylor's order to "Put away those slingshots"; and never, *never* to sass old "Maggie Bonhomme." None of us wanted to go to Spanish any more than we wanted to go to hell or a concentration camp.

Though we didn't know for certain what Spanish represented, our fear of it was not without foundation. Many of our parents had gone to the institution — or one like it. But they did not share with us their knowledge of Spanish or Mount Elgin or the Mohawk Institute or Shingwauk. Spanish! It was a word synonymous with residential school, penitentiary, reformatory, exile, dungeon, whippings, kicks, slaps, all rolled into one. "Spanish" for us came to mean only one thing: "the school," known as St. Peter Claver's Indian Residential School and then later, from 1945, as the Garnier Residential School.

Spanish was but one of seventy-six such institutions, with a combined total of 8,000 students, that operated in the 1940s throughout Canada. Such institutions, funded by the federal government, were administered by sundry religious denominations. Spanish must have been like Shingwauk in purpose. According to the *Ontario Indian* (Vol. 3, No. 10, 1980), "The purpose of the Shingwauk school was to lead the Ojibway from a 'life of poverty, dirt, and ignorance.' It was patterned on other industrial residential schools opening across Canada during this era."

"We don't wish to un-Indianize them," said the Reverend Mr. Wilson, a nineteenth-century commentator, "but for their own good, induce them to lay aside the bow and fish-spear and put their hand to the plough or make them wield the tool of the mechanic. . . ." Four areas of teaching were stressed: good personal habits (such as cleanliness and punctuality); English; reading and writing; and trades (carpentry or farming for the boys and house-keeping for the girls).

But the disclaimer "We don't wish to un-Indianize them" was soon forgotten. The line generally taken by the instructors was that Indian culture was inferior, and Wilson boasted that "not a word of Indian is heard from our boys after six months." This was achieved through strict discipline and rigorous punishment. Punishment was given every night at seven to those who broke any of the rules.

When "integration" became the popular philosophy in the late 1880s and 1890s, Wilson began to preach that the Indians and whites should become "one in language, one in pursuits, tastes, ambitions, and hopes . . . we want them [the Indian residents] to become apprenticed out to white people and to become in fact, Canadians."

Bad as we may have imagined Spanish to be, it was not the worst of the residential schools. It was reported that at Shingwauk Residential School little boys were forced to stand in line, hands joined, to receive shocks from an electric socket.

Even if by comparison with the abuse and maltreatment inflicted upon little boys in other institutions, the boys at Spanish received less malevolent treatment, the sense of hurt and alienation was not in any proportion diminished. Most of the boys were already hurt; they were orphans, waifs, cast-offs, exiles from family and home, who needed less of a heavy hand, a heavy foot, heavy words, and more of affection, approbation, companionship, praise, guidance, trust, laughter, regard, love, tenderness.

Now, if the priests and brothers, but especially the prefects, could not extend the warmth, sympathy and affection that were necessary, it was because their system, the system of the Jesuits, prevented them from doing so. For upon entry into the Order of the Society of Jesus young men had to renounce the world and worldliness; they had as well to repudiate worldly feelings and demonstrations of emotion. Moreover, these young men, or "scholastics" as they were known within the religious community, were under close observation. During their two-year tenure at the school they had to show their suitability to continue their training as candidates for the priesthood. In the case of Father Buck and Father Kehl, they had to bear the extra burden of being aliens in enemy territory. As German nationals, they had been caught on this side of the Atlantic at the outbreak of the war and couldn't go back. To forestall internment, the Order dispatched the two young men to Spanish. In such a system and in the circumstances, it was easier for scholastics and priests to appear to be indifferent, insensitive to and even intolerant of human distress, real or imagined.

Most of the boys were already hurt and wounded on arrival at the institution; to receive a blow, a kick, or a t'rashing merely aggravated and opened the sores and the wounds . . . and kindled resentment and enmity for prefects, priests, religion, church, authority, rules and regulations.

The women, mothers in their early twenties and thirties, along with the grandmothers, must have suffered as much anguish as their sons and daughters. Many did not speak English, many had little more than Grade 3 education, and even those with Grades 7 and 8 could not understand the Indian Act and the powers that it conferred upon the Indian agent, who one day, any day, could come to a house to announce, "We've decided that it's best for you and your children that they be sent to Spanish. There they'll be well taken care of, clothed, fed and educated. Here, they have little to eat and little to wear. Get them ready. The priest has already made arrangements for their admission to Spanish. I'll come for them next Monday. Now, if you and your husband should get back together. . . ."

The mothers and grandmothers cried and wept, as mine did, in helplessness and in heartache. There was nothing, absolutely nothing, that they could do, as women and as Indians, to reverse the decision of "the Department." Already they had suffered the anguish of separation from husbands; now they had to suffer further the anguish of being dispossessed of their children; later, they would have to endure alienation from the children who were sent away to Spanish. It is no wonder then that when my mother, during a visit to a hospital in Owen Sound, saw the Cape Croker agent who was convalescing there, she expressed the sentiment that she wouldn't give two hoots if he never got better.

Spanish, the Garnier Residential School, along with its "sister," St. Joseph's Residential School for Indian Girls, were originally one school located on Manitoulin Island.

Established at Wikwemikong in 1825 by secular priests of the Roman Catholic Church as part of an extensive missionary effort to convert the Indians of Manitoulin Island, the school was operated there for almost 100 years before being transferred to a site on the north shore of the Spanish River where it empties into Georgian Bay. . . .

. . . [T]he Jesuit Fathers finally decided that if the school was to achieve what it had set out to accomplish it must be removed from the Reserve and from the parents. A tract of 1,000 acres was purchased in 1913 at the mouth of the Spanish River. . . .

Under the driving force of Rev. Joseph Sauve, of Wikwemikong, and ably assisted by Father Paquin, the Garnier school was launched. Father Paquin, a builder of note, designed the building, drew all the plans and supervised the construction.

The first students were selected by Indian agents throughout the province from those who had shown the greatest talent and were the most deserving. . . .[1]

The practice of selecting students throughout the province continued into the 1940s and 1950s, but the basis of selection was modified somewhat in preference of cast-offs. No matter where the students came from, however, they all had difficulties with the correct pronunciation and enunciation of the English language. The tribal language operated quite well without the letters "r," "l," "f," "v," "x" and "th." Thus when the boys attempted these strange sounds they stuttered and muttered and made substitutions. "Xavier" became "Zubyeah"; "never" became "neber"; "Virginia" became "Bayzhinee"; "father" became "fauder"; "Cameron" became "camel"; "three" and "through" were pronounced "tree" and "true." And having at the school German and French priests and brothers who also had problems pronouncing the ubiquitous "th" did not help. From the tribal tongue and from the influence of the French teachers,

---

[1] From "The Garnier Residential School for Indian Boys," school brochure, 1950.

the boys developed their own slang and dialect with a strong Gallic bias and flavour. In addition we all had some trouble with the English practice of separating the pronouns "he" and "she" in speech. It was hard to get away from tribal syntax in which "he" or "she" was embodied in the word and structure. We also had difficulty with the English practice of chaining adjectives and adverbs to nouns and pronouns; it was difficult to break away from tribal diction. Most of the dialect and the slang have been removed from the text to oblige readers who may not readily grasp the auditory incongruities of Ojibway, Cree and Mohawk trying to speak English.

In 1973 I went to St. Regis to deliver talks on "Indian culture and history" to the students in the public-school system. At the same time it was a good opportunity to call on some of the students I had gone to school with in Spanish. In Cornwall I found Jake Thompson's number and called.

"Jake Thompson, there?"

"Yeah! What can I do for you?"

"It's me, Basil Johnston, number 43. I went to school in Spanish with you; we worked in the chicken coop. . . ."

"Well! . . . Can you beat that. Out of the damn past just like that! Where are you?"

"In Cornwall. I'm calling you from a restaurant."

"Well, holy hell. What you doing in town? Where are you staying? Well, you get your butt over to the reserve right now. You're having supper with me and the Mrs., and you're staying with us while you're here. How would you like to go fishing tonight?"

Later that evening I found myself in Jake's company with rod and reel, fishing in the St. Lawrence River for pickerel and catfish. Right off the bat my rod bent as if there were a lunker at the end of the line. "By Jupiter, you got one. Careful now! Take your time. Don't want to lose him."

I took great care playing this monstrous pickerel, careful not to lose him. At last after a ten-minute struggle, during which time Jake caught three pickerel, I saw the sinkers in the dark above the water line. "Jake, better get the net ready." I stood up, to get better control of the rod and to guide my lunker toward the dip net. But as I lifted my rod to steer my fish over to Jake, I saw to my horror not a fish but a snake two feet in length and a good two and a half inches in diameter dangling and writhing at the end of the line. My knees buckled. I almost dropped the rod.

"A water s-s-s-snake! Jake!"

Jake roared. "Can't you recognize an eel when you see one? Just like the rest of you Adirondacks," (the Mohawk term for my tribe, Bark-eaters). And Jake continued to roar while I struggled to get that eel off my hook. "Serves you right for making me do all that work in the chicken coop," he chortled.

When we entered Jake's house to the welcoming committee of former Spanish inmates led by Antoine Lafrance (Big Bar Poot) and his brother John (Li'l Bar Poot), I realized why Jake had taken me fishing for eels.

The meeting then was like any other meeting of former Spanish students. It was an evening of recollection, of reliving the days in Spanish by recalling not the dark and dismal, but the incidents that brought a little cheer and relief to a bleak existence. I share some of these with you.

None of the stories recounted in the text will be found recorded in any official or unofficial journals of the Garnier Residential School for Boys. In setting down some of the stories I have had to rely on my own memory and on the memories of my colleagues: Eugene (Captain) Keeshig, Charlie Shoot (Akiwenzie), Hector (Kitchi-meeshi Hec) Lavalley, Cecil King, Maxie Simon, Ernie (The Wrestler) Nadjiwon, and many, many more. This account of Garnier covering two periods, 1939–44 and 1947–50, is as accurate as memory and effort and bias will allow. I hope as well that it is fair.

I dedicate this work to all the boys who preceded us and bequeathed their maroon sweaters to us, to all of my colleagues with whom I endured the hurts and shared the laughter, to those who inherited our maroon sweaters and wore them every Sunday until Garnier was closed in 1958, and to all the prefects and priests and teachers who tried to instruct us and made possible the events herein recorded. But I dedicate this work most expecially to Boozo, friend, raconteur, fellow resident of Toronto, and teammate in an Indian hockey club, whose "Haw! Haw! Haw!" brought a sense of fun to our teammates, twenty to twenty-five years younger than we were. He is now probably regaling St. Peter with tales from Spanish.

The *Sudbury Star* of June 8, 1950 reported that I had said in my closing remarks as valedictorian: "Only through having the courage to continue our studies and determination to use the talents we have for advancement can our Indian people become true citizens of Canada." We were "wards of the Crown," not citizens of Canada. Under the Treaties, Indians were constituted "wards of the Crown," according to the Submission of the Union of Saskatchewan Indians of December 1946 to the Special Joint Committee of the Senate and the House of Commons appointed to examine and consider the Indian Act. It was not until 1960 that Indians were allowed to vote in federal elections in Canada. And having been committed to the care of the Jesuits at Garnier Residential School for Boys we were "wards of the church" as well.

Lastly, in reply to the inevitable question, "Is there a place for residential schools in the educational system?", I respond with a qualified yes. Some who attended Garnier after 1946 have said, "It was probably the best thing that could have happened to me." However, for those going to St. Peter Claver's in the pre-Garnier days, it was "the worst possible experience." Just as private schools have a place in the educational system, so too do the residential schools, but under vastly different terms, conditions and formats from those that existed in the residential school as I first encountered it.

Spanish!

"Come on! Let's go hunting," Charlie Shoot suggested boldly. "I got my slingshot."

I started at the daring of the idea. Charlie and I, lounging beneath an apple tree that stood twenty feet or so from the school, were waiting for the teacher to ring the bell that would summon us to classes for the day.

"Hunting?" I could scarcely utter the word. As pleasant as the idea was, going hunting meant skipping school. Never having done anything that reckless, I could not conceive what the penalty might be. A presentiment made me hesitate. "Hunting?" I repeated.

"Yeah! Up on top of Peter Nadjiwon's hill. Lots of squirrels up there."

"But won't Miss Burke get mad?" I asked Charlie. I wasn't really concerned about school, but I had a respectful fear of Miss Burke, who was merely waiting for one of her students to make one small mistake.

"Such a nice day," Charlie observed wistfully. "Nobody should be inside on a day like this . . . especially in a school." And it was true. It was a glorious day in May. Everyone should have been outside, in the woods, at the beach or in the meadows.

I wasn't against hunting or anything like that; in fact I was decidedly in favour of it. Almost anything was preferable to drawing flowers and learning the names of the parts of plants and other useless bits of information. To go hunting was a powerful temptation.

"Yeah. Would be good to go hunting, but what about Miss Burke?" I asked again.

"Well! We'll just say that we were sick."

I had not thought of that. I admired Charlie all the more for his thoroughness.

"But I didn't bring my slingshot." I wished now that I had stuffed it into my lunch bag.

"I got a couple more at home. Come on."

I needed no further urging. I gathered my lunch bag and books and followed Charlie to his home, a tarpaper shack about three times as long as it was wide, situated beneath a canopy of immense elm trees. The shack was no more than 150 yards from the school. We left our books at Charlie's and made straight for Peter Nadjiwon's sugar bush.

Along the way Charlie shot several sparrows, cedar wax-wings and a chipmunk, as well as shattering several insulators, just for practice.

"Charlie Shoot" or "Chaulie Shoot" or "Chaulie Shot" was born Charles Akiwenzie. But he never bore the name Akiwenzie, preferring either Shoot or Shot. No one, not even his parents, knew the origin of the name, but it was apt. Chaulie always had a slingshot, and he was always shooting at something: crows, cats, dogs, bottles, tin cans and insulators. Insulators were his favourite targets for their pleasing shattering sound when struck by a pebble. "Shoot" for shooting; "Shoot" for accuracy.

He could hit a sparrow on the wing at fifty yards, deliberately graze a rabbit's ear at twenty-five paces, and on the run pick an apple off a tree by hitting the stem without damaging the apple. Later, the force with which he could fire a hockey puck reinforced the reputation that had first earned him the name.

"Shoot" was apt, and Chaulie answered to it more readily than to Akiwenzie. It is still so today.

On top of Peter Nadjiwon's hill was a sugar bush fifteen acres or so in extent, its maples towering fifty, sixty and seventy feet into the air, a haven for squirrels, black, red and grey, and a paradise for young hunters. By noon Chaulie had brought down ten fat black squirrels, which he skinned and gutted and then roasted. After a feast, Chaulie and I had a nap.

Around two in the afternoon we woke up refreshed, ready for more hunting. I watched clouds forming images in the sky.

"Perch be biting good this afternoon," Chaulie observed, looking at the same clouds. "Be mighty hungry, them. Bes' time to go fishing. Come on, 'fore someone takes our fishing spot." I followed.

Down Peter Nadjiwon's hill, left at Edgar Jones's place, target shooting along the way at posts, sparrows, king birds, goldfinches, insulatorless brackets that pinged. At Shawnee's (Charlie Jones's) I stopped.

"Don't you think we should go around by Shawnee's field an' down along the crick to your place so's the teacher won't see us?"

"What you scared of? We'll go right by the school, sneak under the windows. Won't see us, her; too busy teaching. Never looks out anyway."

"Whadayadoin' out on the road? Why aren't you in school? I'm going to tell on you!" Liza, Shawnee's white woman, shrieked out, her voice and words echoing a good mile in every direction, such was the power of her lungs.

We ran, clambered over the stile and hunched our backs as we sneaked by the school. We made it to Chaulie's home.

"We'll make a lunch first an' then go fishing. How'd you like some scone and salt pork?"

We were sitting on blocks of wood in the shade of the elms eating our sandwiches buttered with lard when Stella, my Grade 7 cousin, hailed us from the road. "Miss Burke wants you at school. . . . Right now."

"Tell her we're not here," Chaulie yelled back. Stella left. We resumed eating, with only thoughts of fishing filling our minds.

"Hey! Miss Burke wants you in school this instant," Stella shouted from the road on her return not more than five minutes later.

"Didn'tcha tell her we're not here?" Chaulie demanded.

"But she can see you plain as day, and she's getting very vexed." "Vexed" was Miss Burke's favourite word for losing her temper.

And it was true. From where we were sitting we could see the school plainly, and anyone looking from the school could see us just as plainly. In fact, we could see Miss Burke plainly, and she was plainly looking in our direction.

"Tell her to go to hell. Tell her we're gone," Chaulie said, getting up. "Come on." And we went around the corner of the building, out of sight of the school.

"You're going to get it," Stella warned as she left.

"You shouldn'a tol' her to go to hell," I gasped. I was scandalized by my friend's sentiments and language. "She'll tell on us."

"Nah!" Chaulie spat out. "Stella never say anything like that to the teacher; too scared, her."

Uneasy, I looked around the corner, down the road toward the school.

"Hey! Chaulie! Valerie [a Grade 8 cousin] is coming."

"Take your pants down," Chaulie commanded.

Down went my pants, almost automatically, as if it were a natural reflex action. It was not until my pants were at half-mast, coiled around my knees, that I asked for an explanation. "What for?"

"Shut up."

I began to feel silly and sheepish with my pants half off.

"Hey! Miss Burke . . . Oh! . . . Oh! . . ." Valerie did not finish, for just as she began to speak, Chaulie placed his hands on my shoulders and pressed me down so that my stern was upturned. From between my legs I got an upside-down view of Valerie's horror-stricken face. With another "Oh! Oh! Oh!", she fled.

"Haw, haw, haw! Ho, ho, ho! Hee, hee, hee!" Chaulie guffawed. He was shaking and crying and dancing, all at the same time. "You . . ." and he doubled over again. "Haw, haw, haw . . . shoulda seen her face. Ho, ho!"

I was angry. I was scared. I was embarrassed. But there was nothing I could do to retaliate. Chaulie was older, bigger and stronger. I could only rage.

"Haw. Haw, ho, hee. Come on, pull your pants up. You look silly standing there with your pants down. Haw, haw, haw." I hitched up my pants; I hadn't realized, in my rage, that they were still unfurled.

"You shouldn'a done that, Chaulie," I remonstrated. "She'll tell on us, and Miss Burke will be vexed."

"Nah! Valerie'd never say anything like that to the teacher; too scared."

I didn't know if that were true about Valerie, but I felt a bit less uneasy about either girl's telling on us. With Chaulie's assurances my spirits picked up. He was in Grade 6, more experienced and learned about life than I. He explained that Stella would never, never utter the word "hell" under any circumstances; nor would Miss Burke allow the dread word to be repeated. It was a blasphemous term, a sin; Stella was a good girl and would never suffer the word to sully her lips. And if she did, she herself would be punished for scandalizing Miss Burke. There was not, in Chaulie's mind, the slightest chance that either Stella or Valerie would tell Miss Burke anything other than "They're gone."

Chaulie and I went fishing at the point in McGregor Bay until sunset. As he had predicted, we caught a pile of perch.

Next day I went to school with little remorse and less anxiety, though I avoided looking at Stella and Valerie, especially Valerie. There was little to fear. Had I not a good excuse?

The bell rang. We all filed into school and sat down.

"Cut out the talking, Ronald. I'm already vexed. Basil Johnston! Come here and go directly into the vestibule and wait there for me. Charles Akiwenzie! Get into the other vestibule and wait for me there."

I went into the girls' vestibule. From the tone of Miss Burke's voice I began to suspect that something was very wrong. Stella must have snitched; or maybe Valerie. By the time the Lord's Prayer had ended, I was trembling. Miss Burke came in. Her nostrils were twitching as she caressed and flexed a strap in her hands.

"Where . . . were . . . you . . . yesterday?"

"Sick, Miss. I was sick."

"Jesus, Mary, Joseph! Have mercy on his soul," Miss Burke implored, looking upward and crossing herself at the same time for my salvation. "A lie; a bald-faced lie! Have mercy on this boy!" And then she snarled. "You scalawag. You liar. You weren't sick. You played hooky. I saw you with my own eyes. Mrs. Charles Jones saw you and that . . . Charles Akiwenzie up the road. How dare you tell me that you were sick? What do you take me for, a fool? Come now; the truth." And Miss Burke bent the strap, back and forth.

I knew when the jig was up.

"Chaulie Shoot!" I blurted out. "Chaulie tol' me to say I was sick. He made me go hunting with him! I didn't wanna go, but he made me; said he was going to fight me. I hadda go."

"Lord have mercy on your souls! You both deserve to be in *Spanish*." At the word "*Spanish*" I quaked even more. Was it hell?

"Put your hand out."

Wham! God, it stung.

"Now the other hand."

Wham! My left hand burned.

Wham, wham, wham. First one hand and then the other, until both my hands were thick and on fire and I was howling with each blow. After eighteen lashes, Miss Burke was puffing and sweating . . . and weakening.

"Let that," she panted, "be a lesson . . . and don't you ever play hooky again, or *lie*." Miss Burke shoved me back into the classroom to face the stares and grins of my classmates.

Miss Burke glared at the class. She didn't have to say anything to command silence. She marched to the other vestibule. We strained our ears to hear what Miss Burke was saying to my friend, but all we heard were muffled sounds and the crack of the strap. They sounded weaker with each delivery, twenty-four in all, the greatest number ever administered to any student. Still there was not a whimper, not even an "eeeyow."

The door opened. Chaulie, shoved in violently, stumbled, but he kept his balance, blowing as hard as a young bull into his hands. He held back the tears that welled up in his eyes; he wouldn't cry.

Miss Burke was panting from her exertions; beads of perspiration were breaking out on her brow and running down the side of her nose. She sat down to get her breath back and to wipe her glasses and face.

When she at last recovered her breath and herself, she managed: "I'm vexed! I'm very vexed. You belong in *Spanish*."

The very word made me cower and quiver.

Sentenced to Spanish

Most of the 135 inmates of Spanish, ranging in age from four to sixteen, with the occasional seventeen-year-old, came from broken homes; some were orphans, having lost one or both parents; others were committed to the institution as punishment for some misdemeanor; and a few were enrolled by their parents in order to receive some education and training.

The reason for and the mode of my own committal were typical. My parents had separated, and, following the break-up, Mother, my four sisters and I lived with my grandmother for a while.

But unknown to either my mother or my grandmother, the Indian agent and the priest had conferred — with nothing but our welfare in mind, of course — and decided that not even the combined efforts of Grandmother and Mother were enough to look after five children and that they ought to be relieved of two of their burdens.

The decision must have been relayed to Mother, for she told me that I would soon be going on a short trip. So ecstatic was I at the prospect of going abroad that I immediately made preparations and grew more impatient with each passing day. My sister Gladys was to have accompanied me, but two days before departure, much to her dismay and discomfort, she succeeded in getting contaminated by poison ivy.

On the fateful day, Grandmother and Mother wept as they scrubbed and polished and clothed me in the finest second-hand clothing that they had been able to scrounge at the bazaar. I could not understand why they did not share my pleasure at my good fortune. I tried reassuring them with their own assurances that I would return shortly, but it made little difference. There was something final in their tears and caresses that was lost on me at that moment. Anxious to leave, I waited outside for the car and chauffeur.

He eventually came around the corner dragging a cloud of dust behind him on the dirt road. I waited at the door and loudly announced his arrival. I jammed my cap on, ready to leave forthwith.

Mr. F. Tuffnel did not come in as invited; instead he stood at the doorway, glowering through his rimless glasses and pursing his mouth as if afraid to open it lest he be contaminated.

Mr. Tuffnel unstitched his lips after looking at me and rasped, "Well! Where's the other one?"

"She's sick," Mother replied in her best English. "Got poison ivy, her . . . in bed."

"You sure?" the agent asked, peering inside.

"Yeah, you wanna see?" Mother countered. "You don' believe me, you?"

The agent flinched, perhaps not wanting to catch poison ivy. "Well, gotta take two at least," he said, showing that dispensing pills at the agency wasn't his only skill; he could also count. "How about her?" he rasped, pointing at Marilyn, my four-year-old sister, who came running into the house to find out what was going on. "She can go; old enough . . . and that'll make two!" Once more he demonstrated that he could count.

Mother and Grandmother were both appalled. "No! She's too young," they wailed. "She can't go to school yet, she's only four. No!"

But the agent knew how to handle Indians, especially Indian women. "Well! If you don't want her to go, we'll take the whole family. Now! Get her ready. Hurry up!"

Mother and Grandmother whimpered as they washed and clothed my sister.

"Hurry up or we'll miss the ferry!" Mr. Tuffnel urged, looking at his watch and down the road.

When my sister was ready, Mr. Tuffnel placed us in the back seat of his car. We made the ferry at Tobermory in ample time. On board the *Normac*, the agent put us on chairs in the cabin with the order, "Don't you move." By this time, I was getting frightened, not only of the man but of my circumstances as well. Moreover, I was getting downright uncomfortable.

Nature would not leave me alone, and I went in search of the "poop house," which fortunately was just around the corner. But before I got there, I was collared by the agent.

"Where do you think you're going? Didn't I tell you not to move?" And I was shoved and pushed back to my chair. "Now! Don't you move. Do you understand?" The agent wagged a finger in front of my nose for emphasis before he withdrew. Though I could not see him I was certain that he kept an eye on us through narrow crevices from below, above and behind.

Worse, the passengers who were sitting in the cabin began regarding my sister and me as if we were fugitives or dangerous felons. I now began desperately to wish that I had not come on this journey. What my sister's thoughts were I do not know; she just sat and stared ahead.

At this moment of desolation an old man, or so he seemed to me, asked if we wanted anything. I told him that I wanted to go to the toilet and that my sister wanted a drink. Now, I don't know if she did want anything, but I nevertheless spoke on her behalf.

The old man went around the corner and reappeared with the agent, who looked dour.

"Okay! You can go to the toilet," he said in a tone that suggested he would have preferred not to let me go; and to make sure that I did not make a getaway, the agent took my arm and conducted me to the lavatory. At the doorway he warned me: "Don't try anything funny!"

Such was my alarm that I could not relieve myself properly; I was certain the squint-eyed agent was peering at me. Finished, I went out, only to be accosted by my captor at the door for escort back to my seat. "Don't move; I'll be watching you," were his words as he slithered around the corner.

The old man came back with two bottles of pop, which my sister and I drank with relish.

"Where'd you get that? Where'd you get those? Where'd you get the money?" Sharp and biting the questions. I almost dropped my pop. It was a good thing that Sis did not understand English, otherwise she would have cried, I'm sure.

"I bought them," the old man said, coming forward and standing beside us. "Anything wrong with that?" he asked pugnaciously.

The agent's lips quivered while some of the ruddiness receded from his face. Gone was the firmness of tone with which he had addressed my mother and grandmother; instead, his voice weakened till it resembled a bleat. "They are my charges. I'm responsible for them. I have to watch . . . because . . . you never know what these two may do."

"What did they do? What can they do? Where are you taking them?" the man demanded.

"I . . . I . . . I'm taking them to Spanish . . . a . . . it's a school for bad kids," the agent stammered.

"I know the school," the old man said. "The kids up there are not a bad bunch; in fact, they're a good bunch of kids, so don't give me any baloney about bad kids. Let me look after these two for a while — you don't know how."

The agent slunk out of the cabin under the accusatory stares and whispers of the passengers.

With the old man as our guardian, Sis and I had a pleasant voyage, promenading on the decks and sightseeing while gobbling ice cream, sipping pop and eating chocolate bars. But the agent was in the background lurking — or so it seemed — behind lifeboats and smokestacks or underneath stairwells.

The next thing I remember with clarity was our arrival in the late afternoon at the schools. After my sister was deposited at St. Joseph's, I did not see her for another six weeks. As for me . . . I was driven to St. Peter Claver's school. No sooner did the car stop at the south-west corner of the school than the boys — all of them, it seemed — assembled on the veranda and around the agent's car. Many more had their noses pressed against the school's windows, which were barred by strong-meshed screens bolted to the bricks with heavy-duty eye-bolts.

All the boys were dressed alike in beige corduroy riding breeches, beige shirts, grey woollen socks and black leather work boots; all were dark and dirty, their heads shaved bald. Every one of them stared and grinned.

Through this crowd a priest made his way to the car. The agent told him who I was and where I came from. "I'm Father Book!" he said. "Come with me."

With fear and misgiving I followed the priest to the third floor, where he ordered me to shed my clothing. He handed me a bar of carbolic soap and shoved me into a shower. "Scrub. Scrub hard." The shower hissed and then stopped. The curtain opened. Father Book (it was really Father Buck, but because of his German accent I first heard it as "Book") poured some vile-smelling substance on my head that smelled like turpentine and gasoline and coal oil combined. "Wash! Wash good!" The shower resumed. I washed good!

When I emerged from this purge, Father Buck gave me a small green bag with my uniform inside and a pair of work boots. After I had dressed, my guide led me to the dormitory where he assigned me a bed in the junior section. It smelled of piss.

"You are number forty-three," he informed me, prodding me downstairs, so that I stumbled on the metal-topped risers and almost fell. In the recreation hall a large crowd of boys waited, curious to know who the newest inmate might be.

With the command "Outside! Outside!" Father Buck dispersed the boys, who, on their way out, yelled, "German! German! Johnsh [Ojibway for Nose]!"

"Here!" Father Buck growled, shoving me toward a thirteen-year-old boy armed with a pair of clippers.

"Numudubin [Sit down]!" the Indian boy said, pointing to the bench he had dragged out. "Aneesh abi-ondjibauyin [Where are you from]?"

"Nayausheenagameeng [Cape Croker]."

"That's where I'm from," he chirped, flitting from behind to the front of me and examining me from nose to eyeball. "Yeaaaah! I remember you. Geee! I didn't recognize you!" and he laughed as he clipped my hair, which fell in chunks to the floor.

Cheered a little, I looked at him more closely, but I could not recall ever having seen him before.

"What's your name?" I asked him.

"Euge! Eugene! Eugene Keeshig!" he warbled, looking at me from side to side.

"Come on, Keeshig! Hurry up! What's the hold-up?" Father Buck inquired from the doorway.

"Awright, Father." Euge's visage darkened as every muscle stiffened. Almost involuntarily he clenched his fists till his knuckles whitened. "Don' hurry me up. Take my time if I wan' to. No white man's gonna make me hurry . . . this guy's hair is tough, like wires." Euge was defiant, born ready to fight and capable. As bears the badger, so did Father Buck leave Keeshig alone.

"No pries' ain' gonna boss me aroun'," Euge declared, looking at the door as if he were about to run after Father Buck. Then just as quickly as he'd flared up, he calmed down and his expression brightened. "You're my cousin. My Grandma Christine and your Grandma Rosa are sisters." He chatted on, clipping and snipping and shearing. "You know who else is here?"

"No."

"There's Charlie Shoot."

"Yeah?" So that's where my old hunting buddy had disappeared to, just as Miss Burke had predicted — probably for the hunting episode.

"An' there's Hector." I wondered what he was in for.

"That's four of us from the Cape," Euge said. "I better cut your hair 'fore that pries' come back. Never know what he's gonna do. Might hit you with a bat or a strap." Euge clipped and sheared.

Father Buck came back. "You finished?"

"Yeah! I'm finished," Euge replied, his tone and manner surly and disrespectful.

"Come here!" Father Buck said, beckoning with his forefinger. He led me outside toward the north-east corner of the building, where a group of boys about my age were busy shelling peas. He made me sit down on a bench and shoved a bushel of peas in front of me. "Shell these peas! Fast. These are the Canadiens. You are on their team." Father left.

I did not like the Canadiens. I would have preferred to be a Ranger, but I didn't have any choice; moreover, it made no difference.

None of my teammates introduced himself to me; each was too preoccupied with shelling peas; cursing and heaping damnation on all peas. For my part, I was too engrossed with other thoughts — how long I would be in the accursed institution; when I would get home. The more I thought about home and my little sister in "the other place," the more lonesome I became. I guess my thoughts must have slowed my rate of shelling peas, which displeased the teammate next to me. He thumped me between my shoulder blades. "Hurry up! The Maple Leafs an' the Rangers an' the Black Hawks is ahead of us."

Not caring about the Leafs or Rangers or Black Hawks, I promptly belted my teammate in the beak, and the fight was on. But I had the advantage, for when I biffed my teammate, he fell backwards off the bench. I immediately leaped on him, fists flailing; in the assault, we knocked over a couple of bushel baskets of peas.

There were yelps and shouts of, "Come on, Simon [Martin]! Get up! Give it to him!" No one was cheering for me, and that made me angrier. I pummelled Simon even harder until his nose was bloody.

"What means this?" the gruff voice of Father Buck inquired. I felt myself lifted by the collar.

"He started it. He hit me first; he hit me for nothin'," I hastily explained.

"He was jus' sittin' there; he wasn' doin' no work, and the Rangers an' the Leafs an' the Hawks was beatin' us. It was his fault. I jis' tol' 'im to hurry up," Simon countered through puffed lips.

"Aha! You like fights, no? But no like work?" Father Buck smirked. "Then you shell Simon's peas, too . . . no? And no supper until all peas finished. Come on, boys; get back to work."

Through tears I looked into the grinning faces of all the Canadiens, Black Hawks, Rangers and Maple Leafs. No doubt the enemy were happy at the dissension within the ranks of the Canadiens. I sat down with my bushel of peas and Simon's half bushel.

While I was shelling peas, Simon came back and shook a fist in my face, threatening, "I'll get you after." The other Canadiens heartily endorsed Simon's intentions with, "Yeah, Simon, get him good. He don' fight fair. He hit you when you wasn' ready. He's a coward!"

Fortunately for me, Euge came back. He sat down with me, cursed the peas with me and helped me shell them. He told the Canadiens who I was and that I was his cousin. The Canadiens were impressed. "Holy Moses, he can fight," they murmured in admiration. With Euge as my protector, I was safe from Simon . . . for a while. But I had thereafter to fight my own battles.

Such was my induction to St. Peter Claver's school. Originally, the Indian residential school had been situated in Wikwemikong on Manitoulin Island, but the building had burned down in 1913 or 1914 and a new school had been constructed in Spanish, Ontario, at the mouth of and on the banks of the Spanish River.

The school itself was located about a mile from Highway 17 and from the town. It was owned, operated and managed by the Jesuits. Across the dirt road was St. Joseph's, a girls' residential school run by a non-accredited order known as the Daughters of Mary.

St. Peter Claver's was more than a school; it was an institution. The main building, a three-storied structure, contained dormitories, class-rooms, a study hall, a recreation hall, dining rooms, several lavatories, chapels, a kitchen, a scullery, a pantry, a refrigerated area, corridors, offices, a cloistered area, a laundry room, an infirmary, a bakery and a tailor shop. In the cellar were huge furnaces surrounded by cords of wood, sacks of potatoes, beans and other produce, coal, paint, pipes, boards and other supplies. Near the school were clustered a windmill, a power house and a shoe shop. Close to the river were a mill and storage shed where wheat, corn and anything else that could be milled were milled. There was also an immense barn that sheltered a herd of cows, several teams of horses, a bull of immense carnality for the greater joy of the cows, a dairy operation and, of course, tons of hay and straw and assorted feeds and equipment. Between the barn and the mill were a blacksmith shop, a piggery and a sheepery. In the north-west corner of the complex was the chicken coop, which harboured four hundred chickens and one forlorn and harried rooster. Between the buildings was a playground, bare and hard-packed from years of baseball games and running feet. Fenced off from the playground and stretching from mill to school was the Garden of McLaren (Brother McLaren) yielding tomatoes, cucumbers and boundless temptations. At the wharf were tethered the Garnier, a thirty-foot cruiser-like vessel; the Iron Boat, a former lifeboat, now an all-purpose vessel; the Red Bug, an open-topped row-boat-styled ark used for transporting cattle, boys and girls, and cordwood or heavy equipment under tow by either the Garnier or the Iron Boat; a scow; and several punts. In addition, there were nearly a thousand acres of land in Spanish and in Walford.

The entire institution was as nearly self-sufficient as the mid-north would allow. Under the guidance of priests and brothers, between 130 and 135 boys, with the exception of the four- and five-years-olds, ploughed, seeded and harvested potatoes, beans and other produce; milled the wheat and corn and baked the bread; forged the shoes and shod the horses; mixed the paints and painted the buildings; measured planks and repaired floors; cut the hides and made shoes; cut the bolts of textiles and tailored shirts and pants and pyjamas; fed and tended cows, horses, sheep and swine and even slaughtered them; and swept, dusted and polished floors and furniture. There was little in the entire institution that was not done by the inmates.

For our shelter, food, clothing and education the government doled out forty cents per student per day. Hockey sticks, balls, hats and coats came from donors.

St. Peter Claver's existed for two reasons. One was to train Indian youth for some vocation: tailoring, milling, blacksmithing, shoemaking, tinsmithing, painting, carpentry, baking, cooking, plumbing, welding, gardening, sheep and swine herding, animal husbandry and poultry care. Alas, while there were some accomplished chicken farmers and shoemakers, no graduate went into business; the trades for which we had been trained were rendered obsolete by new technology. The school's other purpose was to foster religious vocations by frequent prayer and adoration. But all the prayers, masses, novenas and benedictions could not overcome the natural resistance of most boys to a career in holy orders. The school produced neither tradesmen nor priests.

A Day in the Life of Spanish

6:15 A.M. Clang! Clang! Clang! I was nearly clanged out of my wits and out of bed at the same time. Never had anything — not wind, not thunder — awakened me with quite the same shock and fright.

Clang! Clang! Clang!

"Come on! Up! Up! Up! What's the hold-up? Not want to get up? Come on, Pius! What's wrong, Henry? You no like get up?"

Clang! Clang! Clang! Up and down the aisles between the beds Father Buck walked, swinging the bell as if he wanted to shake it from its handle.

"You deaf? You no can hear? Hmmm? You like sleep? No?" Father Buck asked as he stood beside Simon Martin's bed. He rang the bell even harder. There was no sign of movement from the still form. "Soooo! you won't get up, Simon!" And Father Buck seized one side of the mattress and lifted and overturned Simon, bedding and mattress together. Simon stirred.

"Ah! Come on, Father," Simon complained, articulating the expression in current usage at the school for "All right! Knock it off. Enough's enough."

Simon sat up, rubbing his eyes. He was taking far too much time to please the young scholastic.

"You! You want see Father Hawkins?" Father Buck asked.

Not wishing to see Father Hawkins, S.J., Simon got up — as slowly as he dared.

From the other end of the dormitory came a muffled and disrespectful challenge. "Whyn'tcha pick on someone your own size, Father?"

The reaction was instantaneous. "Who says this? Who says this?" demanded Father Buck, red in the face and redder still in the ears.

While Father's attention was elsewhere, Simon, now remarkably wide awake, stuck out his tongue and shook his fist at Father Buck, much to the delight and amusement of the boys in the immediate vicinity. Father Buck, guessing Simon's conduct behind his back, spun around, but Simon, knowing the tactics of adults in games of this kind and having considerable skill in outwitting the enemy, was instantly transformed into a groggy sleepy boy, all angelic innocence, struggling to replace his rebellious mattress, sheets and blankets back on his bed.

Meanwhile, during Simon's mutinous behaviour and irreverent charade, most of the boys, some fully awake others partly awake, and a few in a trance-like state, carried on as if nothing unusual were taking place, folding their pajamas, tucking them under the pillow and then rolling back the top sheet and blanket to air the bed. Not until they had performed these steps did anyone proceed to the washstand.

Clank! Clank! Clank! went the washbasins as they were flipped right side up on the bottom of a long shallow sink that resembled a cattle-feeding trough. To the clatter of basins was added a hiss as water gushed from many spigots into basins or streamed over toothbrushes that were then thrust into little round tins of tooth powder. Clank! Hiss! Gargle! Scrub-a-dub! Scrape! Choo-choo-choo! were the only sounds heard from the washing area.

Occasionally there was a complaint. "Come on, hurry up!" Lawrence Bisto or some other student would growl. "Ain't got all day." And, to lend force to the demand, he would prod the laggard.

"Hold your horses! Can't you see I ain't finished. What's a matter, you blind?" the laggard would retort, his tone of voice signalling that he was prepared to fight.

Clang! Clang! Clang!

"*Line up!*"

Two serpentine columns of listless boys formed.

"*Okay! Quietly!*"

But though tongues were quiet, boots beat down on the metal stairs, so that stairs, windows and railings rattled and reverberated from the bottom of the stairwell to the ceiling on the third floor.

In the recreation hall downstairs the boys either stood around in knots or sat slouched on the top board that served as a bench as well as a lid for the boxes that were built into the wall. But as I was to learn later, the boys were not really waiting in the commonly understood sense of the word "wait." Though they may have appeared to be waiting, the boys were in reality exercising a form of quiet disobedience directed against bells, priests, school and, in the abstract, all authority, civil and religious.

Since the boys could not openly defy authority either by walking out of the school and marching north or south on Highway 17 or by flatly refusing to follow an order, they turned to the only means available to them: passive resistance, which took the form of dawdling.

Only once in my eight years of residence did I witness the phenomenon of boys racing to line up and then maintaining the strictest monastic silence when no bell had rung. As well as I can remember, the incident occurred in the following manner:

"Ice cream!" someone yelled.

"Ice cream! Ice cream! Ice cream!" was repeated a dozen times across the playground.

Well, the announcement "ice cream" uttered either by La Marr (Antoine Lafrance) or Neeyauss (Angus Pitwaniquot) had the same effect as the cry of "Fire!" except that in this instance it operated in reverse. As the magic words "ice cream" went echoing from mouth to mouth across the yard, bats, baseballs and scoreboards were abandoned and 130 boys rushed to line up in front of the veranda, where goodies such as ice cream and candies were often distributed to mark some special feast or event.

Prefects, too, clutching the hems of their soutanes, sprinted across the yard in pursuit of the boys.

Panting and flushed with impotent rage, Father Buck demanded to know: "Who says this?" Back and forth in front of the twelve rows of boys, every one of whom was anticipating the issue of ice cream, strode Father Buck, looking darkly into the faces of the boys as if he could discern the look of guilt. He paused directly in front of Donald Fox and Joe Coocoo, two of our fellow inmates, already well known for their habitual disregard for rules, regulations, laws and the Ten Commandments. He peered into their faces.

"You!" Father Buck snapped at Donald Fox. "Did you say this?"

Donald was deeply pained. In his most aggrieved tone he said, "Not me, Father. Honest to God. You always blaming me for nothing."

Father Buck continued to stare at Donald, dumbfounded that Donald should deny his guilt. Only Donald would sabotage a ball game and circulate false rumours. But before the young scholastic could do anything rash, such as sending Donald to Father Hawkins for a thrashing, Father Buck's fellow teachers, Father Kehl and Father Mayhew, moved to his side. After a brief whispered consultation and a quick glance at his watch, Father Buck commanded, "You go back and play, until this bell she rings."

6:45 A.M. Clang! Clang! Clang!

Boys shuffled into lines as slowly as they dared without having their names inscribed in the prefects' little black books. It would have been easier to line up immediately without waiting for the bell, but that would have been seen as surrender.

Father Buck must have imagined himself a commander and we his soldiers as he stood in front and stared us into silence. Even when there was silence all around, he still felt constrained to command it. "*Quiet!*" It was not until he had obtained a sepulchral silence that he nodded to his colleague, Father Kehl, to open the door. "Okay! And no talking."

Our route from the recreation hall to the chapel was not direct, through the first corridor, but round about outside, along the south side of the building. We trod it in hail, sleet, blizzard and deluge. Had there been fire and brimstone, we would have walked in that as well.

At the word "okay," the teams proceeded outside, where they converged into two columns, with the youngest and smallest in front and the oldest and biggest boys at the back. When the two columns shuffled to a halt in the left aisle, they stood at reverent attention.

"Clap," snapped the clapper in Father Kehl's hand. Down on one knee we dropped in united genuflection, remaining in that position until the clapper clapped a second time in signal for us to rise and to stand once more at attention. Only after one more clap did we slide into our assigned places in the pews.

Moments later, under the heavy escort of Miss Strain and Miss Chabot and wearing pretty hats and dresses, the girls from St. Joseph's entered the chapel in much the same way as we had done except in one particular. Their movements, pace, halting, genuflecting, rising and entering the pews from the right aisle were regulated not by a wooden clapper but by the clapping of the hands of female prefects who glowered and frowned just as severely as our own keepers, in an effort to make sure the girls did not cast lustful glances at the boys or receive similar glances.

When mass was over, we were ushered out with the same order and precision as we had entered . . . clack! clack! clack! We went directly back upstairs to make our beds according to a pattern more than likely of Jesuit invention. The dormitory, even though the beds had received a thorough airing, was rank with the smell of piss from the "pisskers' section." Once the beds were made we were led downstairs.

7:25 A.M. Clang! Clang! Clang!

For once the prefect did not have to yell to bring about peace and order. The older boys, anxious to eat, assumed the role of enforcement officers, delivering what were called "rabbit punches" to those who persisted in talking, as samples of what was to come if the talker did not at once desist.

Silently we filed into the refectory, which, from the state of the furnishings and settings, was a more appropriate term than "dining room." There were sixteen long tables of an uncertain green flanked by benches of the same green. On each table were eight place settings, consisting of a tin pie plact, a tablespoon and a chipped granite cup. In the middle were two platters of porridge, which, owing to its indifferent preparation, was referred to as "mush" by the boys; there were also a box containing sixteen slices of bread, a round dish bearing eight spoons of lard (Fluffo brand), and a huge jug of milk. It was mush, mush, mush, sometimes lumpy, sometimes watery, with monotonous regularity every Monday, Wednesday, Friday and Saturday. The boys would have vastly preferred the Boston baked beans that, along with a spoonful of butter, were served on Tuesdays, Thursdays and Sundays.

Not until we had said grace — "Bless this mush," some boys said in secret, "I hope it doesn't doesn't kill us" — could we begin. But no matter how indifferent the quality, no boy, to my recollection, ever refused his portion of mush. During the meal there was little conversation except for the occasional "Pass the mush" or "Pass the milk" and the clatter of spoons, which served as knives and forks as well.

7:55 A.M. Clang! Clang! Clang!

After grace of thanksgiving, it was outside to the recreation hall. Except for the lucky ones in Grades 1, 2 and 3, everyone went to his assigned place of work. The seniors, in Grades 6, 7 and 8, went to their permanent occupations: to the barn, to tend horses, cows, sheep, pigs and all their products; to the chicken coop, to look after chickens; to the tailor shop, shoe shop, electrical shop, carpentry shop, blacksmith shop, mill or plumber's shack. These were jobs of standing and responsibility in the adolescent community. The other boys, from grades that had no status, waited outside the storeroom for the issue of mops, pails, sponges, soap, rags, brooms, dustpans, dust-bane and other janitorial paraphernalia for performing the menial tasks of washing, sweeping, mopping, dusting, polishing toilets, corridors, refectory, chapels, kitchen, dormitory, scullery, every conceivable area.

"*Johnston!* Number *forty-three!*"

"Yes, Father."

"I have special job for you," Father said, handing me a mop, pail, soap and a peculiar, curved oval brush such as I had never before seen. Up to this time in my life the hardest and most detestable forms of work that I had performed were reluctantly carrying either wood or water for my mother. I really didn't want to work but, if work I must, it was better to begin with something special rather than with some plebeian labour.

"Come with me!"

Father Buck led me directly to the toilets, which were so vile with the reek of human waste that I nearly choked and disgorged my mush. Even Father Buck, who must have been aged about twenty-three or twenty-four, gasped as he issued his instructions: "Wash the bowls with this and the walls with this, and the urinals with this, and the floors with this, no? . . . And make clean and smell good . . . no? I come back." I thought that Father Buck staggered slightly as he went out and breathed deeply to cleanse his lungs.

I too had to go out to avoid being overcome. While I stood outside breathing in oxygen, I developed a stratagem for cleaning up the toilets without collapsing. For self-preservation the job had to be done in stages. Flush the toilets, run outside. Wash the bowls, run outside. Hold breath, wash urinals, run outside. Hold breath, wash partitions, run outside. Spread sawdust on the floor, run outside. Sweep up sawdust, run outside. The toilets may not have completely lost their miasma of dung as I swept up the last pile of sawdust, but they at least looked vastly cleaner. I staggered out, inhaling huge quantities of the "breath of life," and waited, proud of my labours . . . almost.

"Achtung! You finish this, already?" Father asked as if he were astounded.

"Yes," I replied with a considerable burst of pride.

"Well! We shall see."

Father Buck didn't have to go into the lavatory to reach the conclusion that, "They not smell good." I was going to say that the smell was stuck in the walls, in the ceiling, on the floor, in the corners, everywhere, but I didn't get a chance. Father entered the lavatory and went directly into a compartment. Inside, he bent down in order to run his finger in the back of and under the bowl. He showed me a black fingertip.

"Sooooo! You like this fight but no like it work. Then you work extra week in these toilets until you learn it like work or until you learn it meaning of clean."

It was back to work.

8:50 A.M. Clang! Clang! Clang!

"Put it away tools."

From every part of the institution and the grounds boys scurried back to the recreation hall with their equipment.

8:55 A.M. Clang! Clang! Clang!

Line up again. According to the system then in operation half the senior boys went to class, while the other half went to work not only to practise a trade but also to provide the labour needed to run the institution. In the afternoon the seniors switched shifts. The younger boys went to classes the entire day.

"Number forty-*three*!"

There was no answer.

"Number forty-*three*!" A little louder.

Silence.

"You! Johnston!"

"Yes, Father!"

"You are number *forty-three*! Do you understand?"

I nodded.

"You answer, when I call *forty-three*!"

"Yes, Father."

"Now, you go with this Grade 5 to Father Mayhew's class."

"But Father, I'm supposed to be in Grade 6. I was in Grade 5 last year."

"Sooooo! You like it fight, you no like it work, and you like it argue!
. . . sooooo!" And Father Buck fished out of his cassock pocket a black
book in which he scribbled something while looking severely at me.
"Soooo, you say you in Grade 6. That's what they all say. Now you be
quiet. And no more trouble. You go with this Grade 5."

On the way upstairs, Ovilla Trudeau commented with a snicker,
"You didn't think you'd get away with that, did you?"

"What's that teacher's name? I can't understand dat pries'."

"Father Mayhew."

After the Lord's Prayer I went directly to the teacher's desk.

"Father. Someone made a mistake. I'm supposed to be in Grade 6. I
passed Grade 5 already. I tol' Father Buck, but he won't believe me."

Father Mayhew just looked at me. "I'm told you're in Grade 5.
There's nothing that you can do about it."

But my appointment to Grade 5, as I learned years later, was not a
product of misunderstanding but a coldly calculated decision made
"for my own good." For if I had been allowed to proceed to Grade 6 as
I should have been, it would have disrupted the entire promotion and
graduation schedule that decreed that all boys committed to a residential school remain in the institution until age sixteen, or until their
parents, if living together, arranged an early parole. If I had pro-
gressed at my normal rate through the elementary school I would
have been ready for "entrance examinations" by age twelve. According to the administration it would not have been appropriate or in the
best interests of society to release me or any one of my colleagues prior
to age sixteen. The only solution was to have a boy repeat grades until
Grade 8 and age sixteen were synchronized. I was not the only one to
be so penalized.

Hence I was mired in Grade 5, forced to listen to dull and boring
lessons rendered even duller and more boring by my sense of unjust
treatment. What unspeakable fate I might have suffered had it not
been for a collection of Tom Swift books and other volumes of
doubtful merit, it is hard to say. That Father Mayhew turned a blind
eye to my reading in class helped enormously; he didn't seem to mind
as long as I didn't disturb the class and passed the tests. The only time
I paid attention was during the reading of *The Song of Hiawatha*,
whose Indian words Father Mayhew mangled and garbled. Inspired
by the success of *Hiawatha*, Father Mayhew next tried to inflict
Winnie the Pooh and *Anne of Green Gables* on us, but we denounced

them as insipid so frequently that eventually Father Mayhew stopped reading them.

11:55 A.M. Clang! Clang! Clang!

Father Mayhew closed his book, looking relieved that the morning had finally come to an end. Wearily he made his way to the door, which he opened. Protocol decreed that he had to wait for Brother O'Keeffe to dismiss his class, the seniors, first. Only after Brother O'Keeffe and the seniors had gone out did Father Mayhew issue the order: "Okay!" As he did so, he stepped back to avoid being trampled by a rush of boys who leaped over desks and shoved one another in their anxiety to get out of the classroom. Moments later the "little shots" came down.

12:00 noon. Clang! Clang! Clang!

"*Line up! Shut up!*" The command need not have been shouted, but it was nevertheless bellowed, in the belief that a shout always obtained quicker compliance.

"Shshshshsh."

For dinner there was barley soup with other ingredients, including chunks of fat and gristle, floating about in it. Finding a chunk of fat in one's soup was like receiving a gift of manna, for it could be used to garnish the two slices of bread that came with the meal if one had lacked the foresight or the prudence to hide a chunk of lard from breakfast for one's dinner needs by sticking the lard under the table. Barley soup, pea soup (not the French or Quebec variety), green and yellow, vegetable soup, onion soup, for dinner and supper. Barley soup prepared in a hundred different combinations. "Barley soup! Don't that cook have no imagination?" Barley soup in the fall. "Hope they run outa that stuff pretty soon." Barley soup in the spring. "How much o' this stuff they plant, anyways? Hope a plague o' locusts eat all the barley this summer." Besides the soup there was a large jug of green tea diluted with milk. Clatter, clatter. "Pass the tea." Shuffle, scrape.

12:30 P.M. Clang! Clang! Clang!

After grace, except for the team scheduled to clean the refectory and wash dishes that week, everyone congregated near "the store" for the issue of baseball equipment before proceeding to one of the three baseball diamonds to play until 1:10, the seniors to the diamond hard by the chicken coop, the intermediates to the diamond near the horse barn and the juniors to the diamond near the windmill.

The only ones excluded from playing were the dishwashers, and the team not scheduled to play that day. The latter was required to provide umpiring, score-keeping and cheering services. Otherwise, there was no exemption for anyone. Cripples like Sam Paul were expected to, and did, derive as much fun and benefit from baseball, softball, touch football, basketball and hockey as Benjamin Buzwa and Eddie Coocoo; the stiff-jointed, like Reuben Bisto and David Jocko, were required to pursue fly balls or give chase to grounders with as much diligence if not grace as the more agile, like Steve Lazore and Tony Angus.

1:10 P.M. Clang! Clang! Clang!

This bell was harsher and therefore even more resented than the previous bells, for it put an end to forty minutes of relative freedom and distraction from sorrows. Hence bases, balls, bats, gloves and score-cards were collected — slowly — and returned to "the store" without haste. For the seniors, or the "big shots," as the intermediates sometimes referred to them, it was time to change shifts; for the rest of us, it was back to the dreary classroom with its dreary lessons . . . or to look out over the Spanish River, across the far portage at Little Detroit and beyond, into the dim shapes and shadows of the past or the physically distant, of mother and father and grandmother, of sisters and brothers and friends, of aunts and uncles and their friends, of happiness and freedom and affection . . . somewhere beyond Little Detroit . . . as distant as the stars.

4:15 P.M. Clang! Clang! Clang!

By now our sole preoccupation, as hunger displaced the shapes and shadows, was food. On our way downstairs one of our colleagues expressed our collective fear: "If I starve to death, it's going to be their fault; we never have enough but they have lots for themselves."

In the recreation hall a line formed bearing in the direction of the refectory, in front of whose doors was set one of the refectory tables. Behind this makeshift counter were two boys, one of whom was lopping off the green tops of carrots with a large butcher knife which he handled like a machete, while the other distributed two raw carrots to each customer. "Collation" they called this lunch. Today it was carrots; tomorrow it would be a wedge of raw cabbage; the day after, a turnip, raw like everything else. As each boy received his ration he was directed to take his collation outside. Despite its lofty name, collation was regarded as little better than animal fodder. Nevertheless, every boy ate the fodder to stave off starvation.

Collation was intended, I guess, not only to allay hunger pains, but also to restore flagging energies. It was our first real period of leisure in a day that had begun at 6:15 A.M., but if anyone hoped for or expected an extended period of idleness, as I then did, he was soon set straight by the sight of the accursed bell in Father Buck's hand.

"Hey! Father!" an anonymous voice called out. "How come you not eating carrots like us?" To which there was no answer.

4:30 P.M. Clang! Clang! Clang!

"Time for work, boys."

For me it was back to the lavatory. But with the five compartments or stalls in continuous occupation, as if most of the boys had suddenly been afflicted with a particularly virulent strain of diarrhea, I could not easily carry out Father Buck's instruction to "clean good." Even a lineup of boys outside commanding the occupants to "Hurry up! Ain't got all day!" could not make the incumbents accelerate the defecatory process. Sometimes threats worked. "Wait till you come out." Or, if threats and exhortations did not work, there was always "the drench," carried out by means of a wet rag squeezed over the top of the stall onto the incumbent. But this method of encouraging haste in the patrons only made my job worse.

4:55 P.M. Clang! Clang! Clang!

"*Line up! . . . Quiet.*"

After quiet was established the prefects counted heads in each line by waggling a pencil and mouthing numbers.

"Where's Shaggy [Joe Missabe]?"

"Helping Brother Grubb."

"Where's Cabootch?"

"Working for Brother Van der Moor."

The young priest made a notation in his little black book, frowning in worry as he did so. Later, he would check the work schedule and consult the brothers to verify the information given him. Woe betide the student who gave false information; double woe betide the absentee.

"All right! Upstairs, and no talking." Father Buck hated talking.

5:00 P.M. As we filed into the study hall, there was Brother Manseau from Asbestos, Quebec, standing to one side of the doorway, greeting the boys by name — or names. "Ah, Ti Phonse! Ti Bar Poot! Moustaffa! Monsieur le Snowball! Ti Blue!" Brother Manseau was of medium height, almost but not quite dark enough to be regarded as swarthy, with a light five o'clock shadow beclouding his face. His hair was grey and frizzy, swept back from his temples and from a point of recession at about the middle of his head, something like Harpo Marx's hair.

To the boys, Brother J.B. Manseau was B. J. or "Beedj-mauss" or "Beedj," from a reversal of his initials, which stood for "Jean-Baptiste." The "Beedj-mauss" also represented a play on words, which, if pronounced with the proper accent and inflection, would mean in our tribal language (Anishinaubae or Ojibway), "He comes reeking of the smell of smoke," a reference to Brother Manseau's pipe-smoking habit. He did not seem to mind "Hey Beedj!", just as he never seemed to mind too much a thumbtack on his seat. To my knowledge he never sent a boy to see Father Hawkins for punishment.

When he had settled down, Brother Manseau reminded us not to disturb him and, as an afterthought, gave us a verbal abstract of the book that he was then reading, *Twenty Thousand Leagues under the Sea*, by Jules Verne. After recommending that we read it, he warned us, "Now I don't want anybody to disturb me; I don't care what you do but don't bother me, otherwise, I kick his ass." And though Beedj had one short leg, he could deliver a mean kick, especially with the discarded Mountie's riding boots that he wore.

No one wanted his ass kicked, or to serve "jug" on Thursday; everyone settled down to do homework, draw, snooze or read, leaving Beedj-mauss to read his book undisturbed.

5:55 P.M. Father Buck slipped into the study hall almost as noiselessly as a ghost. He nodded for Brother Manseau to close his book, and Brother Manseau promptly disappeared. Believing that study was now over, many of us, in imitation of Brother Manseau, closed our books and put them away.

"STUDY IS NOT OVER! PUT THESE BOOKS BACK! AND NOT PUT AWAY TILL I TELL YOU!"

Father Buck looked at his watch. Not until the malefactors had reopened their books and resumed study, or appeared to do so, did the prefect dismiss us. Everything was by the clock, by the book, by regulations.

"Downstairs!"

6:00 P.M. Not one second before the minute or the hour would Father ring that bell, Clang! Clang! Clang! Clangity-clang! "Hurry up! Shshshsh!" There was silence, almost absolute except for the scuffle of boots and the odd sniffle and cough. This is the way it should have been, the way that it was intended to be, the way that would have gratified and edified the prefects and the way that would have pleased Father Buck.

Father Buck nodded, as he always did, to his colleague, Father Kehl, to open the door. In we filed and, for the next twenty minutes or a little longer, gave ourselves wholeheartedly to pea soup, bread, lard and green tea from Java. In quantity served there was just enough food to blunt the sharp edge of hunger for three or four hours, never enough to dispel hunger completely until the next meal. Every crumb was eaten, and the last morsel of bread was used to sponge up any residue of soup that might still be clinging to the sides or to the bottom of the plates, thereby leaving the plates clean and dry, the way puppies lick their dishes clean. There was the same quantity for every boy, regardless of size or need. Yet not even the "little shots," whose ingestive capacities were considerably less than those of their elders and who therefore should have required and received less, were ever heard to extol a meal with "I'm full." "I'm full" was an expression alien in our world and to our experience.

Never having the luxury of a second serving or an extra slice, the boys formed a healthy regard for food that bordered on reverence that shaped their eating habits. If they could not glut themselves, they could at least prolong the eating by carnally indulging in every morsel of food. To eat with such carnality may have constituted a sin, but we never considered it as such. Meals became rituals almost as solemn as religious services in their intensity, the only sounds the clatter of spoons on plates and mugs and the muted "Pass the mush" or "You owe me a slice"; "When you going to pay me that lard you owe me?"

"I'm so hungry right now, can you wait till tomorrow?"

As deliberate as the boys were at table, few could match the solemnity or the sensuousness with which "That's the Kind" (Jim Wemigwans) presided over his meal. During the entire course of supper "That's the Kind" broke his bread, one pinch at a time, as one might nip petals off a bloom; each pinch was then deposited with delicacy on his tongue. Our colleague ate every morsel, be it barley, green beans, peas, onions, potatoes — every spoonful of every meal — with as much deliberation and relish as if it were manna or ambrosia . . . or his last meal prior to execution.

6:30 to 7:30 P.M. If the prefects had not prearranged some event — swimming, a short walk, a choir practice, a game, a play practice — the hour was relatively free for the boys to do what they felt like doing. But it was during this free time that mischief and misdeeds were perpetrated and fights most often broke out. Hence, it was to forestall the commission of mischief and to reduce the number of fights that the administration planned each day — each hour — so that there was as little free time as possible.

Now such fights as did break out from time to time were in the main instigated merely to infuse some excitement into the monotony of institutional life, a monotony that may have suited the clergy, but was not to the liking of the boys.

Like many other pursuits and diversions in the school, fights were conducted according to certain customs and codes. They never broke out amid the shouts and accusations that usually precede fights, nor did one aggressor, as from ambush, spring upon his victim to deliver the coup de grace with one blow. Nor yet was a fight conducted to the finish. Not allowed during the course of a fight were kicking, biting, hitting an opponent from behind or striking an opponent while he was on the ground. No one was allowed to interfere on behalf of a friend or brother; every boy was expected to fight his own battles. Fights were to be fair and square.

By custom, the challenger, usually one of the intermediates anxious to prove his worth or to avenge some wrong, would deliberately seek out his foe with a wood chip or a flat stone on his shoulder, placed there either by his own hand or by that of someone else. In the school, "walking around with a chip on his shoulder" was not merely an expression but a literal reality. Some challengers, not satisfied with the obvious meaning of the act, issued a dare in addition: "Betcha too scairt to knock it off."

But no one was "too scairt" ever to refuse such a challenge, even if he knew from previous experience that he could never win in the proverbial "hundred years." For among the boys it had long been established that refusal was a sign of cowardice, and boys would sooner suffer a black eye, a bloodied nose or puffed lips than bear a reputation of being "yellow." Hence, it was a matter of honour for the challenged to rise to the dare and, with as much scorn and delibera- tion as he could muster, knock the chip off the challenger's shoulder. And there was no greater sign of contempt than, in knocking the chip off the shoulder, to brush the cheek of the challenger at the same time; to do so was comparable to a slap on the cheek with a pair of white gloves. In more formal fights, if there could be such things as more formal or less formal fights, a "second" would retrieve the chip and hand it to the challenged, who in his turn placed the object on his shoulder to make certain that the challenge was no bluff.

"Fight! Fight!" resounded throughout the recreation hall as the adversaries stood up to square off like boxers. The words were mag- netic, at once drawing an audience, prefects included, who formed a ring around the contestants.

It was Eugene Keeshig and Michael Taylor, two senior students (Grade 6) who could never see eye to eye on anything. They circled each other like professional boxers.

All of a sudden there was a "pow, pow, pow," and the next moment Mike was on the ground, stricken by three blows delivered with lightning speed by Eugene, who had launched himself forward with the suddenness of a panther. Eugene now stepped back to allow his opponent to get back on his feet. Once Mike was upright the fight resumed, arms flailing and fists driving forward like pistons, with some grunts and growls. The skirmish was spirited but brief. Down went Michael who, in a kneeling position, held up one hand as a sign of submission; with the other he held his nose to stanch the flow of blood.

The fight was over in five minutes, but not the feud. Mike would never yield to anyone — or to anything, for that matter. In his ongoing feud with Eugene and Charlie Shoot, Mike took many lumps in living up to the basic principles of survival at the school: "taking it like a man" and "toughing it out."

Sometimes in the cold dreary evenings of October and November, when the weather was too inclement for playing outside, the call "mushpot" rang out. Instantly, all the boys, including those well settled on the pottie, suspended their operations to answer the summons. No fireman or soldier responded to a call more quickly. No one wanted to be "it," "mushpot." Hence, when the cry was uttered, everyone scrambled for a place in the circle — seniors, intermediates and juniors, all except the babies.

The last to arrive, the one who was "it," fashioned a mushpot from an old rag or a handful of toilet tissue soaked in water, the soggier the better. With the dripping mushpot, the boy who was "it" ran around the perimeter of the circle proposing to plant the soggy object behind somebody. This was difficult to accomplish, because the boys in the circle kept a watchful eye on "it." For if one of the players failed to notice the mushpot behind him by the time "it" came back around, "it" was entitled by tradition to bash the victim over the head with the mushpot and to kick him "in de hass" at the same time. The boy so walloped now became "it." However, if the intended victim noticed the "plant" behind him, he instantly took up the mushpot and gave chase and, if he overtook the planter, was allowed by the rules to wallop him over the head with the mushpot, causing "it" to continue to be "it." Some mushpots couldn't take it. As well as being mushpots, they were soreheads.

"Come on, Father! You ring that bell too soon . . . jis' when we were having fun. You don' want us to have fun."

Bells and whistles, gongs and clappers represent everything connected with sound management — order, authority, discipline, efficiency, system, organization, schedule, regimentation, conformity — and may in themselves be necessary and desirable. But they also symbolize conditions, harmony and states that must be established in order to have efficient management: obedience, conformity, dependence, subservience, uniformity, docility, surrender. In the end it is the individual who must be made to conform, who must be made to bend to the will of another.

And because prefects were our constant attendants and superintendents, regulating our time and motions, scheduling our comings and goings, supervising our work and play, keeping surveillance over deeds and words, enforcing the rules and maintaining discipline with the help of two instruments of control and oppression — bells and the black book — we came to dislike and to distrust these young men. Most were in their early twenties and had completed their novitiate of four years' study at Guelph, Ontario. Regardless of their dispositions or their attitudes toward us, they were the archenemies, simply because they held the upper hand both by virtue of their calling and by the exercise of threats. If one of our fellow inmates grew too contumacious even for the strap there was always the "reform school."

While most of these young novices (referred to as first, second or third prefects) superintended our lives by the book, a few possessed a degree of compassion. But even they were helpless to show their sympathy in a tangible way, for the prefects, too, were under the close and keen observation of the Father Superior and "the Minister," the administrator of the school. During their regency, the prefects, sometimes called "scholastics" by the priests, had to demonstrate that they had the stuff to be Jesuits.

Once one of the boys, after being warned to "*Shut up!*," continued to whisper, or perhaps just uttered one more word, which, if left unsaid, would have rendered his entire message meaningless. It must have been a very important word to risk its utterance in the presence of Father Buck. Anyway, the prefect flew into a rage and struck the offender on the head with the bell. At least, it appeared as if Father Buck had clouted the offender with the bell, for he struck our colleague with the same hand in which he held the bell — not hard enough to draw blood but forcefully enough to raise a contusion and to elicit an "Eeeeeyow!" and cause the victim to clutch his head in pain.

Even before the outcry had subsided, the senior boys at the back — Renee Cada, Tom White, Louis Mitchell, Jim Coocoo, John Latour and Louis Francis — protested: "Come on, Father! That's going too far." They wrenched the bell from Father Buck's hand and threatened to knock him on the head to "See how you'd like it. . . ."

The boy who had seized the bell raised his hand as if to strike . . . but, instead of bringing it down on Father Buck's head, returned the instrument to the disconcerted young prefect, whose face turned from ash to crimson and then back again. Had our colleague carried out his threat, he would most likely have been committed to the nearest reformatory, and also excommunicated from the church. There was a hushed silence throughout the recreation hall, both at the moment the bell was suspended over the prefect's head and afterward.

Father Buck opened the door in silence. What saved the senior boys then and other boys on other occasions from retribution was the prefect's own uneasiness about his superiors. Of course, we knew nothing of the prefects' fears.

9:00 P.M. At that hour we were dismissed from study (the babies having gone to bed at 7:30) to retire to the dormitory where everyone — or nearly everyone — loitered around the washing area, either brushing his teeth or washing . . . or just pretending to wash. Anything to waste time. While many boys dallied near and around the trough, others made their way to the infirmary, there to linger and to have their pains, bruises, aches and cuts attended to by Brother Laflamme.

9:25 P.M. The lights were switched on and off in a radical departure from bell clanging as a signal for all the boys to return to their bedsides.

"Kneel down and say your prayers."

We prayed, imploring God to allow us release from Spanish the very next day.

9:30 P.M. "All right! Get in bed . . . and no noise!"

The lights went out. The only illumination in the dormitory came from two night lights glowing red like coals at either end of the ceiling of the huge sleeping quarters. In the silence and the darkness it was a time for remembrance and reflection. But thoughts of family and home did not yield much comfort and strength; instead such memories as one had served to inflame the feelings of alienation and abandonment and to fan the flames of resentment. Soon the silence was broken by the sobs and whimpers of boys who gave way to misery and sadness, dejection and melancholy, heartache and gloom.

Besides the sobs and whimpers, which would come to an end by the finish of a boy's first week at the school, there were the muted fall of footsteps and the faint motion of the phantom form of the prefect as he patrolled the dormitory.

"Shut up!"

But the dormitory was not always given to either golden or angelic silence or to the frigid winds that blew in through the open windows or to maudlin whimperings. More often there were muted whispers commingled with muffled giggles from the various regions of the dormitory. Sometimes one boy would cup his hand under his armpit and bring his arm down abruptly to produce a most obscene backfire, such as one would hear in a horse barn produced by an overwrought horse. Within moments there would be similar eruptions all over the dormitory.

For the prefects, who had a highly developed sense of law and regulation and of what was proper and improper, these night watches must have been harrowing. They were ever on the prowl to quell sobs, whispers or whatever disturbed the silence. They dashed from one side to the other in a vain attempt to catch the guilty party by asking for a confession. "Who makes thees noise?" For all the good their investigations did, they might as well have tried to quell spring peepers in a pond in May.

But there were times when Father Buck and Father Kehl brought the harassment on themselves.

Late at night they would sometimes confer in hushed but excited tones.

"Father! Did you hear the news today? The Fatherland sunk two hundred thousand tons of these enemy ships. Heil Hitler."

There was always someone awake, someone to hear, someone to whisper aloud, "Nazi"; and the word "Nazi" echoed and re-echoed throughout the dormitory.

"Who says thees?"

"Nazi," in the north corner.

"Who says thees?"

"Nazi," in the south end.

"Who says thees?"

"Nazi."

Eventually the two prefects would have to terminate the search and punish everyone by making us all stand stock still by our bedsides for half an hour.

Then to prevent being understood they spoke in German, with even worse results.

Eventually they stopped talking to one another in the dormitory; and finally they learned that it was better to grit their teeth and to bear whatever names the boys called them. And in due time, the boys too desisted in their practice of calling names.

For some, sleep, the friend of the weary and troubled, came soon; for others, later.

Though some days were eventful and were memorable for some reason, most passed by as the seconds, the minutes and the hours mark the passage of time, in work, study, prayer and proper play. Were it not for the spirit of the boys, every day would have passed according to plan and schedule, and there would have been no story.

6:15	Rise
6:45-7:25	Mass
7:30-8:00	Breakfast
8:05-8:55	Work
9:00-11:55	Class/work
12:00-12:25	Dinner
12:30-1:10	Sports/games/rehearsal
1:15-4:15	Class/work
4:15-4:30	Collation
4:30-4:55	Work/chores
5:00-5:55	Study
6:00-6:25	Supper
6:30-7:25	Sports/games/rehearsal
7:30-10:00	Study and prepare for bed

Holidays and Holy Days

"Holiday tomorrow."

"Tomorrow? But it's only Thursday. . . . Whoever heard of a holiday on Thursday?"

"That's when there's holidays here, don't you know?"

"That's good!"

"You won't think it's so good tomorrow," Bearskin (Norman Simon) warned a newcomer, Irvin Contin.

"How long you been here?"

"Two years."

"And you don't have a holiday on Saturday?"

"No! It's so's we won't meet the girls, who have their holidays on Saturdays."

Bearskin was right. Thursday was not a holiday in the ordinary sense of the word; it was not spent in the way most people spend their time off — sleeping in, fishing, hunting, picnicking or simply doing nothing. No! Thursday was not really a day off, except for the teachers. It's true that we slept in for half an hour or so, and that we were served Boston baked beans, and that there were no classes, but Thursday was chiefly a day of labour that was almost as rigidly scheduled and regimented as any other day, apart from a few minor adjustments in time. Only three to four hours of Thursday could be regarded as time off.

After breakfast it was off to work till noon or until excused, with each one going to his appointed place of labour. Tailors went to the tailor shop, shoemakers to the shoe shop, farmhands to the cow barn or the horse barn, swineherds and shepherds to the pens, electricians, plumbers, carpenters and painters to report to one of the laymen — Gerry Labelle, Joe Albo or Clem Eicheldinger — for assignment. Intermediates and juniors collected their janitorial apparatus to scrub, scour and shine the building from top to bottom, from stem to stern.

During this work period there were frequent inspections conducted by Father Hawkins, the administrator (or "Minister") of the school, who made his rounds to check up on the work and on the labourers. Lucky were the janitors who, when they were finished and their work was judged satisfactory, were excused and allowed to play ball or skate until noon. From the time work commenced till 10:00 or 10:30 (or until the house-keeping chores were completed), the janitors worked diligently. But for those on lavatory detail there was no early reprieve, because lavatory duty was used as a means of straightening someone's attitude, especially that of newcomers, and as a means of punishment for the hard-headed; scrubbing toilet bowls and urinals was degrading and torturous. No early reprieve could be expected until one was properly penitent and determined to mend his attitude.

Of all the menial jobs, the most sought after were those of bull cook in the kitchen and cleaner of the priests' refectory. There, in either place, one could eat leftovers — bacon, eggs, toast, jam, roast beef, roast pork. And if there were no leftovers, the kitchen help and the fathers' refectory workers had a system of signals (which worked in the mornings only) for ordering an extra service of food.

One stratagem was for the fathers' refectory workers to send down one plate instead of the entire collection of dirty dishes on the dumbwaiter. One of the bull cooks' duties was to unload the dumbwaiter; seeing a single plate, they would relay an order to the cook for poached, fried or scrambled eggs. The other ploy was simple and direct. One of the refectory boys would whip the dumbwaiter rope against the passageway and order breakfast from his accomplice downstairs.

On Thursdays, work in the kitchen, for which the workers had to get up earlier than other boys, was wearying. Not only had the bull cooks to slice bread, cut butter, scoop out spoons of lard from pails, wash pots and pans, peel potatoes, carrots and other monstrosities and wash same, they also had to scrub the floors. But at least the kitchen workers didn't have to eat "sad ol' mush" or "barley soup" for an entire week.

After having served various terms in recreation hall, corridors, dormitory and chapels, I was finally detailed to kitchen duty, along with Tommy Diabo, Norbert Debossige and Martin Assiniwe.

On this particular Thursday, by working diligently, we completed our chores by 10:30 A.M. and received permission from Mr. Robert Pilon, the school's Ojibway cook, to be excused until 11:30, along with a warning to keep out of sight.

There was no better place to keep out of sight than in the cellar playing war, we decided after a brief consultation. With ample ammunition in the form of rotten potatoes, we could wage a fine long war behind walls, pillars, piles of wood and other natural fortifications. To decide who would be the Germans and who the English, we drew lots. Tommy and I were to be the Germans. Once war got underway in the gloom of the cellar there were only muffled footsteps, scurrying shadows and the hiss and splat of flying missiles.

It was at this most feverish pitch of battle that Father Buck stealthily opened the door that connected the main cellar to the kitchen storeroom, gingerly stepped over the threshold and pussyfooted forward, directly into the line of fire. We had neither the time nor the means to warn our colleagues. I was wedged behind the door.

The British had suspended their fire for a while, waiting for the right moment. All at once there was a shout of "Fire!," followed by a barrage of missiles and cries of "Take that, you Hun" and "One for Hitler" as they scored direct hits. One missile struck Father Buck full in the head before he let loose a torrent of what sounded like German blasphemy. Neither Tommy nor I remained on the battlefield to assess the damage done to Father Buck, much as we would have liked to see the gore of mushy potatoes. As soon as I had a chance, I retreated to the kitchen and found a clean pot, which I began to scrub fervently.

Within moments Father Buck bounded into the kitchen, not quite out of breath but breathing hard. Had he been a dragon, he would have been breathing flames. His hair was matted, his sweater was polluted with potato mush, and his eyes were aflame with vengeance and destruction. He seized the cook's puddling paddle, which he brandished like a war club.

I took instant flight to the opposite side of the great butcher's table to keep out of range and to stave off destruction as long as possible. Twice we ran around the table. Unable to close the gap between us, Father Buck mounted the table. I dove under so that I was looking right side up at Father Buck, who was looking upside down at me. Anyone seeing us would have thought we were at play, instead of engaged in a deadly business.

It was at this moment, fortunately as it turned out for me, that Bob Pilon returned to the kitchen. I had been thinking of throwing myself on the mercy of Father Buck.

"Heeeeey! Get off my table!" Bob cried out.

Father Buck dismounted and, without a word to Mr. Pilon, collared me. I put my arms over my head and closed my eyes. "Leave him alone, Father. Not in my kitchen." It is significant that by saying "Not in my kitchen," Bob was consenting to my destruction elsewhere.

"*Just you wait! I fix you!*" Father Buck snarled at me on his way out.

As the door to the scullery closed behind the prefect's departing figure, Norbert, Martin and Tommy skulked back into the kitchen, looking worried and guilty.

"What were you boys up to, anyway?" Bob Pilon asked. "I thought I told you to keep out of sight."

"Well, we didn't know it was him. I thought it was Tommy, or Basil here, an' we let 'im have it," Norbert explained. Martin giggled as if he didn't have a care in the world. "We didn't mean it, honest," Norbert continued. "We was having a war with potatoes, the rotten ones . . . an' he jis' got in the way. It was his own fault for sneaking around."

"I don't like to say it, an' it's even less nice to think it," Bob said, "but it couldn't happen to a nicer guy."

It was comforting, but not by much, to have Mr. Pilon almost approve of what we had done. Bleakly we resumed our chores, peeling potatoes and vegetables in preparation for supper.

"Do you know what these boys did?" Bob asked his wife when she came back in.

"No. I can't imagine."

"They ambushed Father Buck and pelted him with rotten potatoes. Ha! ha! ha! ha!"

"Oh, my God!" Mrs. Pilon gasped, putting a hand over her mouth in horror.

What hope was there for reprieve from reformatory? From a thrashing? From excommunication? Might Father Buck somehow forget, or maybe relent? Never. Our only hope, Tommy's and mine, was for Norbert and Martin both to confess at once.

"Hey, Norbert. Whyncha go to Father Buck and tell him that you hit 'im?"

"Whatcha think? I'm crazy?" That ended that hope.

We worked during the entire lunch hour without the usual banter, fully expecting Father Hawkins to make his appearance at any moment. Before going out to the yard, we waited until the last moment, just as the bell was ringing, then, as quickly as we could, we mingled with the crowd, standing behind bigger boys to avoid detection.

"Well! Where you want to go today?" Father Buck asked the seniors. Such a question was more form than a genuine exercise of the democratic process, for what possible consensus could there be, when there were so many factions and preferences? There was a babel of choices . . . "Rangers' Camp! . . . Maple Leafs' Camp . . . No! Canadiens' Camp . . . Black Hawks' Camp . . . Let's go to Smith's Lake . . . Brennan Harbour . . . Toward Walford . . . Naw! Let's go toward Cutler . . . There's nothin' there. . . ."

Then there was Charlie Shoot's gang — Angus Pitwaniquot, Eugene Keeshig, Johnny Migwans, Antoine Lafrance — all of them chanting, "Canadiens' Camp! Canadiens' Camp! Canadiens' Camp!"

In days gone by these camps had actually been camps with buildings on them serving as quarters for the teams. But now these places were camps in name only; the buildings, through neglect, had collapsed into heaps of weathered planks and boards. Still, staff and boys continued to refer to these sites as camps, and used them as assembly points on Thursday walks.

For Charlie and his gang of hunters, there was only one place . . . Canadiens' Camp, which was infested with rabbits. To go to Canadiens' Camp meant for Charlie and his gang a chance to do what they most preferred to do, and, if they were lucky, to come by a meal for themselves. In this the cooks at the school always obliged enterprising boys by cooking a rabbit or a partridge or a fish. On more than one occasion this group, armed with slingshots and lead pellets, had killed enough rabbits — between forty and fifty — to feed the entire student body and faculty. But much as the rest of the boys were obliged to the hunters for the occasional feast, they did not regard Thursday afternoon primarily as a time for hunting expeditions. There were other things to be done.

"Smith's Lake," Father Buck declared without counting either heads or hands. It was all democratic. Grumbles of "There's nothing there!" and "Can't hunt there!" greeted the decision.

"Okay, boys! Let's go."

During the election I fully expected my name and number to be called out in order for me to remain behind and to report to Father Hawkins. But there was no summons, and it was with a little relief that we set out with our companions. Even though our names were not called out I remained full of misgivings, and I proceeded to the head of the column to be as distant from the prefect as possible.

At Smith's Lake the boys dispersed, friends gathering in small clutches and knots to exchange tales of injustice, recount humorous incidents that had occurred during the past week, or scheme how best to get revenge on a prefect or relive the last baseball game. To talk, as I imagine other boys our age did, about the latest adventure of Batman or the exploits of the Shadow; or to compare the relative merits of a Packard and a Studebaker; or to speculate on the earning powers of lawyers, doctors and engineers; or even to contemplate our future careers, professional or otherwise, was beyond our experience and imagination. Our sole aspiration was to be rescued or released (it didn't much matter which) from Spanish, and to be restored to our families and homes. That was the sum total of our ambitions. Our vision did not extend beyond the horizon; our world was confined to the playground and the west wing of the building enclosed by fences and walls. The outer world and events taking place therein were as distant and as alien as Mars. The future was tomorrow; beyond that we could not see. But there were some lucky ones — Tom White, Louis Mitchell, John Latour, James Coocoo, Tom Sarazin, Harpie Penassie, Joe Thompson, Renee Cada, Louis Francis — who had a future and who could look ahead and see beyond tomorrow. During the coming months they would be sixteen and allowed to leave Spanish. Everything else, the war included, found no place in our minds or in our discussions.

While the rest of us sat or lounged under a tree, Paul Migwanabe was putting the finishing touches on his latest carving — a boat, a plane, a car, a tank, a jeep, a toy house, a truck or some other article. If he wasn't whittling something, he was looking for a piece of wood; he was always carving. Same with Joe Thompson. Joe was a Mohawk from St. Regis, who, from Brother O'Keeffe's descriptions of a crossbow, had made several of these weapons. Only after Joe and his companions were caught slaughtering chickens and had riddled one wall of the recreation hall in target practice were the crossbows confiscated, and Joe was forbidden to make more of these deadly instruments.

At 3:20 the whistle sounded to recall the boys to assembly. It was an anxious time for the prefect, the interval after blowing his whistle until the boys returned and were all accounted for. That some boy or boys might make their escape during the afternoon must have been constantly on his mind. He must have speculated about what penalty he would have to pay for his negligence. And he must often have wished he were elsewhere: Montreal, Kingston, Halifax, Winnipeg, Regina ... India ... Iran — any place but Spanish. Spanish was known as an institution that made or unmade priests, and young men who had just completed four years of their novitiate at Guelph must have dreaded assignment in northern Ontario. Father Buck counted the boys, not once but twice. He even smiled.

So meticulous was the timing that we arrived back at the school in roaring hunger at 4:15, just in time for collation. Afterwards it was back to schedule: work, study and supper.

After supper there was still no summons for any of us, but there was not much relief in this. Always there was the next hour, and the next. Sooner or later what we had done would catch up to us.

Every Thursday night there were confessions to be made, regardless of guilt or innocence. Everyone was expected to go: the sinner who had sinned and needed to be shriven, and he who had followed instructions the previous week to "go my son and sin no more." Everyone had to go on the premise that no one was perfect; all were sinners. But if we felt aggrieved by the frequency of our confessions we were lucky compared to our predecessors of just two years before who, we never knew why, had been required to go to confession not only on Thursdays but on Tuesdays and Saturdays as well. Perhaps they were more sinful than we.

To purge us of our sins there were four resident confessors, fathers Richard, Dufresne, Belanger and Vandriessch, often assisted by a visiting missionary priest, fathers Barker, Rolland, Dwyer or O'Flaherty.

Of these confessors fathers Richard and Belanger were to be avoided. When the confessors entered the confessionals, therefore, the boys quickly formed lines outside the cubicles of the "easy" priests who, for penance, directed penitents to say "One Our Father, one Hail Mary and one Glory Be. . . ." The prefect did his best to ensure that each confessor had his fair share of sinners; but of course as soon as the prefect had gone from the chapel to attend to his other duties the boys returned to their former places, or to some other line, where they commenced impious shoving and pushing to gain some advantage in a line. The object was to be neither too near the front nor too far to the rear; the closer to the front, the sooner one would have to report to study; the closer to the back, the greater the risk of ending up in Father Richard's confessional.

Father Richard had his own means of getting his fair workload. If there were a noticeable decline in the rate of entry of sinners to his confessional, Father would come out of the small chapel to summon the wicked.

"Any more sinners?"

If sinners did not voluntarily accept his invitation, Father Richard, though very old (in his late eighties) and half blind and frail, would shuffle to the longest line to relieve an easy confessor of half his burden, always the hind end. "You come with me." And heaven help the sinner who returned to his line or took refuge in some other line. Despite his failing sight, Father Richard knew the boys well.

Sinner and innocent alike, we soon got the hang of confessing.

It would never do to go into the confessional, as Donald Fox once did, and say "Father, I didn't do nothing bad . . . an' I didn't think of nothing bad all week."

"How dare you say such a thing, *you sinner, you*. Only the angels and the saints can say that. You don't expect me to believe what you told me! You must have done or said or thought something wrong. Come now. You are a sinner just like everyone else. No one can go without sin for a week. You are not perfect. I know that, me."

Nor would it do to own up to too many lapses. "Father! Forgive me for I have sinned. Since my last confession one week ago, I got mad seven times, and I lied ten times." To have got mad seven times and to have prevaricated ten times did not reflect a proper degree of remorse and represented little effort to improve.

Three was a good number, neither too pious nor too dissolute. "I fought three times during this past week" was credible and acceptable.

With Father Belanger the most venial of sins contained within it the potential for greater evil that could be transformed into a cardinal sin and ultimately global catastrophe. The confession of anger deserved more than an act of contrition and the assessment of penance; it deserved a sermon.

"Ah! Anger! Not for nothing is it regarded as one of the cardinal sins. Think on it, my son. It is small in itself, no more than a flash, a feeling of doing hurt to someone to get even. Sometimes it flares up and is soon forgotten. Other times it lingers and swells like an abscess, becoming stronger until at last it turns into rage and will not abate. It takes hold of the mind and the spirit and beclouds the judgment; it strangles charity, good will, kindness, and breeds envy, revenge, prejudice, and becomes *hate* . . . *hate* that needs to be fulfilled in the world. Satan himself fuels and fans the flames of *hate* and transforms them into quarrelling, slander, contumely, fighting, hurting, wounding, injuring, maiming, murder . . . and war. That is why there is a war today, my son. It is the cause of war. . . . Do you understand that?

"My son! Don't you see the danger? the potential outcome of even the smallest sin? Don't you see why you must control your passions and pray for grace?" . . . and on and on Father Belanger would talk until the penitent was either thoroughly bored or scared stiff that he would, sooner or later, commit some worse offence if he didn't mend his mind and his ways. And to assist the penitent with remorse, Father Belanger conferred the sentence, "For your penance, you will say the Rosary five times. Go my son, and sin no more."

It was only fitting, then, having had our souls cleansed, that our persons be cleansed as well. After study, commencing with the youngest and ending with the oldest, there were showers and a change of clothing and bedding for everyone.

Still the expected summons didn't come — "Norbert, Martin, Tommy, Basil, go see Father Hawkins."

We went to sleep, the sleep of unease.

On Friday we expressed the hope, "Maybe he'll forget. Maybe Father Hawkins is away. Haven't seen T'in Beak for the last few days." (The boys called Father Hawkins "Thin Beak" from the prominence of his nose, but it wasn't long before Brother Manseau's pronunciation — "T'in Beak" — caught on.)

Saturday, still no words.

At least on Sunday, the other day off, no one but the kitchen and barn workers had to work. But we did spend considerable time in devotions, in our opinion far too much. Now if we thought that we spent too much time in prayer by attending two masses in the morning, one at 7:30, the other at 10:30, plus Benediction in the evening, it was nothing compared to what our predecessors had had to undergo just the year before: two masses in the morning, Benediction in the afternoon and Vespers in the evening.

At 10:15 A.M., we were herded from the study hall to the dormitory to wash, comb our hair and put on over our beige shirts our Sunday best — a faded maroon sweater — in order to be as presentable as possible for High Mass at 10:30.

In the winter months, while the rest of us were labouring over our hair and making such preparations as were required to enhance our appearance, two of our colleagues were dispatched to the girls' school to draw a sled bearing Miss Leutsch, who was unable to navigate in the snow owing to a heavy elevated shoe that she wore to compensate for her short leg.

Like most of her sorority in the Daughters of Mary (an order outlawed in France during the French Revolution), Miss or Sister Leutsch was a very severe woman, a trait that added to our misery during the interminably long and much-too-frequent choir practices. As a musician and an organist, she could not tolerate mistakes, and would make us sing passages again and again until she was satisfied that no note was abused. She also taught music armed with a pointer that served as a baton. With this pointer she would crack the knuckles of Bearskin (Norman Simon) or Boozo (Harold Belleau) if they happened to play fortissimo instead of pianissimo during practice.

The teamsters were usually respectful when they called on the sister. "Good morning, Miss Leutsch." For her mean temper and sour disposition the boys privately called her "Miss Slush" or "Short-Leg."

"Now boys," she would command imperiously, pointing her black cane like a rapier. "I don't want any nonsense, otherwise Father Hawkins will hear about it. Just you remember what happened to those hooligans last week. There is no need to gallop like a team of wild horses." And she would board, with difficulty, the little sled that had a special backrest made just for her.

If Miss Leutsch had not mentioned "horses" and "galloping," it is quite possible that the boys might not have got anything into their heads. But, on the other hand, there was that extra-long practice last week for which she deserved something in return. Hardly had the words "horses" and "galloping" tumbled out of Miss Leutsch's mouth than the teamsters broke into a trot, causing the good sister to raise her voice.

"STOP IT! STOP IT THIS INSTANT, I TELL YOU! I WILL REPORT YOU! STOP IT!"

As if urged on, the teamsters accelerated their pace, running not quite fast enough to capsize the sled when they turned left at the main road, yet fast enough to send the vehicle skidding sideways. To scare Miss Leutsch in this manner did not merit punishment, and it often amused the priests. Now, instead of the imperious command "STOP IT THIS INSTANT," there came a series of moans and whines from the bundle of blankets that covered Miss Leutsch: "Eeeeeee-oooooh-aaaaah."

"Hang on, Sister. Gotta run. It's cold," the boys yelled back as they raced down the short stretch of road from St. Joseph's to St. Peter Claver's. In turning right at the main entrance, the teamsters miscalculated their speed, though they had let up their pace just a little. The little sled bearing Miss Leutsch skidded sideways, mounted the snowbank and turned over in mid-air, dumping the screaming sister in the snow.

The teamsters, like good Samaritans, rushed to the sister's side and encumbered her with aid and solicitous inquiries: "Are you okay, Miss Leutsch? We didn't mean to; it was a accident."

Through snow-encrusted lips Miss Leutsch sputtered, "I'm reporting you. Just you wait and see."

Though every trip from school to church and back again must have been like a roller-coaster ride for Miss Leutsch, not all of them ended in an accident. The careening rides that the sister endured from time to time were about the only thrills that she must have had in decades of pious existence.

From 10:30 till 12:00 noon we prayed and chanted lustily one of the several styles of Gregorian chants that we had got to know through hours of practice under the direction of Miss Leutsch.

While Mass was a solemn occasion in the exercise of piety, it was also a time for indulging in impious thoughts. Only a few sidelong glances at the girls gave us reason enough to "bemoan our outcast state and trouble deaf heaven with our bootless cries." The girls wore fine dresses, fine coats, fine hats, fine shoes; some even wore gloves and carried little handbags. On the other hand, our finest garment was a faded maroon sweater handed down from previous generations. The girls, we had heard, ate Corn Flakes, Puffed Rice and Rice Krispies; all we could look forward to was "sad ol' mush." No wonder, then, that the girls were plump. Instead of being thankful for our blessings, as we were encouraged to be, we were incited to envy; often did we wish we were under the care of nuns or that the priests had been endowed with as much humanity, understanding and compassion as the Daughters of Mary.

Besides stirring in us thoughts or feelings of envy during mass, the girls inspired in some of our more imaginative colleagues bursts of creativity. One poor girl whose hair had been completely shorn, for "hygienic reasons," upon her arrival in Spanish, was promptly and permanently nicknamed "Haircut." From her height, Tillie Lavalley was known as "Tall Indian." For wearing a pink-ribboned straw hat Angeline Trudeau earned the name "Farmer's Hat." Because their father, David Solomon, was in the habit of chewing tobacco and was commonly referred to as Dave Plug, all his daughters — Eleanor, Doris, Lillian and Joyce — were christened "Plugs." Besides being a "Plug," Lillian, someone noticed, had a cute turned-up nose. Thereafter, she was "Up-shoot." A few girls derived their names from their brothers. Joe Cameron, whose tribal language operated well without the "x", "l", "r", "v" and "f", had difficulty in twisting his tongue around these strange and peculiar consonants; when asked his name, he could do no better than "Camelon," which was abbreviated to Camel. Joe's sister became She-camel. The moment Alex Restoule stepped into the recreation hall as a new student he became "Mars" to betoken his distinctive ears. His sister was henceforward Miss Mars. The villagers who attended our chapel also received names. There were two young ladies whose legs were as thick and as shapely as cedar trunks; they became simply "Logs." Another young lady became "Pau-pau-sae" (Woodpecker) for the sharpness of her nose and other facial features. Then there was poor old "Kiss-ass," an older man whose Indian name, Keezis (sun), was corrupted. Mass was not always spent in worship.

After mass it was back upstairs to put away our "Sunday best" and to settle down in our beds as if we were fast asleep, in preparation for the weekly fire drill. As soon as the fire alarm gonged, the senior boys, each of whom was assigned to rescue one of the "babies," collected their wards and, bearing them koala-bear style, slid down the metal poles from the third storey to the second-floor landing, then transferred themselves and their burdens to another pole and slid on down to the ground, a distance of fifteen metres. After them came the rest of the boys, who turned the drill for life into an exercise in survival; they dropped from landing to landing to ground one after another as linemen or lumberjacks do from poles and posts. The idea, developed long before our time by other boys, was to parachute as fast as possible without being crowned by the next evacuee. No matter how agile the boys, there were accidents: bruised shoulders, scraped heads, but nothing serious.

A collision was always followed by a grumble: "Come on! Watch out!"

As usual in accidents of this kind, the accused pleaded innocence or offered an excuse. "It was jis' a accident. Anyways it's your fault for being too slow. You should git outta the way fas'er than that."

"Nah! You musta jis' been 'meaning it,' " the injured one would complain, articulating an expression in use at the time that could mean one of two things; when it didn't mean "on purpose intentionally, deliberately," as it did on this occasion, it meant the opposite, "pretending."

From the bottom of the fire escapes the boys ran to the front of the recreation hall, where they lined up to be counted. There would hardly have been time to escape during the short interval between the end of mass and the end of the fire drill, but counted we nevertheless were.

Meanwhile "the babies" gathered around Father Mayhew as chicks gather around their mother, cheeping "Father! Father! Father!" and following him around wherever he went. They were a sad lot, this little crowd of babies; they seldom laughed or smiled and often cried and whimpered during the day and at night. Having no one in this world, in this institution, except this young scholastic to look to, to call for, to touch, to hold, these little waifs were even more wretched than we were. If they weren't huddled around the young scholastic's knee, they were hunched in their wretchedness and misery in a corner of the recreation hall, their outsized boots dangling several inches above the asphalt floor. And though Paul Migwanabe and Joe Thompson and other carvers made toys for them, the babies didn't play with their cars and boats; they just held on to them, hugged them and took them to bed at night, for that was all they had in the world when the lights went out, and they dared not let it go. On occasion the older boys acted as guardians or as big brothers to these cast-offs, holding their hands and comforting them with, "What's wrong?" "Don't cry," "It's going to be all right." But the burden of care for these babies fell on the young scholastics, who had a much more fatherly air than the senior boys in Grades 7 and 8.

There were two young men who, by disposition and temperament, were well suited to look after the little ones. The first was Father "Barney" Mayhew, S.J., a man of tremendous compassion and understanding, who served the "natives" until his recent retirement. During those years of ministry, he even acquired an "Indian outlook." He was always like an indulgent uncle.

The other, Father Schretlin, S.J., who came some years later, was made of sterner stuff, with a strong predilection for law, order and discipline. In no time after his appointment to Spanish, Father Schretlin had the little guys organized. From the way he had his charges standing at attention and in soldierly posture and formation we believed that he had a military background. But from the way the little shots cheerfully stood at attention on command, "forward marched" and followed him around, Father Schretlin must have been father, brother and uncle all rolled into one.

Though Father Schretlin had abundant patience with the young, he had not the same forbearance with the high-school-age boys. Just how short his patience was we didn't know until Dominic McComber, our Mohawk friend from Caughnawaga, put it to the test. It happened in the following manner.

We had already been counted after the Sunday fire drill and dismissed, when Dominic stepped forward, remaining on the grounds to observe the "little shots" who were then standing at attention while undergoing inspection.

Just from the way Dominic was standing reviewing the inspection of the "troops" we knew that something heavy was on his mind.

"*Charge, men! Charge!*" he bellowed all at once, like a sergeant.

There was a pause, a moment of suspense, as the "little shots" stood open-mouthed, not knowing quite what to do, whether to charge or not. Father Schretlin stood speechless, transfixed by Dominic's audacity. But the suspense lasted no more than three seconds. The next thing we saw was Father Schretlin, soutane flapping, in full and instant pursuit. Astonished by the sudden onslaught, Dominic wasted not a moment in beating a retreat toward the chicken coop.

"Well, gentlemen," Cec King observed, "you are about to witness the martyrdom of a Mohawk at the hands of a Jesuit," showing his command of the language and grasp of the situation. Even Frank Commanda, preoccupied though he was with the forthcoming game, had to laugh.

But before they reached the coop Father Schretlin broke off the pursuit, unable to close in on Dominic. Never had we seen our colleague run faster.

On the father's return to his undismissed squad, we struggled to wipe the smiles and grins from our faces and to don suitably grave expressions. Our demeanour would have compared favourably to that of the most severe Baptist or Puritan.

"Dismissed," said Father Schretlin curtly, omitting all intermediate commands.

With Dominic we had a field day of teasing. Julius Niganigijig promised that we would all pray while Dominic was being burned at the stake. Cec assured Dominic that the Ojibways would never surrender a Mohawk to the enemy — so long as Dominic sacrificed a chunk of lard for his safety.

While Sunday mornings were reserved for prayer and study, the afternoons — weather permitting — were set aside for baseball, softball or hockey, depending on the season. For weather to permit we prayed·mightily to Kitchi-Manitou in the firm conviction that He would withhold rain, brimstone and snow until after the games had been played.

It had long been a tradition to play Sunday-afternoon exhibition games with the staff or teams from Spanish, Cutler, Sagamok, Little Current, Massey and Espanola. The names White, Latour, Mitchell, Francis, Lazore, Penassie, Keeshig and Akiwenzie were already legend. Boys and staff recounted with awe Sa-faw-saw's (Louis Francis's) feat of striking out fourteen of the eighteen batters he faced in one game.

In those days, when our predecessors were establishing a reputation for skill and sportsmanship, travel in the north was by train or bus over milk-route railway runs and roads that were little better than wagon trails. These sometimes interfered with games. Once, just to play a baseball game with the Timiskaming team in Cutler, the boys walked from the school to Cutler, a distance of better than six miles. The Timiskaming team didn't show up, owing to a series of flat tires their bus suffered. Back walked the boys.

Among the opposing teams there was only one right-hander, a tall good-natured young man who could "burn them in" in the general direction of home plate. When he was pitching it was standard practice to be ready to "bail out" in self-preservation, otherwise someone might have been maimed by a burner. In a way it was a good thing that the young man pitched wild, otherwise it is doubtful that our seniors could have scored runs; our seniors walked. And when our team had walked in enough runs, the young man's team urged him to "let them hit it." They had come to have fun.

The rest of the pitchers were left-handers. Spanish had one, Lefty (Loftus) Pilon, and, when his cousin Ernie came home from Sudbury, two. Cutler had the Day brothers, Joe and Alex, and Mike Jacobs. We used to envy the seniors and dreamed that when we too came to their age and size we would play against the men from Cutler and Sagamok and Spanish. Until then we could only watch and cheer. Maxie Simon, Adam Roy, Eugene Fox, Rudy Rice, Julius Niganigijig, Alfred Cooper, Frank Syrette, Harold Belleau. Our time would come.

Later, when our turn came we went further abroad and far more frequently. Blind River, Echo Bay, Thessalon, Bruce Mines, Sault Ste. Marie, Webbwood, Sudbury.

The senior team, whose members wore purple sweaters with the letters SPC (for St. Peter Claver's) imprinted on an orange diamond crest, belonged to the boys. But the boys had to share ownership with the girls from St. Joseph's and with the people of the village of Spanish, who adopted the team that nearly always won. For the boys the team was a symbol for winning; a catalyst that created a bond of friendship and brotherhood; the medium by which they inspired one another.

There was one event that took place on Sunday evenings that made the week worthwhile in these early days, an event that we looked forward to.

In an institution where there was little amusement and entertainment other than the exhibition games and the infrequent silent movies of cowboys and Indians with Hoot Gibson, Tom Mix, Ken Maynard and Charlie Chaplin and "the Cheese-eaters," the hourlong stories recounted by Brother Edmund O'Keeffe meant a great deal to the seniors.

As the senior boys followed Brother O'Keeffe into the senior classrooms, the intermediates and juniors, who had to do homework in the study hall, cast envious glances at their elders. Despite all their efforts, they could never completely suppress the envy that flared up anew each time a burst of laughter exploded within the sanctuary of the senior classroom.

Of all the staff, priests included, Brother O'Keeffe was probably the most gifted and accomplished. We had heard that, before the First World War, Edmund O'Keeffe had been a professor of English in a military academy in Munich; according to another story, Brother O'Keeffe had been a private tutor to the Kaiser's family. Some time before the outbreak of the war he had made his way out of Germany to Britain, where he joined the British army. During the war he advanced to the rank of Major, serving on General Allenby's staff in Palestine. Following the war, Edmund O'Keeffe (who spoke six languages) had worked for British Intelligence for some years, during which he travelled the world; eventually, however, he had realized that there was more to life than spying on one's fellow human beings. Rather than devote the rest of his life to the destruction of his fellow men, he had joined the Jesuits as a brother to serve his God and humanity. Brother O'Keeffe had ended up in Spanish, far from his homeland and from the grave of his wife (she had died within months of their marriage).

The boys who studied under Brother O'Keeffe were twice fortunate; once, to have learned reading, writing and arithmetic from him, and again to have heard him narrate stories. There was not a boy who was not influenced or enriched by Brother O'Keeffe's knowledge and love of and reverence for the word.

It was from him rather from our own reading that we got to know *The White Company*, *The Exploits of Brigadier Gerard*, *The Hound of the Baskervilles*, *The Adventures of Sherlock Holmes*, *King Solomon's Mines*, *The Talisman*, *The Black Arrow*, *Kidnapped*, *Ivanhoe*, *Robin Hood*, *Treasure Island*, *The Knights of the Round Table*, *Great Expectations* and episodes from *The Pickwick Papers*.

For an hour the boys sat spellbound as Brother O'Keeffe told stories of daring, adventure and intrigue or described in the most graphic terms a venomous snake coiled on top of a man's head ready to strike. He spoke English with the delivery of an actor and the polish of an orator. Had Edmund O'Keeffe not become a Jesuit he might have been another Laurence Olivier or a renowned barrister, a Rufus Isaacs.

Besides entertaining us and at the same time teaching us something of the worth of the ideas and ideals embodied in literature, he sought to instil in us the same respect for the spoken and written word that inspired him.

"My gallant Henry [Webkamigad]," Brother O'Keeffe once interrupted a classmate as he stumbled over a passage he was reading. Henry stopped, probably wondering how he had now mangled the English language. "My dear Mr. Weeboo-kemi-gad! The word is 'greeezee,' not 'gree-sea.' Try it again. Enunciate the word as a learned man would, and not as some illiterate might. Enunciate the word with tone, inflection and feeling in order to convey the meaning and the revulsion that the term 'greeezee' is supposed to impart. Try it once more, my good lad. Utter the word with as much disgust as you can possibly muster for an object that is slippery, slimy and . . . unclean."

Henry made a gallant effort, which earned him a "Well done! A noble effort."

Brother O'Keeffe taught reading, penmanship, Bible history, arithmetic, English and history. With only half a day set aside for academic instruction, Brother O'Keeffe did not have the time to teach more than the basics. Still he managed to teach some geography, not formally but quite casually. Right after opening exercises he would unfurl wall maps of Europe and of the world and review for us events in Europe and around the globe. Once in a while he distributed copies of the *Illustrated London News* as a reward for our diligence and good behaviour. Maybe, on the other hand, he wanted us to acquire a broader knowledge than we were getting. Of the policies, causes, strategies, tactics, logistics and wars and places that we discussed, we remembered little; but we did get to know the countries of the world, oceans, seas, bays, mountains, passes, marshes, plains, hills, rivers; von Bock, von Rundsdet, von Leeb, Keitel, Guderian, List, Kleist, von Manstein, Gestapo, Panzers, Brown Shirts. The boys probably learned more about geography than their contemporaries elsewhere, who were still memorizing the counties of Ontario.

Never did Brother O'Keeffe have to lose his temper or punish anyone to maintain order. On the few occasions when he got angry, he was deliberately provoked, set up by boys who wanted a little excitement and to hear English as he spoke it. When angered, Brother O'Keeffe would rise to his feet — he was a tall man — and tower over one of our colleagues. He might commence his prosecution with

"You little scalawag. . . ." And then his words poured out, eloquent and damning. It was delicious to listen to Brother O'Keeffe speak English the way it ought to be spoken.

By comparison with courses of study in other schools, our curriculum would have been regarded as below standard. It's true that we did not have access to a well-stocked library, or attend classes from 9:00 A.M. to 4:00 P.M. It's also true that we were taught to know what to do with what little we knew; we were taught to be resourceful. But unless one has a sense of worth and dignity, resourcefulness, intelligence and shrewdness are of little advantage. Brother O'Keeffe, in the little time that he had to teach us, instilled in us intangibles that were far more important than mountains of facts.

In the dark after lights out we wondered how the man with the snake on his head was going to escape; in the days that followed we speculated wildly.

The Year Round

The Jesuits could regulate the day and the week with precision and guarantee that what had been planned and scheduled would come to pass as planned and scheduled. If they'd been able, they would have governed the year with the same precision, but, like everybody else, they had to abide by the seasons and cope with all sorts of unforeseen events. And though they may have been rigid in some respects, they were flexible in others. They had to be, in order to administer a school that was about as self-sufficient as an institution in the mid-north could be.

Six brothers were responsible for making the school as self-sustaining as possible. Brothers O'Keeffe, Manseau, Grubb, Van der Moor, Laflamme and McLaren looked after the practical operations of the institution, assisted at various times by laymen Gerry Labelle, Joe Albo, Joe Savoie and Clem Eicheldinger.

As the boys, old and new, began to arrive at the school during the last week in August and the first week in September, it was time to harvest the rich crop of beans, carrots, peas, squashes, pumpkins, cabbages, cucumbers and tomatoes that had been planted and tended affectionately by Brother McLaren the summer through.

In those first few weeks of the school year and continuing until the entire crop was harvested, there were many calls for volunteers.

"Who wants to help Brother McLaren?"

"Me! Me! Me!" forty to fifty voices piped up while hands stabbed and jabbed the air. "Me! Me! Me!"

"You! You! You!" Father Buck snapped, pointing out the volunteers, basing his choice on the good behaviour of the boys. Were the scene in the Garden of McLaren beheld from the clouds, the volunteers picking the vegetables and then bearing them to the school's kitchen or just outside the doors might have appeared as a moving chain of little ants scuttling back and forth between home and workplace, or wherever ants scuttle to and from.

As the produce was shelled or husked, more volunteers were solicited. "Who wants to help Brother McLaren can?"

"Me! Me! Me!" was repeated many times over as boys offered their services to escape the drudgery of cleaning toilets.

With the help of volunteers Brother McLaren canned peas, tomatoes, green and yellow beans, corn and meat, and made barrels of sauerkraut.

"Who wants to help Brother McLaren bake?"

"Me! Me! Me!"

Every Thursday Brother McLaren baked bread, thousands of loaves it seemed, both brown and white, but mainly brown; their aroma aroused 130 overpowering urges of hunger and visions of thick crusts of bread dripping with lard. Like bees, the boys swarmed near the bake shop to inhale the ambrosial scent.

Gardening and canning and baking were not Brother McLaren's only talents or portfolios. Just as essential as these duties were chanting, tending to the huge furnaces in the winter, and making and repairing shoes the year round.

Brother McLaren may have been a jack-of-all-trades and many things to the staff, but to the boys he was first and foremost a cobbler, a man who made shoes and mended soles and heels; patched baseball gloves, hockey gauntlets and skate boots; soldered broken skate blades and sharpened them.

When Brother McLaren was absent from the shoe shop in tending to his other duties, one of the senior boys in apprenticeship was left in charge. Probably no student learned the trade of shoemaking better than Joe Thompson or "Gistigly," as his fellow Mohawk tribesmen from St. Regis called him. While Brother McLaren was away from the shop, Joe not only superintended the repair work of his colleagues, but himself made new boots and "oxfords" to add to the inventory.

According to the boys who worked in the shoe shop and who helped him in the garden on occasion, it was good to work for Brother McLaren. As evidence of Brother McLaren's compassion, it was said that he would allow the volunteers a tomato or a cucumber to alleviate their hunger. The reason, if a reason were needed, for this compassion may have been his own experiences as an orphan or of having to scrounge for a meal as a hobo.

And how did Brother McLaren come by his talent for making the soil yield such harvests, repairing and making shoes, preserving fruits and vegetables, reading music and chanting the most difficult passages, and looking after the furnaces? Did he enter the Society of Jesus as a shoemaker, baker, gardener, chanter, stationary engineer? Or did he develop these talents and crafts with the same spirit, good will and diligence with which he read the dictionary — as he was peremptorily instructed to do when he asked what he ought to read for the improvement of his mind? Soon Brother McLaren had become a walking dictionary, reading and willing to provide definitions of words to priests and laymen alike.

Brother McLaren had one habit — talking to himself — that might be regarded as odd. But he was no different in this respect from Charles Dickens, who talked out his sentences as he was writing. Brother McLaren was expressing his ideas aloud. Anyway, the boys found this habit amusing and entertaining, and it enhanced his reputation. Brother McLaren would talk to anything. Some of his more memorable conversations were with piano keys and cord wood.

Difficulty with piano keys during the practice of a chant never failed to initiate a discourse. When Brother McLaren missed a note he would suspend his practice for some moments to reprimand the offending key. "Ha! You dodged, didn't you, you little beggar. That's why I missed. Don't you want to help me make music? Or do you want me to make mistakes? . . . Well! You're not going to get away with it. Come! Come! Let me hear you sing." And here he would strike the key several times. "Ha! Got you! There! Now wasn't that easy? Don't be shy; you have a wonderful voice. Don't you want to make music for God? Come! Let's try again." Ting! Ting! Ting! And on getting the passage right, Brother McLaren would once more address the key: "Now! Wasn't that easy? Wonderful? God will be pleased with you."

For four-foot lengths of firewood that would not readily slide into the bowels of the furnace, Brother McLaren had words of understanding that he delivered in a tone that was supposed to be soothing. "Hmmmph! So! . . . You don't want to go in, do you? I guess I can't really blame you. I wouldn't want to go in there myself. I even hate having to do this to you. Hmm! Hummph! You must know something about fire that I don't know. If hell fire is anything like that fire in that little furnace I often wonder why people don't strive harder to keep out of hell." Brother grunted as he rammed the obstinate log with another. "Hmmm! Why don't you go in? I'll wager that Lucifer doesn't have to labour quite this hard to keep hell's fires stoked.

Wonder what he uses: wood, coal, oil? Get in there, you little devil . . . Umph . . . About time!"

The wood that Brother McLaren used to fuel his furnace fires was cut and drawn by the seniors during their regular work days in the fall. But sometimes there was one special day set aside for cutting wood. For days there was talk of a picnic for seniors and intermediates. In the morning boys and prefects boarded the Red Bug, along with a cargo of Boston baked beans, loaves of bread, butter, Freshie, ladles, spoons, mugs and pie plates, to be towed up river by the Garnier to "the farm." No one minded the hard work so long as there was a good meal during the day and so long as it was far from the school. Later the seniors would return to deliver the wood to the school.

Some days later there were rumours that there was yet another picnic in the works. But these were rumours only, exciting at first, then growing sour as they remained unconfirmed, until Father Buck announced one day in October that there would be "a special holiday tomorrow . . . if you are good."

And good as angels the boys were the entire evening. None of the troublemakers did anything to upset Father Buck. Next morning after breakfast we set out for Walford five miles away, mostly on foot, but occasionally riding one of the three wagons drawn by three teams of horses: Jack and Dan, Prince and Jim, Bill and Queen. In the lead wagon were the two tubs of beans, loaves of bread and Freshie to tempt us to greater heights of industry. And there were further rumours that, if we picked the entire crop of potatoes planted by Brother Van der Moor in the spring, there would be a special treat when we returned to the school that evening. There were all kinds of wild guesses as to the nature of the special treat. And though the odd rotten potato flew through the air, the pickers dug potatoes with diligence. For our reward we were served johnnycake.

In previous years, under the command of Father Hawkins, the Garnier, towing the Red Bug, used to go all the way to Manitowaning to pick up 350 bags of potatoes and then back again, all within a forty-eight-hour period. Once or twice the two boats had to drop anchor in a cove in the North Channel or behind some island to wait out a storm. When the imports of potatoes from Wikwemikong were discontinued, it was not because of the hazards of autumn navigation in the North Channel; most likely for reasons of economy, land was bought or leased in the potato belt in Walford for growing our own potatoes.

Both Father Buck and Father Kehl were in their glory as their "fatherland" scored triumphs on land and at sea. Out of naked spite rather than any real conviction, we prayed even louder and with greater fervour during mass when prayers for an Allied victory were solicited. No doubt the two young Germans must have prayed to the same God with equal devotion for victory for their homeland.

October was a particularly busy time, with its endless preparations for the coming winter. While Brother McLaren was canning and preserving, Brother Van der Moor (in appearance as dour a Dutchman as there ever was) and his farmer apprentices were milling flour and ploughing the fields to make them ready for the spring. When the farmhands had finished milling and ploughing, they turned in the equipment, lit the forge and took up the tongs, the hammer and the anvil to repair horseshoes, ploughshares, discs, mowers, harrows, rakes . . . all the equipment. Afterwards these same boys assisted in the slaughtering of heifers, steers, pigs and sheep.

While all of this was going on and when the last cabbage had barely been put away, a small crew of six boys was conscripted to pick apples in Gore Bay. The select few earned spasms of jealousy from everyone else, along with the epithet "Pets!"

The pickers went by a Model-T, open-sided Ford that had cost the school the princely sum of fifty dollars two years before. To go from Spanish to Gore Bay was an adventure in itself, especially between Espanola and Little Current, a route so engineered that it contained only one straight stretch of no more than 500 yards in length. The rest of the road was a series of curves and bends, scales and slopes. When the pickers returned from their "picnic," a crew of bigger boys was taken on board the Garnier and the Red Bug and ferried to Gore Bay across the channel to take delivery of barrels of apples and to bring them back to the school. The apples were promptly stored under lock and key in a special section in the cellar for distribution three times a week and on special feasts and holidays.

One Sunday afternoon, brothers and sisters met for their regular monthly visit of one hour in the recreation hall of the boys' school. Other than "Ahnee" ("Hi"), I had nothing to say to my sister Marilyn, and she nothing to me. It wasn't that I didn't try, but she was absolutely uninterested in my toilet-cleaning skills and in my pea-shelling exploits. If Sis and I said few words during that hour and subsequent rendezvous, and if we had little to discuss, the only explanation may be found in the barrier in communication that often exists between ten-year-old boys and four-year-old girls. For the first few moments, all Sis did was to look up at me, her eyes black and misty with sadness and bewilderment at being wrenched from her mother and sisters and transported to an alien place where "suffer the little children to come unto me" was largely forgotten by sisters and priests. After the greeting of "Ahnee," and some questioning glances between us, Sis snuggled up against my leg. An hour later we said " 'Bye."

As October ebbed slowly into the past, the days grew shorter and colder. Boys complained: "When we gonna get coats, anyway? Not till somebody freezes to death or gets sick?" They hunched their shoulders and blew into their hands for added emphasis.

Or they taunted the tailors: "What's the matter with youse guys, anyway? Can't you make them coats an' mitts on time? We got our winter stuff last year 'fore this. What youse guys doin' in the tailor shop anyways . . . playing?"

But though the issue of winter clothing was late, Brother Manseau's tailors were not to blame. They were as busy a crew as any in the entire institution. Already they had made the requisite number of pairs of mittens from old coats that had been donated to the schools. Partly from Jesuit custom and partly because of the small per capita grant for each student, little was wasted. Besides the special assignments, every week there were bags of socks, pyjamas, underwear, shirts, trousers, overalls and coveralls sent down by Brother Laflamme from the clothes shop to be repaired before Thursday's change of clothing. When repairs to worn and torn garments were complete, there were new ones to be made from bolts of blue denim, beige corduroy and beige flannel. Except for the coveralls and overalls, all trousers were cut and sewn from corduroy in the riding-breeches style. The tailor shop fairly hummed as eight tailors pedalled eight machines in a contest to see who could make the most shirts or pants in a morning of work. Though Brother Manseau spent the greater part of the work period tending to his chickens, leaving ample opportunity for play, one never knew when Father Hawkins might be lurking in the immediate area and might abruptly swing open the door to conduct a spot check.

Only after Father Hawkins had come and gone did any or all of the tailors yield to the temptation to play. Even then there was a risk that

Father Hawkins would double back. One of the more favoured tricks
— and also the riskiest, in the event of Father Hawkins's unexpected
return — was the baptism trick perpetrated on new tailors and on
those who had gone to the toilet. In the colleague's absence one of the
tailors put a quantity of water in a pail, which he then set at an angle
against the door and the door frame and balanced at the tip of a broom.
It was a booby trap that produced considerable tension and laughter.
If, instead of the intended victim, some other person walked in, that
person would get water and bucket . . . and there would be damnation
to pay. If Beedj-mauss were the victim, it wasn't so bad. Other than
spewing forth a blue streak of French and English swearing, Beedj-
mauss would do little against a G-d d----d jack-hass.

Tee-deet (Herbie Beaudry) once set up the booby trap for Ivan
Kanasawe but got Father Hawkins instead. In addition to receiving a
severe thrashing, Herbie was banished from the warmth of the tailor
shop to the cow barn to shovel manure.

"Hey, Stiff [David Jocko], we're having a race; see who can make
most shirts afore ten . . . we was jus' waiting for you. You in?"

"Okay."

"Ready? One . . . two . . . three . . . go!"

Whirrrr went the Singers, like motorcycles. Whirrrr, clack, clack,
thump, thump, boomp went David's machine, as it bounced over a
fist-sized rock that someone had planted behind the treadle and then
drawn forward with a piece of thread when David was pedalling at a
furious pace.

Beedj-mauss frequently disappeared for a week at a time and then
just as mysteriously reappeared. "On retreat" was the explanation
given if a tailor or a chicken farmer inquired about Brother Manseau's
whereabouts. "On retreat" was a euphemism for "confined to his
room" for a week for swearing. And after a while, judging from the
frequency of his retreats, and knowing the rigours of seclusion and
religious meditation, the boys began to think that Brother Manseau
must be far more virtuous than they had at first believed him to be.
The other brothers went only once a year.

But no matter how often Beedj-mauss was exiled, or for how long,
he never got over the habit of cussing. "Where's dat G-d d----d
Hannin [Father Dan Hannin, S.J.]," Brother Manseau asked in exasperation — and within hearing of Father Hannin, who happened to
be standing just around the corner of the school.

Brother Manseau turned on his Gallic charm — "It's a nice day, Father. How are you? I was jus' looking for you" — but it was too late.

Father Hannin was scandalized as well as offended. "Get to your room!" he commanded, pointing a finger of damnation in the general direction of "out of sight."

Like the boys, brothers had to toe the line and hold their tongues in check.

At last one morning we received word that coats were to be issued after classes that day; new coats, someone said, causing great excitement. New coats! However excited most of the boys were, a few skeptics among them insisted that "them priests wouldn' buy anything new."

Instead of having collation at 4:15 we were directed to go outside and there to wait until summoned. On the way out and through the recreation hall the boys marched past a mountain of coats whose vintage and origin was the subject of much speculation in the cold outside. At least they were coats.

"Seniors first." It was always "Seniors first."

As the seniors burst through the door opened by Father Buck, the rest of the boys hurled the worst insult they could imagine, "Pets! Pets! Pets! Always first, them," and then crowded to the wire-mesh-protected windows to watch the seniors swarm around the pile of coats as seagulls swarm, squawk and squabble over the remains of fish. Coats were snatched up, tried on and flung to one side; too big. Another, too big also. Like old women inspecting the quality of yarn, the seniors took an interminably long time to make their selections. From outside came howls of protest, of "Hurry up! Hurry up, we're freezing!" From further back came other voices: "I can't see. What's taking them so long anyways? Gimme a chance, so's I can see."

"Holy Gee! Them coats, most o' them is too big! Even most o' the seniors can' fit them!" one of the window observers groaned. After that the demands of "Hurry up" dwindled. Nevertheless, the intermediates, when called, swarmed into the recreation hall as eager as the seniors.

For the next few days the boys resembled a rag-tag mob of ragamuffins or even a colony of scarecrows in the oversized coats that, Brother O'Keeffe declared, had been tailored from some of the finest fabrics, for the soldiers fighting in the Boer War. Ovilla Trudeau wanted to know why the British Army had not kept the garments if they were of such exceptional quality.

For some time after the issue of new coats, the tailors conducted a profitable business in illicit alterations. They struck hard bargains.

"Shorten my sleeves? Give you a slice for your beans on Thursday."

"No! . . . Don't think so, me. . . . I don't wan' a thrashing, if I get caught . . . can't do nothing else, except the work that we're supposed to do."

"Give you two slices then, one on Thursday and one on Sunday."

"If you throw in butter, I'll think about it."

"Heck with that. Too much. . . . Hey, Stiff!" (This to David Jocko, another tailor.) But the customer requiring and requesting an alteration didn't need to finish.

"Okay! Okay! A slice then," Ivan Kanasawe agreed, "but don't you change you min'."

In this way were business deals and simple contracts struck; though for most of the boys lard, butter and a slice were commodities too precious to barter. It was cheaper to roll up one's sleeves and hold them up with a pin or a nail.

Hats, also of Boer War origin and quality, arrived a little later and were distributed in the same way as the coats. Except for a few of us with large heads, we found the hats as ill-fitting as the coats. A few enterprising boys like Paul Migwanabe cut out the coats-of-arms crests engraved on tobacco-can lids and attached them to the front of their hats to restore their military look.

The boys were now prepared for winter. But after the crops had been stored there was an interval commencing in late October and lasting until the river froze over when few sports could be played inside and none outside. It was a particularly trying time for everybody — boys, prefects and priests. The boys wanted free time, their own games to organize and to play. The prefects could think of nothing better than choir practices — or play rehearsals, if a stage play were planned for Christmas. In those days and weeks, when free time was spent in choir practices, every boy prayed powerfully for the snow that would deliver us from singing for Miss Leutsch and bring hockey instead. And until the boards were installed there was little relief.

As always, Brother Van der Moor was tardy in installing the boards;

worried that he might forget, the boys reminded him that winter was coming each time he shuffled from the school across the yard to the barn. "Hey, Brother, when youse going to put up the boards?" Brother Van der Moor, who was regarded as the tardiest man alive, never appeared to hear; he waited until the last possible moment.

One morning in late November Father Buck announced the happy news as he clanged the wake-up bell. "Snow, boys! Just what you wanted." In an instant everyone was awake, at the windows, happy. The day couldn't go by quickly enough. After supper in the twilight, three lines of boys, arms linked at the elbows, marched back and forth over the surface of the rink from one end to the other, stamping their feet to pack down the snow. Later the flooders, senior boys as usual, poured hundreds of gallons of water in two, three, four and sometimes five floodings to produce ice level enough for skating.

For a change, the boys were occasionally taken to Brennan Harbour or down to the river to skate.

Few events were more keenly awaited than the issue of hockey sticks, which came bound in neat bundles from some generous donor. On the day of issue the senior boys who played on the school team had first choice. While the hockey team tested the sticks, the rest of the boys looked on in envy and impatience through the windows from the veranda. Before checking the other properties of a hockey stick, the players first examined the grain of the wood for knots or curvatures. They looked at the trueness of the shaft as a hunter looks down the barrel of a rifle to check the alignment of the sights; they bent the shaft this way and that to test the flexibility of both shaft and blade, and they hefted the stick for balance. Slow they were and inconsiderate. By the time the team players, followed by the rest of the seniors, had made their selections, only the rejects were left, scattered all over the floor.

The call "Intermediates next" was more like a call of "Break in and charge." Unlike the seniors, the intermediates could not afford the luxury of slow, considered selection. The object now was to grab a stick of the proper lie and angle. Except for the school-team players, who got an extra stick, every boy got one stick and one stick only, and that had to last the winter. No chattel was more cherished or better cared for than a hockey stick.

As may be expected there were sticks that survived use and abuse for some time and "sad ol' sticks" that broke within days of issue. The boys used all their ingenuity to try to repair broken hockey sticks with leather, tin or wood, but those sad ol' sticks would never be the same again.

A popular, regularly used description, the phrase "sad old" reflected the overall condition and outlook of the boys. A low-grade warped stick was a "sad ol' stick"; a torn mitten was a "sad ol' mitt." A rainy or stormy day was a "sad ol' day." The expression may not have been as precisely descriptive as another word or especially pleasing to grammarians, but it was apt. Most of our equipment and clothing was old, nearly ancient, and frequently on the verge of ruin and decay, which made us all very sad.

From the time hockey sticks were issued till the last patch of ice ended in a puddle, the rink was in constant occupation; there were boys on the rink playing "hog the puck" or shooting from one side of the rink to the other to develop the hard shot and accuracy of a Joe Lazore.

On the evening before an exhibition game some of the hockey players gave their sticks "special treatment." They soaked the blades in water and bent them in the grilles of the hot-water radiators to "give them a hook."

Blizzards occasionally interrupted hockey. One blizzard covered over the entire rink one night. Every boy and prefect, including Brother Manseau, shovelled and scraped for two days to clear the beloved rink.

Christmas is supposed to be a time of great joy and rejoicing. The very thought is supposed to send one into transports of anticipation. It may have been so for people with families and homes, but it was not so for the boys at Spanish. The coming of Christmas only served to increase the sense of alienation and the general loneliness. As best they could the priests and brothers tried to impart the meaning of the birth of Christ and the significance of Christmas for all of mankind, but the feast and the season served only to deepen the general dejection. There was one comfort, however — at least, for ten days, there would be no classes.

To transform the bleak school into something bright and cheerful, squads of boys went to the Rangers' camp to cut cedar boughs and bring them back to other squads of boys who transformed them with wire and string into wreaths and streamers to decorate the refectory, the recreation hall and the main chapel. After the rooms were decorated, Christmas trees were delivered and erected. Another squad of boys, artists led by Paul Nowigijig, were supplied with coloured construction paper and crepe paper, scissors, pencils and glue. They drew and sketched stars, camels, sheep, donkeys, dogs, cats, pigs, horses, cows, snow-covered hills and villages, a caravan of wise men, stables, angels with trumpets and nativity scenes. These works of art were mounted on windows to give the windows a strained-glass effect; or affixed to lamps or over bulbs to create imitation Tiffany lampshades. It took the better part of three weeks, but the school was actually converted into something less bleak and dreary.

In the fall of 1942 Eugene Keeshig, our friend and compatriot from Cape Croker, received a letter from his sister Delina. His eyes lit up as he read the letter and got progressively brighter the further he went along. "I'm going home," he blurted out, and he said it again, as if he needed to convince himself; or maybe he repeated "I'm going home" because it was delicious to say and to hear. "Come on! Read it!" Charlie, Hector and I begged Euge.

Eugene reopened his letter and read: "Dear Brother. We just received the good news that you are coming home for Christmas, for good. We all miss you, Donald and Luke especially. It will be so good to see you again and we'll have loads of fun when you get home."

"Gee, you're lucky!" we said in envy and in sadness.

Eugene had received the kind of letter that every boy anticipated every day. His sister had remembered. Somehow she knew the importance of a letter from home and a word of encouragement; perhaps it was because she herself had spent some years at St. Joseph's.

We were envious. Our friend had received the kind of letter we longed to receive. From the day of our committal to the final day of our release our one abiding aspiration was to get out of Spanish and go home. Every boy understood that he was to remain in the school until age sixteen or until his earlier release had been arranged by his parents with the concurrence of the Indian agent; every boy hoped that he would be sprung loose any time, the sooner the better. For a lucky few, it was only seven months to freedom and restoration to homes; for the rest it was years away — ten or even twelve years for some.

If the boys frequently nourished the hope of early release, parents and sisters encouraged it just as often.

Dear Son.

This is to let you know that we all fine and hope you are the same. The weather has been real good hear.

We are trying to get you home. I spoke to the priest and the agent and they said that they going help.

That's all for now and be a good boy and do what the priests tell you. I pray for you every night for you come home.

Love, Mom.

Such a letter gave a boy hope and inspiration and the strength to go on from month to month, from year to year. It was for such a letter that boys with parents who were literate congregated around the prefect at mail call. Orphans and boys whose parents could not write did not bother, and it was easy to tell that they were sad.

For those of us from Cape Croker, it was our custom to retire to a corner whenever one of us received a letter, to share the news from home. The recipient first read the letter silently, usually skimming over the news of deaths, births, weddings and other irrelevant news to bore in on the sweet passages that promised "You are coming home." After the silent reading, the lucky recipient read his letter aloud to his compatriots, and then passed it on to his friends.

When Eugene received his letter he was ecstatic, while Charlie, Hector and I were downcast. Our friend, quick to anger, quick to fight, quick to talk back, suddenly underwent a remarkable reformation. He now held his anger, fists and tongue, lest the priests withhold their consent to let him go home. Though not exactly angelic, he was the next thing to it, almost saintly. From around mid-November, when he received the good news, Eugene resisted temptations to which he would willingly have yielded before. He resisted Charlie's invitation to make wine; he even refused Charlie's offer of a drink of "mash," much as he would have liked to sample a cup.

The days passed slowly, but Eugene didn't care; he was going home. It was easy to wait now.

December 1 came. Eugene too, perhaps more eagerly than the rest, stood near the prefect at mail call, waiting for his name to be uttered. He wanted to know on what day and date he would be going home; he wanted to know if the train fare or ticket had arrived. "Hey! Father! Any mail for me?" Eugene asked, darkly and suspiciously.

"No!"

Well, there was ample time, a whole three and a half weeks. Maybe tomorrow or next week. December 5: "Any letter?" . . . "No!" . . . "You sure?" December 10: "Any letter?" . . . "No!" . . . "Prob'ly got it, them priests, but jis' don' want me to know." December 15: No letter, no ticket. December 23: still no letter, no money, no ticket.

December 24: "It's them priests' fault. All right then, from now on they're going to be my enemies. I'm going to tough it out . . . they're not going to make me beg or nothing."

Eugene did not go home. Probably, when his sister wrote the letter, she had got carried away by a desire to raise his spirits. Whatever the case, Eugene believed the priests had kept him from going.

December 24, Christmas Eve. It was early to bed tonight, at 8:30, in order to get at least two hours of sleep before midnight mass; with the exception of the smaller boys, few slept. And those who remained awake did not have visions of sugar plums, pudding, turkey and toys; or of uncles and aunts and grandparents and parents; or of reindeer and sleighs and jolly old St. Nick; instead they had visions of the last farewell with granddad who had died during the summer and whom they would never see again; or of the last thrashing; or of the last fight; or of the Indian agent's face; or of *"Line up! Stand up straight! Shut up!"*

The feeling of abandonment, never far from the surface, now welled up and was intensified by each boy's inability to understand why his parents had given him up and turned him over to the priests. No one had bothered to explain, "You're here because your parents are dead and we've been asked to look after you until . . . "; or, "You were sent to us to look after because your father is dead and your mother cannot care for you"; or, "Your parents are no longer living together. We're going to look after you until they are reconciled." Even if such explanations had been given, it is doubtful that the hurts felt on Christmas would have been assuaged by one degree.

At 11:30 we went down to the chapel to sing carols in preparation for the celebration of a solemn High Mass. Also in attendance, mainly to hear the boys' and girls' choir, were many people from the village, Kellys, McGraths, Trudeaus, McLeods, Pilons, Solomons, Gignacs, Sauvés, Greniers, Joncases, Descouteaus, St. Denis, Bishops, Beauchamps. We derived some comfort and hope from the words, "And it came to pass that the days of Mary were numbered when she was to be delivered of her first-born son. . . ."

Mass over, it was back to bed. Twice more in the morning did the boys attend mass. Afterward they skated till noon, uplifted and sustained by a bellyful of beans.

While others at home and abroad sat down to feasts and banquets, we sat down at noon to nothing special; just "that sad ol' barley soup. You'd o' thought they could o' killed some o' them chickens," Archie Pancake complained. On this day "sad old" took on its deepest and most accurate meaning.

On another day the boys would have grumbled a good deal more about the food and barley, but today no one belaboured the point. There were other matters to think of — the presents after lunch, the feast in the evening, maybe more beans.

For each boy there was a gift bag containing a handful of peanuts, a handful of jawbreakers, a small bag of mixed candies, a bag of mixed nuts, an orange, two Gore Bay apples, religious cards, medals and a toy or two; marbles, a yo-yo, a water pistol, a cap pistol, a car, a truck, Parcheesi, crayons, a drawing book, a big-little book, a kaleidoscope — most articles donated by the T. Eaton Company. And for the next hour the boys shared in the spirit of Christmas by gorging themselves on candies while at the same time conducting a brisk trade in the exchange of articles. Luckiest of all were those who had received parcels from home, who had been remembered. Besides candies, they received cookies and chocolate bars, a good pair of mitts, a warm cap.

Later in the afternoon boys with sisters received a rare invitation to visit their siblings at St. Joseph's. There they got first-hand evidence of how much better the girls lived and of the vastly superior care they received from the good sisters. By comparison with our quarters their rooms were clinically clean. And their food, the cookies and the cake, were far more nourishing and appetizing.

When we expressed our envy for their style and affluence with "Gee, you girls are lucky," the girls snorted. They said that they would gladly and willingly trade their corn flakes and puffed rice for something more substantial and for some of our freedoms.

For our feast in the evening the cooks prepared hamburger meat, mashed potatoes, green beans, butter, gravy, cake and blueberry preserve.

To follow Benediction at 7:30, a special excursion had been arranged. Three sleighs drawn by three teams superintended by Brother Van der Moor took the boys on a sleigh ride toward Walford.

On the way there and back, boys alternately rode on or ran alongside the sleighs to keep warm. Back at the school there was one more surprise, a collation of johnnycake and hot chocolate.

From Christmas to the New Year it was skate, skate, skate after work and between chores. But after the New Year it was a return to the same daily routine, as monotonous and as regular as the spasmodic motion of a minute hand.

Though we were ill-fed, ill-clothed, ill-sheltered, and attended by only a good-hearted "infirmarian," Brother Laflamme, we were as healthy as young oxen, seldom seriously sick. But it had not always been so. There had been one terrible period in the fall of 1918 when many boys died in the dread flu epidemic that gripped the world. There was one pathetic entry in the journal, "*Personne mourit aujourd'hui* [No one died today]." There were other epidemics, less deadly than the 1918 variety, that occasionally felled anywhere between thirty to fifty boys at a time: chicken pox, measles and mumps were the most common of these.

Patients were thought to be lucky both for their quarantine and for the special menu that Brother Laflamme prepared for them. The healthy boys were not only envious of the patients, but also resented them for the extra work their sickness meant for their colleagues. These boys weren't really sick, they were just "meaning it." They didn't look sick, and they didn't act sick. Whenever the healthy boys went upstairs to make their beds, they could hear peals of laughter ringing from every corner of the dormitory and actually see boys run and leap about, in and out of bed. Some sickness, that chicken pox. The patients didn't have to go to church, they didn't have to go to classes, and they didn't have to go to work.

"Keep away from them," we were warned. "Don't touch them. You don't want to catch their germs. You don't want to get sick, do you? And spend twenty-one to twenty-eight days in bed?"

"No!" we lied, trying to hide the fact that we desperately wanted to get sick, not for sickness' sake, but to escape the tedium of a regimented life. To get sick we sat on the beds of the sick, shook their hands, patted their backs, felt their foreheads for fever and breathed in deeply the air around them.

Brother Laflamme and the infirmary had always been a popular spot to visit before lights out to have one's hurts and pains attended to as well as to delay going to bed. But during the epidemic the line of boys outside the infirmary was even longer than usual, despite the depleted ranks of the healthy.

"Ah! My doodlebug, what seems to be the matter?"

"It's sore, Brother," a patient might say, holding up a hand, which Brother Laflamme would examine with a kind and critical eye. Usually there was nothing. The patient knew it, Brother Laflamme knew it. But Brother Laflamme sensed that what the boy needed was not medical treatment so much as a kind word and a pat on the head before going to bed.

"Hmmm! Hurt here? . . . There?" the brother asked while he gingerly pressed here and then there.

"Eeeeeyow."

"I'm sorry, Doodlebug! At least it's not broken. Here's something that'll make you feel better." And he would anoint the wounded finger with a tincture of Bededine.

"Feel better?"

"Yeah, Brother."

"Now, that's a good Doodlebug."

Each night numerous fingers, thumbs, hands, wrists, arms, elbows, jaws, foreheads and joints of Doodlebugs and Little Fatheads were remedied by Bededine or by an application of sulfathiazole. Whatever its properties Bededine possessed remarkable curative and restorative powers.

During epidemics there were new and exotic symptoms.

"Brother! I got sore throat, me. . . . I think I got a fever, me. I'm itchy here behin' my shoulder."

"Open your mouth. Stick out your tongue and say aaaah."

"Aaaaah!"

"Hmmm . . . let me see . . . Wider! . . . I don't think it's chicken pox, but I can see a touch of a cold. . . . I'd better give you an aspirin before it gets worse. You take this aspirin with a glass of water."

"It's not chicken pox, Brother?"

"No!"

"Gee, but it shore feels like it."

While most ills were either imaginary or minor, there were injuries that were very real and serious, the results of accidents that no quantity of Bededine or sulfathiazole could remedy.

White Man (Ernest Pelletier) suffered such an injury. One fall White Man was running while pushing a hoop with an inverted T-frame. He was having a good time propelling his hoop, guiding it around sharp bends and clumps of dirt. Well, White Man tripped and, in trying to break his fall, thrust the inverted T-frame in front of him. The T-frame shattered, and a long splinter about the length and thickness of a ruler broke through White Man's cheek and emerged near his right ear. White Man got to his feet holding his cheek and the splinter, which dripped with blood. Without a cry, he staggered to the main building and the infirmary and was rushed instantly to St. Joseph's Hospital in Blind River.

Long before the Spanish River was warm enough for swimming the boys began to agitate for a good swim. "Come on, Father, water should be warm enough for a swim."

When finally the water was deemed warm enough, the boys were warned before going down to the river. "Before you dive in check the water around the wharf for dead-heads." But the boys had ideas other than safety. "Las' one in is a swine." From the moment the challenge was issued the swim became a race.

At the shore boys flung shoes, socks, pants, shirts and underwear in all directions. None cast his garments off faster than Benedict Shig-wadja. Before his shirt had fallen to the ground, he was off like a bolt shot from a bow, racing to the end of the wharf and leaping into the river to claim the honour of being the first one in that year. Just as quickly as he had plunged in, Ben's head broke the surface; on his face was a pained smile of triumph. But instead of returning to the wharf, as he normally would have done, to repeat his performance, he slowly dog-paddled toward the bank, touched bottom, and walked ashore holding his left arm.

All the boys sensed that something was quite wrong, otherwise Ben would have challenged everyone with, "Come on! What's wrong? Scared of a li'l cold water?"

"You'd better go see Brother Laflamme," Father Mayhew advised Ben, who, like all the others, had to receive permission for an appointment with the infirmarian outside regular clinic hours. "Someone help Ben with his pants."

"I can put them on myself," Ben growled. Many times Ben winced as he wiggled into his clothing, but he would not moan and he would not allow others to do what he could do for himself.

Ben was back from Blind River two days later with his arm in a cast.

For ending his swimming season after only one dive Ben hacked the offending dead-head to small pieces, which he cast to the four winds.

In those days just about all a hockey player wore for protection were shin guards with padding consisting of a number of wooden splints inserted into long vertical slots. Above the splints, sewn into the felt, was a hard stiff material to protect the kneecap. With no more protection than shin guards and hockey gloves, a player had to have the good sense to get out of the way of flying pucks and sticks.

Despite his experience and his agility, Charlie Shoot was once struck by a puck fired by Mike Taylor during a warm-up just prior to an exhibition game. Charlie's hand flew to his jaw, and he took a couple of strides toward Mike as if he were going to cuff him around, but then he thought better of it. He could always find Mike after the game.

After the game Charlie complained that he couldn't open his jaw properly. Brother Laflamme sent Charlie to Blind River to have his broken jaw wired up.

It's a wonder that there were not more broken bones, or injuries more serious than broken bones.

In addition to the daily chores, such as milking the cows, cleaning out the barns, feeding the chickens and so on, there were many other tasks required for the general upkeep of the institution. Painters never finished painting. They went from room to room, hallways and corridors, dormitories, chapels, classrooms, windows, barns, mill, powerhouse, shoe shop, the Garnier, everything. Some painting sessions erupted into open warfare in which the enemies, armed with brushes, fought with red paint on a scaffold, no quarter asked or given. One war started because Alvin Nashkewe thought that his partners were dogging it. Victor and vanquished dripped from head to toe in blood incarnadine, and the Spanish River ran red as the warriors attempted to cleanse the gore.

Plumbers armed with wrenches and plungers followed Joe Albo in search of leaks and drips; mostly, though, they spent their time fishing diverse foreign objects out of the drains. Electricians trailed behind Gerry Labelle in his tour of the buildings, replacing burnt-out or broken bulbs, repairing damaged switches, and in general looking after the power-house. Carpenters were as busy as the plumbers and electricians. There was always something broken to repair.

Once when the roof developed several leaks, the carpenters, along with some conscripts — Alfie Cooper, Julius Niganigijig, Boozo (Harold Belleau) and Maxie Simon — were detailed to make the necessary repairs. Like experienced roofers, Department of Highways employees and Hydro workers whom they'd seen during their walks, they stood around looking as if they were busy inspecting the general condition of the roof; they stood around for several days, enjoying not only the bird's-eye view but also the sensation of having some privacy, away from the prying eyes of prefects; only when they could delay no longer did they get down to the serious business of looking for leaks. When asked why it was taking so long to repair the leaks, they replied that the holes were hard to find. Eventually they found the holes, after which they walked along the edge of the roof like high-steel riggers, except that they wore no safety belts. There were more consultations as they estimated how long the repairs ought to take.

While the roofers were conducting one of their conferences, Brother Laflamme espied them.

"Hey! You fatheads, come down here at once."

The crew descended directly.

"What you want, Brother?"

"Just this. I don't want to see you hurt. From the eaves of the roof to the ground is sixty-five feet. If one of you slipped and fell, that's the end. . . . Goodbye. . . . I don't like funerals; they make me sad. So, for your own good and for my own peace of mind, get a rope, a good stout one. Tie one end to something firm — the chimney for instance — and the other end around your waists. Make sure you test the rope first."

"Okay, Brother."

In the attic the crew found a stout rope, long enough to be attached to an anchor while bearing two men at either end. From its weight and density, it appeared stout enough, but it had to be tested. Did not Brother Laflamme so advise?

There followed a discussion as to what would constitute the most effective test for the soundness of the rope. And there was no test more appropriate than for one of the crew, safely and safety bound, to fling himself over the ledge or allow himself to be pitched over the side. No one volunteered, so the crew cast lots. But at the last moment the crew had a slight change of mind and agreed that the volunteer need not hurl himself off the roof; it would be enough to leap from the roof through the skylight to the attic floor below.

Accordingly the rope was secured to the chimney, which was to serve as an anchor, and the other end was wound three times around Boozo's midriff. With considerable foresight the crew shortened the rope.

With his colleagues standing by the skylight offering encouragement — "Come on. Hurry up! . . . You scared, you" — Boozo, after several false starts, closed his eyes and leaped. From the gloom below there came only a grunt, followed by silence.

"You okay? Rope strong enough?"

Not receiving an answer, the roofers above drew up the rope. Boozo was unconscious.

For some moments the roofers squatted around their stricken colleague. While the rest huddled worriedly over their friend, who was not meaning it, Julius scampered down the ladder and returned some minutes later with a bucket of water. When he dashed the water over Boozo's face, Boozo came to at once.

It was never clearly established what had caused Boozo's knockout, but for several days he bore rope-burn marks around his rib cage and had difficulty breathing deeply.

Just around the time the boys' beloved ice began to thaw, a shipment of chicks from Tweddle's Chick Hatchery in Sault Ste. Marie arrived at the chicken coop, and over the next months the chicken boys, under the supervision of Brother Manseau, slaughtered the old chickens in flocks of between twenty and thirty on slaughtering days. By the time the new batch of chickens was ready to replace the old in productivity and usefulness, the old hens were nothing but broilers in the kitchens of hospitals in Sudbury and Sault Ste. Marie. Chickens came, chickens went; none ended up on the boys' plates.

The month from mid-March to mid-April was like a twilight period, with the ground and the grounds too soggy for outdoor play; as in the fall, there were only hours of choir practice and Lenten devotions in preparation for Easter. It was a time of sackcloth, penitence and sobriety.

In keeping with the grave character of Lent, Leon Abraham from St. Regis was properly long-faced, except that he was long-faced not out of any deep sense of penitence but rather out of a powerful sense of grievance over what he considered unnecessary harassment at the hands of Father Rushman. It seems that the father was hounding him: "Come on, Leon, get a move on." "Come on, Leon, hurry up!" or "Come on, Leon, do some work!" Right from the first, Leon resented Father Rushman's reproofs, but there was nothing, absolutely nothing, he could do about it.

Leon's chance finally came when he heard that Father Rushman was leaving.

Instead of asking directly, Leon elected to be cagey. "Heard you're leaving," he remarked while Father Rushman was inspecting the work of the dishwashers in the scullery.

"Why yes, Leon."

"Good! I hope you go to hell — an' I hope you never come back," Leon broke in before Father Rushman had a chance to explain that he was going only to Sudbury.

"Sorry to disappoint you, Leon, but I'm coming back in a couple of days."

As Father Rushman went out, the dishwashers expressed both their admiration and their anxieties for their colleague. "Gee, Leon! You're not scared o' them priests, you. I'm glad you say that . . . but I think you're going to get into trouble."

But there was no summons from Father Hawkins's office, not a word from Father Rushman. For days Leon waited in trepidation — for nothing. The scholastic had chosen to overlook Leon's insolence.

The snow had not quite completely melted from the ground when baseball season opened, with the games played in a field between bushes near the village separate school on top of the hill. The ground was still spongy and soggy in places, and it was difficult to keep one's eye on a fly ball while keeping one's mind on the numerous cow pies that dotted the playing field like big brown mushrooms, but we didn't mind too much; it was vastly preferable to choir practice.

In two and a half months the school year would end. Some boys would go home, never to return; they had served their term. Others would go home for the summer holidays and come back in the fall. A few, those too distant from their homes, would remain in the school for the summer.

Everyone looked forward to the budding of trees and plants, and to the blooming of flowers. Father Dufresne, a retired missionary, was as anxious as any boy for the return of spring. He too had languished the entire winter, and now wanted only to return to the task that he had chosen to perform in his retirement years, that of landscaping the outcrop of the shield on the riverside.

From early spring to late autumn Father Dufresne laboured daily with crowbar, axes, sledge hammer and saw, moving and splintering rocks and trimming and pruning trees and bushes to make grottoes, walkways, flower beds and rock gardens. With his great whiskers and craggy visage Father Dufresne might have passed for the Biblical Moses, except for his size. A miniature Moses.

Two years before, Father Dufresne had been ordered by the Father Superior to stop working. He could not possibly improve the grounds any further; besides, it was altogether too dangerous for an old man. As if he had not understood or even heard the order, Father Dufresne still carried his tools down to the shore every day. A free spirit was Father Dufresne.

Spring is a time for all sorts of things: romance, gardening, painting, mischief and breaking rules and regulations.

Joe Coocoo and Donald Fox were seduced by spring fever into breaking two school rules: they went down to the shore, which was out of bounds, and there had a smoke. Father Dufresne, to their relief, was nowhere to be seen.

Even before they struck a match, the boys heard a feeble "Hooo! Hooo!" At least, whatever it was sounded very much like "Hooo! Hooo!" And there were other words, in a language they could not understand. The voice and the language and their apparently extra-terrestrial origin unnerved both boys. Someone — a saint, an angel, or even Beelzebub himself — was at that moment watching them in the commission of their acts and was now demanding their attention. According to the Bible, on occasion the deity or a spirit might address a human being to deliver good news or to issue dire warnings of impending disaster. Quickly the smokers crushed their cigarettes in a belated attempt to pretend innocence.

"Aidez-moi! Aidez-moi! . . . Help me! Help me!" The voice, without question, came from above. Donald was stricken stiff and speechless. Joe dared to look upward tentatively, half expecting to be blinded by brilliant rays of light. But instead of gazing into the indignant visage of a supernatural being, Joe looked into the face of

Father Dufresne, peering over the ledge of a platform that he had constructed as his own private retreat where he could read his "office" in tranquility.

"Help! Help!" Father Dufresne repeated. Then, motioning with his cane, he added, "Layder! Layder!"

At first Joe didn't understand what Father Dufresne meant by "layder," but when he saw the ladder on the ground he guessed at once that the priest was stranded and wanted only to get down.

"Don't tell on us now; okay, Father?" Joe asked before Joe and Donald restored the ladder.

"Non! Non! Non!" And Father Dufresne was as good as his word.

Reuben Bisto wasn't quite so lucky.

Before the chicken coop crew commenced work, they first took a break to smoke cigarettes made from tobacco supplied by Beedjmauss. After a cigarette each, the boys went to work collecting eggs, feeding the birds and cleaning the roosts.

While his crew was having a break and a smoke, Brother Manseau patrolled the building outside, acting as a lookout under the pretext of examining the eaves and windows. If he saw Father Hawkins, Brother Manseau would deliberately address the priest and talk extremely loudly as a signal for the smokers to disperse.

"Good morning, Father. It's a nice morning. I never saw such a morning for a long time, me," etc.

Reuben didn't hear the signal; he continued to sit at the foot of the stairs after all the other workers had taken themselves off to the various quarters of the chicken coop.

"Good morning, Reuben," Father Hawkins greeted the smoking Reuben. "Good tobacco?"

"Good morning, Father." Reuben returned the greeting. "Good to have a smoke." Only then did the smoker realize he was speaking to Father Hawkins; belatedly Reuben tried to hide the cigarette. Finally, he got up and crushed the butt under his heel; he was shaking.

Snowball (Mitchell Loft) and Tony Angus were caught loitering in the dormitory, red-handed and cold — caught by no less than Father Buck.

"And what," Father Buck asked the classic question that is always asked on such occasions, "are you doing here, Snowball?"

"Nothing, Father," Snowball explained.

"And you, Tony. What are you doing here? You're not supposed to be here."

"Helping Snowball, Father?"

"Go and see Father Hawkins."

Spring was as busy as the fall, especially for the farmers. The cow-barn workers, in addition to the regular chores, now had to care for calves. There were always more than 100 cattle, sometimes as many as 125. Toward the end of June young heifers and steers were transported on a scow to Aird Island where they would graze until autumn. Horse-barn workers ploughed and harrowed and disked. Behind them followed planters with seeds. In the building carpenters hammered and painters painted, winding up the year.

Besides devotions and holidays of obligation, there were baseball schedules to be completed, play-offs to be arranged and exhibition games to be played.

In the last week there were jamborees for the championship teams and tests for all the boys.

On the last day, Tom White, Herbie Penassie, Renee Cada, Tommy Sarazin, Louis Mitchell, Louis Francis, Joe Thompson, Roy Rice, Cabootch and Archie Espaniol went home for good.

"What you gonna do, Renee?"

"Gonna join the army. Fight the damn Germans," Renee replied.

Summer Holidays

For those of us who had to remain in Spanish for the summer, the last week of school was particularly hard. During those final days the boys bound for families and homes laughed constantly as they discussed plans for days of fishing, hunting, sailing, picking berries, riding horses, going to the movies, helping grandparents, gathering birch bark and sweetgrass, accompanying their parents to Manitowaning or to some other equally enchanting place or staying up all night to lie in ambush for strolling paramours alongside Coocoosh Meekun (Hog Boulevard); but mainly they talked about the meals that they were going to eat: salt pork, baloney, potatoes, gravy, bannock, real tea, cake, pie, cookies and jam that would put some fat on and around their bones. And as their spirits took flight into the heights of anticipation, so did ours, in direct proportion, descend to the depths of despondency. For them someone cared; for us . . . we were forgotten.

What was there to look forward to? "Be like last year," Charlie and Eugene and Hector explained. "Older boys will have to help with the haying and other chores around the farm. The smaller boys will go for walks and swims; picnics and fishing; playing catch, maybe go to a bazaar in Cutler; and the best part was camping at Aird Island . . . yeah . . . spent nearly three weeks there."

As bad as the week might have been, it was as nothing compared to the final day in June when our fellow students left. We could only stare with mist in our eyes as we watched parents from Sagamok, Cutler, Mississauga, Garden River and Birch Island arrive and leave with their sons, Skinny Dominic (Eshkakagun) and Skinny's brother, Hubert, Leo Sego and his brother, Leonard; Martin Assiniwe and Clarence and Russel Abitung; Joe and Paul Migwanabe, David and Harry Mitchell, Angus Pitwaniquot and Ernie St. Germaine; the Trudeaus, Wilfred and Ovilla; the Buzwas, Benjamin, Francis, and Dolphus from across the river; Meeshaukoot (Wilfred McCoy). From the village, poor as he was, came David Plug (Solomon) to collect his brood of little "Plugs" who danced and skipped their way to freedom and happiness. All day old Model-Ts and -As came and went, leaving the school just a little emptier each time.

Of the students going home for the summer, the majority from Manitoulin went by boat. At 9:00 A.M. on the day of departure the boys from Wikwemikong, West Bay, Sheguindah, Sheshegwaning and Sucker Creek on Manitoulin Island lined up in the yard in front of the main entrance to be counted, as if anyone would absent himself on this day of days. They were then marched in columns down to the wharf, where they boarded the Red Bug. After them came the Manitoulin girls from St. Joseph's under heavy escort. They too were conducted aboard the Red Bug, to sit on the side opposite the boys. Under command of Father Hawkins, with engineer Gerry Labelle and a small crew, the Garnier towed the Red Bug from Spanish to Gore Bay, a distance of some thirty-five kilometres.

By the end of the day there might have been thirty to thirty-five boys left in the institution, lingering in the shadows and in the silence that now took hold of most of the building; Ojibway or Anishinaubae from Cape Croker, Saugeen, Parry Island, Byng Inlet, Chapleau, Missinabi, Golden Lake, Temagami; Mohawks from St. Regis and Caughnawaga.

In the dormitory that night Father Mayhew announced: "Get your stuff ready — your toothbrushes, toothpowder, everything that you'll need. Tomorrow you're going to Aird Island, where you'll spend the summer." While the announcement did not evoke transports of joy, it did bring some consolation. As Eugene put it, "Beats staying in this place."

Next morning after breakfast we made preparations for our own summer vacation on Aird Island, three and a half kilometres from the mainland. We prepared and packed straw, bedding, clothing, pots, pans, spoons, dishes, cups, ladles, tin cans, pails, baskets, butcher knives, tarpaulins, sails, oars, paddles, boards, tools, ropes, nails, tin, flashlights, beans, peas, tea, oatmeal, bread, pails of lard, beets, onions, beef, pork and a medical kit, all of which we helped load on the democrat. The horse, Pitou, was busy drawing the little wagon back and forth from school to wharf. Usually a cranky beast, he was today almost amiable.

It took the Garnier, cruising leisurely, no more than an hour to tow the Red Bug and the three punts from the wharf to Aird Island.

Hardly had the Red Bug touched the bottom of the sandy bay at the campsite than all the boys leaped off to race to the lean-to that was to be our shelter at night and during rain, in order to claim and to stake out a sleeping place near a friend. During this rush Father Hawkins and the prefects, who were to be our guardians, wardens, cooks and orderlies for the summer, stood indulgently by to allow us to enjoy our freedom. "This is my place. I'm going to sleep beside my friend here . . . an' don' you snore and don' you piss on my blanket or my straw"; the conversation was good-natured. Only after we had staked out our sleeping places did Father Mayhew blow his whistle to summon us to work.

For the next while we were busy unloading the Red Bug, willingly and cheerfully. "Where's you wan' this straw, Father?"; "Where's you put this here pot?"; "Where you wan' us to put this sad ol' mush?"; "Hey, Father, where you gonna keep the candies?" And Father Mayhew, whom we called Joe DiMaggio, grinned as he directed the porters to deliver "Peas over there," "Blankets over there," and "You know where the tarp goes."

When the Red Bug was unloaded and the punts were pulled on shore and tethered, the Garnier steamed back to the mainland, leaving us to all the comforts and freedom that only the forests, winds, waters and rocks can provide, confer and allow.

But before we were allowed to leave camp, there was more work to do.

The lean-to, damaged during the past year by wind, snow and porcupines, had to be repaired. With birch bark, leaves, boards and driftwood, thirty-five boys soon patched all the cracks and chinks and stopped up every hole against wind and rain. Because we constructed our beds with the same ingenuity as loons but with far less care, our sleeping arrangements resembled a series of nests without eggs, or mice's nests. In quick order, after getting our own quarters fit for habitation, we scrubbed the picnic tables, gathered wood, pitched the tent for Father Mayhew and erected the tarpaulin above the tables.

While we were busy putting the camp in order, Father was brewing a meal in an enormous pot. Just what he was doing we did not know, nor did it appear from the results that he knew what he was doing either, but according to his helpers, Father Mayhew had opened jars of cut green beans and sauerkraut and poured the contents into the pot, then spilled peas, beans, carrots, potatoes, onions, bones and meat into the boiling cauldron. As we left camp, he was paddling and puddling the sludge.

At last we were free: free of rules, free to come and go as we pleased, free to eat or to go without. We got to know and cherish freedom as only those who have been denied it can know and cherish it, as only seven- to twelve-year-old boys can exercise it.

There were channels and bays and inlets for sailing and fishing and the islands of Villiers, Passage, Otter, Jackson, Brown and Green a quarter of a mile opposite our campsite for visiting and discovering.

Some of the boys, notably Alvin Nashkewe and his brother, Lloyd, my former confederates at Cape Croker, did nothing but ride the waves and fish. With each flat-bottomed punt equipped with only one oar or paddle, navigation of any kind was almost impossible. Even with oars it was hard to control these craft, which, caught by the winds, slid or slithered sideways on top of the waves. Nevertheless, Alvin and Lloyd claimed one of the better punts for their own use or, in our own vernacular, "just hogging it, them guys."

Use of these punts was supposed to be decided on a first-come, first-served basis for all the boys; but, by getting up before the others, Alvin and Lloyd were well within the rules. Because no one really envied them, no one objected. Besides, having learned the craft of sailing from their father, Enoch, they were skilled sailors and navigators, adept at poling the punts along the shore, paddling to the islands, and even sailing with the use of their blankets or shirts whenever the winds were favourable.

During season there were patches and patches of blueberries, which meant money. For each pail picked and delivered we were credited with twenty-five cents, which was recorded in a little black book in the same manner as our ancestors were credited in trade for beaver pelts. At the end of the picking season, which lasted about three weeks, some of us had amassed what to us was a small fortune, accumulating as much as five dollars in our accounts.

(Our only motive in picking blueberries was to earn money to relieve our hunger during the coming winter by bread–lard–candy trading. At the school there was a little candy store underneath the first-floor stairway that was opened twice daily for fifteen-minute periods at 12:30 and again at 6:30. With a small investment of two or three cents in jawbreakers, licorice twists, bubble gum and suckers, a boy could drive a good bargain with his candy-loving but penniless colleagues who congregated in the recreation hall just outside the doorway, waiting and pleading, "Gimme one, gimme one." Except to friends, no one gave a candy away. The object was to tempt one or several boys to make an offer. Luckily there was always someone who preferred candy to bread or lard. The going rate on the open market was seven jawbreakers for a slice of bread and five for a spoon of lard, to be delivered either at the very next meal or at a time to be decided by the vendor of the candies. It was through this means that we got to eat an extra slice of bread on the odd occasion to allay our hunger.)

Then there was hunting. For Charlie Shoot, of course, there was *only* hunting. It was first and last. He was probably the only boy in camp — in the whole institution — who devoted his entire time from morning to night to hunting rabbits, squirrels, partridges, groundhogs, beavers, skunks — whatever was worth hunting. I very much doubt that he ever went fishing or picking berries. For him the day began at the beach, picking pebbles — round ones that didn't curve. With a pocketful of ammunition, Charlie would be gone for the day.

Charlie preferred to hunt alone rather than invite anyone too heavy-footed or loose-tongued for the silence and stealth that hunting demanded. Still, he asked me to go with him on a number of occasions. Not that I was a good hunter or anything like that; but I was useful either as a decoy or as a porter, for carrying extra ammunition or plucking partridges that he had killed. It was Charlie's habit of walking directly through instead of around swamps, hills, muskegs, ponds and thickets that provided us with excuses not to accompany him. Otherwise we might have gone more frequently and learned something.

Of the many hunting trips with Charlie, I remember one clearly, and one only. That day we were to hunt foxes, wolves and bears, and I think he mentioned eagles and tigers. It was exciting and frightening at the same time. As protection against whatever dangers may have lurked behind rocks, stumps and limbs, I stuck right behind my partner, who, armed with a slingshot, frequently bent down to peer into the bushes or stop to listen for some distant growl. For my part, I was busy checking which spruce or pine would offer the nearest shelter should a bear or a tiger come bursting out from ambush.

Out in front Charlie pushed on, his slingshot ready to fell bear or tiger. He stopped, held up a hand, and then knelt down on one knee. I too heard it: "Cluck, cluck," the sound of the molars of a bear, or was it a tiger? I looked around, behind, and to the front. Charlie was drawing a bead upward, stretching the rubber band of his slingshot well past his ear . . . steady . . . strong . . . dead on. On a pine limb sat an immense snowy owl, its hooded eyes half open in a sultry stare.

Charlie fired. The eyes flew open and the owl teetered on the limb for a couple of moments before tumbling to the ground. He lurched to his feet, wings outspread, beak snapping, eyes rolling, unable to focus. Unsteady, as if drunk, the owl reeled from side to side.

"Got him jis' where I wanted," Charlie chortled. "We'll catch 'im an' take 'im back to camp. . . . Gimme your belt."

I took my belt off without thinking; gave it to Charlie.

"You stay in front o' that owl; don't let 'im turn around. I'll sneak aroun' and catch 'im from behin' by the legs," Charlie instructed me as he circled, crouching low. As if he knew Charlie was up to something, that owl turned his neck, fixing his eyes on my partner. Me, he ignored.

"Hey!" Charlie stopped. He whispered loudly, "He's looking at me. Git 'im to turn aroun' and look at you. Do somethin'." Charlie was angry.

With one hand I held on to the waistband of my pants, already sagging southward; with the other I waved at the owl. I took two steps forward, calling at the same time, "Hoo! Hoo!"

The owl, perhaps perceiving the "Hoo! Hoo!" as a mating call, instantly turned. By now he had recovered most of his senses. When he saw me, he snapped his beak, then charged, half-flying, half-running. I went into reverse. With the owl gaining, I turned to sprint away. In so doing I lost my grip on my pants, which fell to my ankles. I went sprawling. I covered my head.

In his rage the owl pounced on my trousers, ripping at them with his claws and tearing at them with his beak, as if he were slashing at his favourite meal, the skunk.

In this moment of mortal danger Charlie hurled himself upon the owl and me. The next thing I heard in my terror was Charlie yelling, "Grab 'is neck, grab 'is head." I twisted around, got my hands on the owl's neck and applied a choke-hold. By this time Charlie had wound my belt around the owl's legs and had bound the owl's wings with his slingshot. I did not let go of that owl's neck until Charlie told me to.

Like big-game hunters who had bagged a trophy, we bore our prize back to camp in triumph. For all the indignities we had heaped upon him — knocking him down from his perch, wrestling with him, tying him up with belts and slingshot, carrying him all trussed up as a big white bundle through the forest, depositing him on a picnic table for all the boys to see and then tying his one leg to the tree so that he wouldn't fly away — that owl stood on the picnic table with pride and looked upon us as if he would take us all on. Then as if weary of the sight of us, he flew up to the limb of the maple tree directly above the picnic table.

After a couple of days Charlie untied the twine that bound the owl's leg. That owl remained in our camp for a week or more. During his stay we fed him mice, birds, bread, fish and scraps. But one morning our owl wasn't there. He was gone, summoned perhaps by his mate or by the spirit of the north. We twitted the prefect in charge: "Our owl woulda stayed except for the mush you cook."

As happy as the summer days were, as happy as they could be in the circumstances, there was the occasional incident that stirred up repressed despondence and rekindled the urge to get away as fast and as far as one could manage.

Our friend and colleague Hector Lavalley, Kitchi-meeshi Hec, broke an oar and, for his carelessness, received a few cuffs that greatly aggravated his sense of neglect. Then and there Kitchi-meeshi Hec decided to run away; no more would he endure his suffering; he would run back to his family.

To run off or away without saying goodbye would have been quite improper and entirely selfish. Kitchi-meeshi Hec was not that kind of person; he went in search of his friends and found Eugene, just returned from a blueberry-picking expedition, lounging under a tree.

"G-g-goodbye," Kitchi-meeshi Hec sniffed between tears and sobs. "G-g-goodbye! I'm l-l-leaving!"

Eugene was so moved that a lump developed in his own throat. "You goin' home, Hec?"

"Y-y-yeah. I'm goin' run away. I c-c-c-can't stan' it no more. I'm goin' right now. Goodbye."

Eugene was decisive. "Just wait. I'm goin' with you. Come on. We'll go and say goodbye to Charlie. Wouldn't be right to run away without saying goodbye."

They found Charlie beside the communal campfire, just ready to smoke the bass that he had caught.

"G-g-g-goodbye, Charlie!" It was hard to stifle the sobs, hold back tears and keep open a throat that tended to tighten up.

Charlie was astounded. "Where you goin'?" he blurted out.

Eugene acted as the spokesman for Kitchi-meeshi Hec, who was so overcome by the thought of leaving a friend that he could not speak properly. Even Eugene was sniffing. "Kitchi-meeshi Hec here is running away an' . . . an' . . . I'm g-g-goin' with 'im."

Charlie straightened up and grasped Eugene's hand; he was tense and he had that faraway look of longing, as if he were beholding some distant vision. His mind wasn't on the present at all; he wasn't saying goodbye or wishing Kitchi-meeshi Hec and Eugene a safe journey.

Eugene had to repeat Charlie's name to bring him out of his trance-like state. "Hey! Charlie! Did you hear me? We're running away, me an' Hec."

"Yeah, I know. I heard you. But I was just thinking. You guys need somebody like me, otherwise you'll starve an' git lost in the bush. Can I go with youse?"

"Shore!"

Hector and Eugene felt an immense weight removed from their twelve-year-old shoulders and spirits. It didn't matter that they knew nothing of the geography of the area or that they would have to walk for miles through black-fly- and mosquito-infested bushes and swamps; or that they were shaved bald like felons and would be immediately recognized as fugitives; or that they hadn't the foggiest notion how to get back to Cape Croker. Escape first; the rest would follow.

Charlie was so busy making plans he forgot his bass. "Gotta take some string, twine, hooks, borrow a coupla slingshots and each take a blanket." They had to be prepared.

On the rocky banks of the narrows at Little Detroit that separated Aird Island from the mainland, the fugitives stopped to regard the flow and pace of the current and to decide on the best manner of crossing the passage. Though less than a stone's throw in width, the river was deep and swift. Even for strong swimmers the crossing would have been dangerous; for Eugene, small and scarcely able to dog-paddle, it was next to impossible.

According to Eugene, Charlie got that faraway look in his eyes, as if he could see something in the distance that others could not see, except that he was looking directly into the mass of rock on the opposite bank. When the vision passed, Charlie spoke of his revelation.

"We're going to pray for a miracle," he said very solemnly.

Kitchi-meeshi Hec and Eugene were astounded and impressed. That damned Charlie thought of everything; it was a good thing they'd allowed him to come along. They'd heard of miracles, but they'd never thought of praying for one.

Charlie continued: "We're going to pray for a miracle like what St. Christopher done, the time he carried that l'il baby on his back across the river on top the water in a storm late one night."

Yes, Kitchi-meeshi Hec and Eugene remembered.

"Hector! You're going to be St. Christopher," Charlie said, nominating his friend for the principal role in the drama to come. As Charlie saw it, Kitchi-meeshi Hec, for his general sinlessness, was more likely than Eugene to receive grace from on high to enable him to cross the narrows like a modern St. Christopher.

For Kitchi-meeshi Hec the nomination was both moving and humbling.

"When we finish praying, Hector, take Eugene across first, then you come back for me . . . an' after that the blankets." In nominating Eugene to make the first crossing, Charlie showed that there was not a selfish bone in his anatomy.

Eugene laughed when he thought of *whom* he would be representing.

"Gotta be serious or else the miracle won' work," Charlie explained, annoyed.

For a while the fugitives prayed mightily and fervently. At the end of the devotions, which were conducted by Charlie, Kitchi-meeshi Hec dropped down on one knee at the water's edge to allow Eugene to get on his back. Even though Eugene was small and light, Hector's knees almost buckled, and he wobbled as he stepped tentatively forward and into the water. He placed his foot in the water in complete faith and slid forward on the slimy slope of the rock. There was no turning back.

Hector slithered down, down; Eugene struggled to dismount. They yelled at one another, they yelled at Charlie. They sputtered and coughed. The water churned and splashed as St. Christopher and his passenger struggled and sank, surfaced and sank, all the while drifting downriver and out toward Shoepack Bay. Just a little way from where they had fallen in, Kitchi-meeshi Hec and Eugene ran aground and scrambled ashore.

Feeling considerably less pious now, they were eager for revenge on Charlie for having nearly killed them both. But Charlie convinced Kitchi-meeshi Hec and Eugene that they most likely had not prayed with the degree of faith required for the enactment of a miracle. Who of the three had entertained the grave doubts that had aborted the miracle will never be known. It may have been Kitchi-meeshi Hec's surprise at being nominated as St. Christopher that prevented him from praying with due fervour; it may have been Eugene's envy of Hector; or it may have been Charlie's inability to turn his mind from such material and temporal matters as rabbits and moose long enough to dwell on the spiritual.

They returned to camp, having abandoned plans for escape; they would tough it out. That summer was the last vacation that Charlie, Kitchi-meeshi Hec and Eugene spent on Aird Island. Thereafter, as older boys, they remained at the school to assist brothers Van der Moor and Grubb with the chores around the barns.

When no special consideration or concessions in the way of food were forthcoming for those who stayed and worked at the school, Eugene reminded the new prefect who served them "sad ol' mush" that "we're supposed to get bacon and eggs for doin' man's work." For a few days the boys ate bacon and eggs, until the prefect was pulled up short and reprimanded for treating the boys too well.

There may not have been much on Aird Island, but the boys took what little there was and what little they had and made it into something bigger and finer and stronger than they had found. No one could see it, but it was there; no one could express it, but it was there. It was in each boy. With every renewed attempt to achieve, the resourcefulness grew, and as the resourcefulness increased so did the spirit of independence and the passion for personal freedom. The boys may have been deprived or felt deprived, but poor in spirit they never were.

At the end of the summer, maybe a day or so before the boys from Manitoulin Island and nearby reserves came back, we left Aird Island and everything on it and everything that it had come to represent — home, comfort, freedom, a place of growth — to return to exile, loneliness, confinement and repression.

Along with the returning students were new boys, equal in number to those discharged the previous June. The Commandas from Timagami, the Jockos from Golden Lake. The eldest Jocko was asked what his name was. "David" he said, "but the people at home call me Beans." Within days David, or Beans, was rechristened "Stiff Bean" from his muscle-bound movements.

Escape and Near-Escape from Spanish

One year gone. How many more? At least I was now in Grade 6; a senior going to school for only half a day, working in the chicken coop the other half day with Jake Thompson and Reuben Bisto.

By mid-October the school was running as it was intended to run; the new boys had adjusted much better than expected, no problems. Fathers Buck and Kehl had reason to be smug: their fatherland had overrun and occupied most of Europe.

We had just returned from a woodcutting expedition from the farm up the road and were being counted prior to the 5:00 P.M. study period.

"Where is Clarence?" Father Buck asked, extracting his little black book from his soutane pocket and making an entry in it.

There was no answer.

"Where is Clarence Abitung?" he asked again, his face growing crimson.

"I don't know, Father."

"Maybe he's in the 'firmary."

"Maybe he's in the toilets."

There were a lot of whispers and worried glances and nervous twitches.

"Yeah! Where's Clarence?" the boys asked one another.

"I don't know."

"Did you see him?"

"Who's Clarence?"

"Jis' one of those li'l guys, in Grade 5, I think. Jis' came to the school this year. Kinda new."

"No! I don't know what he looks like."

During study Father Buck came in several times to look over the study hall and to whisper violently into the ear of Mr. William

McGrath, one of the local residents who often supervised and super-intended studies in order to sustain himself and to support all the little McGraths, born and unborn, who had come to populate Spanish. Mr. McGrath shook his head in unconcern. With each shake, Father Buck's face grew another shade redder. Tension was mounting.

Again at roll-call and count before supper Father Buck asked, "Where is Clarence? . . . Anybody see Clarence?"

"No, Father. I never seen 'im since this morning afore breakfast."

"Maybe he's in the 'firmary."

"Maybe he's in the toilets."

"I hope he runned away," one boy whispered.

During the meal Father Buck and Father Kehl stood side by side whispering heavily and heatedly. While they were in heavy discus-sion, Father Hawkins, looking even more severe than usual, sum-moned both prefects into the recreation hall. When they returned to their posts both wore worried frowns.

From the end of supper hour until bedtime the rumours flew thick and fast.

"Yeah, I think he's runned away."

"Maybe he's drowned."

"Hope he makes it."

"Where's he from, anyway?"

"From Sagamok."

"Betcha he runned away, 'cause he got a good thrashing t'other day for talking Indian. Father Kehl caught 'im. Betcha he runned away, when we were up at the farm today cutting wood. Sagamok not too far from there."

"But he's jis' a li'l guy, him; he'll get lost in the bush."

"Nah! All's he got to do is follow the shoreline."

"Yeah, but not even the senior boys try that."

"Anyways, I hope he gits away."

"Nah! They'll catch 'im. Do you think them priests gonna let 'im get away so easy? Not them. Jus' watch, they'll go after 'im an' bring 'im back. An poor ol' Clarence. . . . Then they'll thrash 'im an' make 'im work in the toilets an' put 'im in the jug every Thursday an' keep 'im here till he's sixteen."

At 4:15 the next afternoon we were called. "Basil Johnston, Martin Assiniwe, Tommy Diabo, Frank Commanda, David Jocko; Father Hawkins wants see you."

I was seized by a sudden terror. They had not forgotten; he had not forgotten about the potato incident. Why now? What'll I say?

Outside Father Hawkins's office Martin, Tommy and I held a worried consultation. "Where's Norbert? How come he's not here? Maybe he snitched? . . . Frankie, David, what are you here for?"

"I don' know."

Father Hawkins came out of his office. "You speak Indian, Martin?" he asked.

Martin didn't even bat an eye as he shook his head. "No, Father. Not me. You tol' us not to talk Indian. It's against the rules, you said," and Martin continued to shake his head.

I knew Martin wasn't telling the truth. He had helped old Father Richard just the other day with a translation of the Bible. He read the Bible and provided translations and the meanings of words while Father Richard recorded the translations on a drafting board using letter blocks to spell out the words, which he then checked by means of a magnifying glass, so bad had his eyesight become. On the one hand we were forbidden to talk our native language, but on the other hand we were expected to assist Father Richard. It was a rule that was not too easily enforced. Many boys spoke their language without fear beyond the hearing of prefects. Maybe Father Hawkins was asking a trick question. Why?

"David?"

"No."

"Frankie?"

"No."

"Basil?"

"Well . . . er . . . um . . . I remember some, but I don't talk it, like you told us."

"Do you think you can say 'Clarence has to come back to the school'?"

"Yes, I think so."

"And would you understand what was being said?"

"Yes, I think so."

"Very well! You'd better, because we're going up to Sagamok to get Clarence Abitung back, and you're going to be interpreter."

From Massey, Father Hawkins drove downstream along the Spanish River road some four miles or so before he stopped.

"That's the Abitung house," he said, pointing to a log house on the opposite shore. Smoke was wafting from the chimney. "I want you to call Mr. Abitung or whoever's home. Tell them that they must hand over Clarence. Call them first, and I'll tell you what to say."

We all got out of the car and stood on the bank of the river facing the Abitung residence, which, apart from the wisp of smoke curling from the chimney, appeared uninhabited.

"You can call now."

"Heeey! Heeey! Heeey!" we all called.

A man came out of the house.

"Waeginaen baebau-nindoyaek?"

"He says, 'What do you want?' " I told Father Hawkins, not telling him that from the tone of the man's voice he meant, "What the hell do you want?"

"Ask him if he's Clarence's father."

"Keen nah Clarence ossun?"

"Ahneen gayae igoh nauh, ahneen dush?"

"Yes. He wants to know why."

"Tell him I'm Father Hawkins and that I'm here to fetch Clarence."

I relayed the message to Mr. Abitung, who replied that he didn't give a damn who the priest was and that he wasn't about to surrender his son to Spanish again.

Displeased with this insolent reply, the priest next instructed me to let Mr. Abitung know that if he did not produce Clarence within the next few minutes, Father Hawkins would have to return tomorrow with the police.

Mr. Abitung disappeared into the house, emerging a few moments later holding what, from where we were standing, looked like a stick.

"Ahow," Mr. Abitung said. "Tell that priest that I have a rifle and if I don't hear that car running in the next few minutes, I'm going to start firing . . . and you kids better keep out of sight. You've caused me enough trouble for today. I don't want no more. And if that priest comes back tomorrow, I'll be ready for him. I don't care how many policemen he brings."

"Father! He's got a gun! He's going to shoot if we don't leave; he's going to start shooting if he doesn't hear the car." And we took to our heels, with Father Hawkins right behind.

Clarence had accomplished what many other boys had often aspired to do: run away, never to return. It inspired other boys, serving as an example to Gordon Solomon, Benedict Shigwadja and Russel Abitung.

Gordon Solomon had just received a severe thrashing from Father Hawkins and was crying openly and unashamedly, quite unlike most of the other boys, who toughed out strappings and refused to cry out for priest, brother, teacher or any man. Some, like Ben Shigwadja, would suffer cuts and bruises to their hands rather than betray a sign of hurt or pain. Throughout his punishments Ben smiled in defiance, daring his oppressor to make him cry out, curling his mouth contemptuously as if to say, "Though you inflict a hundred lashes, you will not exact one moan from my lips." In frustration and in order to maintain some self-esteem and dignity, the disciplinarian would discontinue thrashing Ben with the dark warning: "It will be worse the next time." Sometimes, just out of mischief, Ben would thank the priest: "Thanks, Father; gotta tough up my hands, might git sof', them."

Even though Ben was tough, he wasn't violent and he avoided fights. A recent arrival at the school challenged Ben to knock a chip off his shoulder in the accepted manner of provoking a fight, but Ben was too busy talking and laughing to be bothered with fighting. Only after the other boy had persisted in his tauntings — "You're scared, eh?" — did Ben rise to his feet. Going to the backstop, he ripped off a half-inch board, clamped his teeth on the board and bent the ends until the board snapped. Then, as he spat out some splinters, he warned his challenger: "That's what I'm goin' to do with youse, if youse don' leave me alone." The boy retreated.

Ben was tough. The only time he had ever showed any sign of suffering was the day he took a running dive into the Spanish River and broke his arm on a submerged dead-head. Even then he had smiled at the priest as he left the dock to report to Brother Laflamme in the infirmary — though he winced as he walked by the other boys.

Gordon was not like Ben; he was anemic and frail and cried easily and loudly whenever he got a thrashing, which was often, because he was always in Ben's company. He was therefore an accessory before, during and after any fact, and held to be guilty of any misdeeds Ben was charged with. Gordon also wore a perpetual guilty look.

"What happen?" Ben asked Gordon, who made no attempt to wipe away the tears that coursed down on either side of his nose and dripped onto the front of his shirt. "Whatcha do?"

"I didn' do nothin': I jis' went up to the dormitory after breakfas' to get a jackknife, an' Father Buck caught me an' sent me to Thin Beak [Father Hawkins]. An' I had to wait outside his office all mornin' an' ... an' ... when he came back jis' now, he didn' even ast me nothin'. He jis' thrashed me," and Gordon put his hands to his mouth, blew into them to cool them and wailed.

Ben put his hand on Gordon's shoulder.

"Ben! I didn' do nothin', I got thrashed for nothin'. You know if you forgit somethin' and you have to go an' git it ... that's nothin', ain't it?"

"That's right, Gordon," Ben agreed, clapping Gordon's shoulder, "Nothin' wrong with that ... do it myself all the time." Ben ground his teeth.

"Always make somethin' out of nothin', them priests. I hate this place. I wanna go home an' never come back.... I'm gonna run away, Ben! I can't take it no more. Maybe I won' see you no more ... waah ... waah."

"Well, I'm goin' witch you," Ben declared, taking hold of Gordon's swollen hands. "Hurt?"

"Yeah."

"Whynch you piss on 'em?"

"*Piss* on them?"

"Yeah. Piss on 'em."

Gordon looked at Ben in disbelief and then at his puffed hands. "That work?"

"Shore! My grandfather showed me that a long time ago. Real good for bee stings ... and for strap stings ... same thing. Go on!" and Ben shoved Gordon around the corner of the chicken coop to administer the medication. It worked, and Gordon sneaked back into the yard.

Gordon felt better, but he was still aggrieved and his belief in his innocence was sustained by Ben. Unfortunately, Gordon *was* guilty of having broken an out-of-bounds regulation — a serious offence, for which an offender was immediately sentenced to a thrashing. Certain areas — the cloister, the wine cellar, the candy shop, the attic, the girls' school across the road, the fields adjacent to the school and, during the growing season, Brother McLaren's beloved tomato and vegetable garden — were out of bounds to all except the workers. Other areas, the dormitory and the rectory, for example, were out of bounds during the day.

No regulation, not even the ones that forbade the speaking of

Ojibway and Mohawk, or prohibited smoking, drinking or swearing, were broken as often as the out-of-bounds rule.

Gordon and Ben lay down on the grass near third base of the senior baseball diamond, just within bounds.

"When we gonna go, Ben?"

"I'm ready anytime; even this afternoon."

That was a little too soon for Gordon. "But we gotta plan the escape. We gotta take some food and figure out the bes' way to go."

"Hell, we jis' walk out behind the barn, round Rangers' Camp, behind Canadiens' Camp an' out on the highway . . . we'll walk."

"But we gotta eat!"

"Jeez, Gordon! Easy. Lotsa farms on the way. Steal some chickens an' eggs an'. . ."

"We need some dishes an' pots, if we gonna eat. Take coupla days to git all that stuff an' hide it someplace. An' besides, don' think we should take the highway, us. People'll know us right away, an' tell on us."

"Well, maybe we'll hop the train . . . be in Sudbury tonight."

"Don' think that's too good, me — shshshsh!"

Russel Abitung sat down. "Hey, Ben! Can you bend this here hoop?" Ben took the warped hoop, strained, grunted, wrestled and straightened it out.

"Hey, Russel! You wanna come with us?" Ben asked. Gordon nudged Ben.

"Where you goin'?"

"We're gonna run away."

"Shore! When?"

"Coupla days."

"Which way you goin'?"

"Through the bushes around Rangers' Camp and behind an' out to the highway."

"That's too far 'round, black-flies and mosquitoes git us before we git too far. There's a easier way."

"Which way is that?" Ben and Gordon asked at the same time.

"Take a boat. Steal one o' them punts and jis' row up to my place or steal Father Hawkins's canoe or maybe Father Vandriessch's ol' sailboat. An' you can stay at my place."

The bell rang for afternoon classes and for work for the afternoon shift.

"We'll talk about that some more after supper," Ben whispered.

After a huge bowl of onion soup (not the French variety), Ben and Gordon returned to their favourite lounging spot to discuss the details of their escape.

"Whatcha ask Russel for?" Gordon asked.

"Cause he don't like it here, an' I feel sorry for him." Russel flopped down beside them.

Gordon, quite doubtful, started the discussion. "I don't know if it's any better to go by boat. Easy for you, Russel, 'cause you live jis' 'bout ten miles up the river [at Sagamok, near Massey, Ontario], but what about us? Me an' Ben here still gotta walk, us."

"Youse guys are dumb," Russel rejoined. "I'll take one boat an' youse guys can take another boat and row to the island."

"Jeez, never thought o' that, me," Gordon said.

Ben clapped Gordon on the shoulder. "You's stupid, anyways," and he laughed.

"But what about Father Dufresne? He's down there all the time."

"Nah!" Ben spat out. "Wouldn't worry about him. He don' care about nothin'; anyways if he ast somethin' we jis' tell 'im we're working for Thin Beak."

If Father Dufresne had little to do with the boys except to hear their confessions, he had as little to do with the administration. The boys did not have to worry about Father Dufresne. Still, they were not about to take unnecessary risks, even with him.

"When we gonna go?" Russel asked.

"Tomorrow afternoon," Ben suggested. "'Bout four clock when everyone's busy. Won't miss us till about six, an' by that time we'll have coupla hours' start."

"But they'll miss us right away at work," Gordon countered.

"Nah! We'll tell the other boys to say we're sick."

"Jeez! That don' give us no time to take some plates an' food."

"You don't need that stuff," Russel advised. "I can git home in three or four hours and youse guys go right across to Li'l Detroit, through them narrows an' across the channel an' youse's on the island. Don' need no food; git lots when youse git home."

Russel's father was a fisherman, and Russel knew something about channels and navigation. He continued: "Youse guys row all night an' you be on the island in the morning — if you row hard, maybe before then."

"Suppose a storm comes up?" Gordon observed nervously.

"Then you stay on Aird Island or at the Buzwas' place at Li'l Detroit until it blows over."

"But how's I git home [to Killarney] from the island?" Gordon inquired, getting nervous because the escape was taking him farther away from home.

"Hey, Gordon, what you worried about that, boy? You jis' wanna git away from here, don't you? Jis' git t'hell outa here an' . . . we'll figure out how you gonna git home after. I'll git my dad to take you home from Wikwemikong."

The bell rang for evening study.

"Okay! Tomorrow at four; we'll meet at the dock. Save some bread and lard tonight," Ben advised.

The next day, shortly after four o'clock, Ben, Gordon and Russel arrived by different routes at the shore, explaining to Father Dufresne, who was painting rocks, that they were doing some work for Father Hawkins. Father Dufresne nodded without looking up.

Russel selected a punt and, with the help of Ben and Gordon, launched the vessel and began to row upstream in the general direction of Sagamok, hugging the shore to avoid observation from any spying eyes.

Gordon, puffing from exertion and anxiety, his eyes round in fright, leaped into the nearest punt.

"Hey, Gordon! Let's take Father Hawkins's canoe; faster and lighter than them old tubs."

Gordon, getting more and more worried by the minute, scampered out of the punt, with a "Let's hurry up," and ran to Father Hawkins's canoe, which was resting upside down on a makeshift rack of logs and poles. He and Ben turned it right side up.

"Ben! There's no paddles!" Gordon wailed in dismay. "Damn canoe's no good without paddles. Why in heck don' that Thin Beak leave the paddles near the canoe? What we gonna do, Ben?"

"Come on, Gordon. Cut out the talk. Go an' git them oars."

While Ben held the bobbing canoe, Gordon fetched the oars. He gave one oar to Ben, then boarded the canoe, almost tipping it over. "Okay?" Ben inquired. Then he pushed the canoe away from shore and leaped into it as he would a rowboat. The canoe bobbed from side to side.

"Ben, do we sit or kneel in this damn thing?" The craft wobbled and pitched and drifted back toward the dock. "We're gonna tip,"

Gordon moaned.

"Steady. Don' move," Ben urged his friend, laughing at the same time. "Paddle!"

As best he could, Gordon dipped the oar into the murk, sending the canoe veering to the left while tilting to the right. Ben dug his own oar into the current and the canoe spun to the right and listed to the left. By lurch and list the canoe moved perilously close to the dock, but then, unwillingly, out toward the open channel. Not having inherited a natural ability to navigate canoes, Ben and Gordon were operating at cross-purposes; still, they managed to reach the channel just beyond the dock, where the current bore them sideways downstream.

By now Ben wasn't laughing or even smiling, while Gordon was barely able to heft the long oar.

"Come on, Gordon, let's head for shore. Have to take a punt instead. This canoe ain't no good."

With mighty efforts, Ben and Gordon attained shore, but while landing they ripped a gash in the hull. They picked up the canoe and, at Ben's suggestion, carried it to the slough, where they concealed it well out of sight, deep in the reeds and thickets. Eugene and Charlie later found it there and, in a fit of revenge, punched holes in it.

Emerging from the chest-high reeds, neither Ben nor Gordon cast a glance in the direction of the school but walked quickly back to the dock, boarded a punt and rowed straight across the mouth of the Spanish River toward the narrows at Little Detroit and beyond, bound for home, freedom and Manitoulin Island some twenty miles away.

Back at the school, Father Buck rang the bell at 5:55 P.M. to summon a mass of hungry boys to supper. On the clap of the bell, the boys lined up, standing as erect as soldiers.

"One, two, three, four, five, six. . . ." The Maple Leafs were counted. Father Buck's face turned white, then crimson, and his mouth quivered. "Where is Benedict Shigwadja?" and he whipped out a little black book and a stubby little pencil. "Come! Donald [Fox]! Where is Benedict?"

"I dunno."

"I come back to you! Just wait!"

Next the Canadiens, who were all accounted for; but when the Rangers were inspected, one was missing.

"Where is Gordon Solomon? Wilfred! Where is Gordon?"

"I din' see him all day, me, Father."

"If you lying, Wilfred, I fix you."

"Maybe he's sick," a voice from the back of the line suggested.

"Who says this?" Father Buck demanded. "Who says this?" and he glowered at the Grade 7 and 8 boys at the back. "Just wait . . . just wait."

After Father Buck had checked the seniors, he inspected the intermediates.

"One, two, three. . . ." A Black Hawk was truant.

"Where is Russel? Eh? Eh? Tell me!" he demanded of Alvin, who mumbled, "I never seen him; I don' know where he is."

"Just wait! You no eat until I found out! No move!" Father Buck scowled.

As he opened the door behind him, one of the seniors, at least it sounded like a senior, muttered something like, "I hope he runned away."

Father Buck's countenance reflected rage. He whirled on his heel and walked beside each line of boys, glaring into each petrified but innocent-looking face. "Who says this? Who says this?" No one answered. "Just wait," and he stalked out.

When Father Buck returned three or four minutes later, the length of time it took to investigate the infirmary and the dormitory on the third floor, his face was as red as a cranberry.

"Okay!" was all he said as he nodded to his colleague, Father Kehl, who opened the doors to the refectory for the boys to file in team by team. During the meal Father Buck and Father Kehl huddled near the doorway talking in low tones in German while the boys discussed the disappearance of their comrades.

Lights were turned off and, as usual, there were muffled whimpers and sobs of boys, especially the smaller ones, crying in loneliness, in longing for home and parents and comfort that many would never again know. In the dark and out of the chorus of sobs a barely audible voice bleated, "I hope them guys don' come back."

Father Buck, who had been moving like a shadow in the dark, exploded. "Who says this? Who says this?" he stormed, switching on his flashlight, beaming it in the general direction of the voice and stomping over. But before he had taken even two steps, another voice in another corner rasped out derisively, "Wanna know where they are, Father?" Father Buck stopped in his tracks, whirled and shone his flashlight in that direction, but each time he did so another voice cleaved the darkness, taunting Father Buck and Father Kehl, who had joined the investigation. "Betcha can't fin' 'em, Father!" Father Buck whirled this way and that, trying to locate and discern voices that were as elusive as the croaks of spring peepers in a midnight pond.

Finally, in exasperation, Father Buck switched on the dormitory lights. "All right, youse! Stand up! And stand till you keep quiet. No noise; no move." We stood up beside our beds for perhaps half an hour before Father Buck relented and commanded us: "Go to bed, and no more talking." We fell asleep feeling triumphant.

But our colleagues did not get away. Russel managed to spend just one glorious night with his parents, where he ate two good meals of potatoes, salt pork, fish and bannock, before Father Hawkins recaptured him and restored him to the school.

Ben and Gordon, after alternately drifting and rowing around and along the McBean Channel, were borne by a north-east wind across the North Channel until, tired and hungry, they hove into Kagawong where they beached their punt. From Kagawong, still dressed in their corduroy riding breeches and beige shirts, they hitchhiked to Little Current and then on to Manitowaning. There, just nine miles from Ben's beloved home, they were apprehended by the local constable on information supplied by an alert citizen whose suspicions were roused by their garments and their conduct. Ben and Gordon were held in custody for Father Hawkins.

On restoration to the rolls, Ben and Gordon were sentenced to latrine duty and confined to the school premises. They also received a severe thrashing from Father Hawkins, which Ben again toughed out. Still, both Ben and Gordon were allowed home for the summer.

This was not the end of the great escape.

During staff dinner one late October evening, Father Dufresne addressed Father Hawkins.

"Father Hawkins! You should takes care better, your canoes. Not good examples for the boys and for the rest. If you leaves that canoes in the swamps, it's goin' to gets rotten an' then you won' have no canoes, you."

Father Hawkins, who had not used his canoe and had not missed it, was flabbergasted. "Where? What are you talking about?"

"In the swamps ... there, by the shores," Father Dufresne enlightened his brother priest.

"Who put it there?"

"Some boys!"

"Who?"

"I don' know, me."

"When?"

"Long times ago . . . las' springs."

Father Hawkins finished his meal hastily, then asked Father Primeau, the Superior, if he could be excused. He found his canoe crawling with insects, the hull partly devoured by cut-worms and other little creatures and partly ravaged by wet rot.

The Cattle Drive

For most of the year, the routine was unchanging for the cow-barn workers. From morning till evening they toiled, milking cows, cleaning out the barn, feeding the cows, separating the milk, putting the cows out to pasture, rounding them up again with the aid of "Buster," an old dog, and then milking again in the evening. The horse-barn workers had a great variety of tasks within the barn, around the institution and beyond — ploughing in Walford, for example, or cutting wood in Brennan Harbour out of sight of prefects. But the cow-barn workers had little to look forward to except driving "steers and heifers" in early summer to Aird Island or to some other island for summer grazing and then retrieving them in September in another "drive." To these occasions, and these only, the cow-barn workers could look forward for a picnic meal and a certain amount of freedom from rules and supervision for one day.

Besides the regulars, that is the older boys, Brother Grubb would ask for volunteers from the intermediate group to assist in the cattle drive.

"Who wants help move little cows to Aird Island tomorrow? We need five boys more."

Of course, everyone volunteered. Eugene Keeshig, Shaggy (Joe Missabe), Angus (Pitwaniquot), La Marr (Antoine Lafrance), Cheeby or Ghost (Alfred Webkamigad), Tony Angus, Alex Manitowabi, Simon Martin and Kitchi-meeshi Hec all waved their hands and pleaded, "Me . . . me . . . me . . . me, Brother."

"Okay! Euchene, Ankus and La Marr," Brother Grubb announced, choosing three of the boys not for their experience or skill in husbandry, or for their good behaviour (the usual norm for selection for special assignments), or out of any particular fondness for any of them, but out of genuine concern for the safety of barn, equipment and livestock. With Eugene, Angus and La Marr nothing was safe. To them work was an unpleasant interruption in what ought to be a blissful state of eternal pleasure. To leave them behind would be tantamount to leaving three cats in a roomful of canaries. Brother Grubb probably selected this trio out of fear for his own safety.

Simon, Tony, Cheeby, Shaggy, Alex, Kitchi-meeshi Hec and the rest of the cow-barn personnel muttered in dismay and envy. "Pets! Grubb's Pets! Always the same ones! Never us! Pets! Pets!" They spat out the most derogatory name that one student could call another: a name ascribed to boys receiving special consideration from a priest or brother.

But the elect refused to rise to the insult. At any other time Eugene would have sprung forward to deliver an uppercut and several lightning jabs to the offender's jaw, while La Marr would have shaken the bones of the same offender into dislocation. Today they were smug and amiable and tolerant of their less-fortunate brethren. "Ah! Youse guys is jis' jealous! Ha! Ha! Gotta take men, him! Gotta take guys who's not scared of them cows!" Alex and Simon and Shaggy continued to grumble, "Pets!"

For his part Father Buck conscripted Boozo, Cigar Butt (Frank Syrette) and Archie Pancake (Francis) from the inferior ranks of the intermediates to assist in the forthcoming cattle drive. They were to report to Brother Grubb in the morning right after breakfast.

Brother Grubb was a short, lean, leather-faced man. Everything about him was diminutive except his arms, which had been stretched by carrying two full milk cans four times daily from the barn to the kitchen, so that his hands oscillated in the vicinity of his kneecaps. Despite his lack of stature, Brother Grubb still managed to superintend a large cow barn, more than a hundred head of cattle, one horny bull, an abbatoir, the dairy operations and an unruly bunch of boys recruited from the august senior ranks. And in the discharge of his temporal stewardship Brother Grubb issued instructions to the boys in a high-pitched voice.

At 6:30 A.M. the cow-barn workers reported to Brother Grubb for briefing before assignment to duty. Such briefings were not really necessary, for the milkers knew that they would milk the cows, and the feeders and the cleaners were already familiar with their routines. But such briefings always represented a ray of hope to the manure slingers, whose job of shovelling cow dung into wheelbarrows and then delivering the cargo to a mountain of manure on the north side of the byre was as disagreeable as any in the entire institution.

Secretly, although it was no secret to anyone, each manure shoveller nursed a hope that one of the milkers or feeders — or anyone for that matter — would be sick on that day and he would be selected as a replacement.

With Eugene, Angus, La Marr and Shaggy gone for the day there were four vacancies representing tasks far better than shovelling dung. Competition was keen. "Brother! Me! Me! Can I milk, me? I never milked yet, an' I wanna learn. Can I churn the butter? Can I feed the cows? Can I work the separator?"

"No!" Brother Grubb declared while shaking his head from side to side for emphasis. "We're not going until after breakfast."

The shovellers muttered as they picked up their implements.

"Brother Van der Moor will be in charge today."

Eugene, Angus, La Marr and Shaggy continued to crowd around Brother Grubb, asking, "What we gonna eat, Brother? Ham? Pork? Beef? Beans? Didja bring some tobaccy?"

"Awright, boys, git to work. Git jobs done first. After breakfas' we go."

The milkers scrambled for their pails while Brother Grubb went on to scrub and scour the separators and their parts.

When Angus brought in a pail of milk he said to Brother Grubb: "Aw, come on Brother, tell me, what we gonna eat?"

Learning that there were to be boiled eggs, roast beef, butter, bread, cheese and honey, Angus relayed the happy information to his partners. In no time every cow-barn worker knew what was on the menu and was muttering in envy, "Them lucky guys." Later, when the intermediates heard the rumours that flew about, they too were envious and nursed ambitions. "Somedays I wanna work in the barns."

At 8:30 the cowboys accompanied Brother Grubb to the back of the field behind the barn, near Rangers' Camp, to round up the steers and heifers that were to be transported to Aird Island and then left for the summer.

On the way to the far end of the field Brother Grubb instructed the drovers, especially the greenhorns, "Don' make liddle cows run. Everything easy; no yelling, no running. Not good for liddle cows get excited; maybe run away and get hurt. Liddle cows mus' be peaceful before they get on this boat."

At their heels plodded Buster, the old dog, occasionally resting his feeble legs. No more would he round up heifers by himself, except perhaps in dreams.

"Hey! Brother Grubb! Can we smoke now?" Angus asked.

"No! No! Too close to school. Father Hawkins might see. Wait till we git on boat."

The cattle drive across the field was unhurried, conducted at heifer's pace. Except for the flies there was nothing to disturb the animals. Even the boys, in imitation of Brother Grubb, addressed the heifers in soothing tones by the names given them by the good brother: Marie, Stella, Ursula, Erna, Wiltrud, Usche, Ulricha and other Teutonic names that may have commemorated various Bavarian beauties. The herd passed the piggery that swelled with the grunts and groans of its tenants; passed the massive barn from which insults were hurled, and the blacksmith shop where the forge whined and the anvil rang as smithies hammered sheets of tin or horseshoes. Not once did the drovers or liddle cows lose their composure.

At the shore, the heifers and steers went straight to the water to drink deeply from the Spanish River, already contaminated by the sewage and chemicals dumped there by the Kalamazoo Vegetable Parchment Company in Espanola.

Meanwhile, Brother Grubb, with an entourage of boys, checked and double-checked the ramp, the dock and the scow. As the captain for the voyage, Brother Manseau was already aboard the Iron Boat, checking the mechanism to see that it was in working order. The Iron Boat would today do tug duty.

Brother Grubb looked at the general condition of the dock that extended from the shore to the point where the river bed fell abruptly away into a deep channel. From its warped and canted condition, the dock appeared to be in danger of imminent collapse, but despite its uncertain architecture — it was hardly more than a boardwalk resting on rock pilings — the structure was fairly sound. Not satisfied from a visual inspection that the dock would support "liddle cows," Brother Grubb and his cowboys took turns jumping on the crossboards to test their firmness. No one fell through.

Nestled against the dock on the downstream side was a scow designed by Brother Van der Moor on the basis of hearsay and his experience of making rough boxes for coffins. The scow had been put together by fifteen- and sixteen-year-old boys armed with hammers, nails and saws; it had then been sealed with axle grease blended with pitch. At one corner of the deck was a trap door. On all voyages a member of the crew was assigned to permanent duty operating a pump or bailing the craft with a bucket to keep it afloat. The pump operator performed his duties through the trap door.

On this voyage there was installed at each corner of the vessel a five-foot birch stave. Three strands of wire connected the staves, thus forming a floating corral. A member of the crew equipped with a short pike was consigned to each corner to keep the passengers amidships. For this expedition Eugene, Angus, La Marr, and Shaggy were to man the corners, while Cigar Butt was delegated to operate the pump, if operational, or to man the bucket.

The scow and its cargo would be towed by the Iron Boat, so called because its entire structure was of metal. It was said that it had formerly served as a lifeboat on an ocean liner; but since its overhaul two years before by Gerry Labelle, it now served the institution as a kind of all-purpose vessel, for transporting boys and equipment and "liddle cows." Because of its shallow draught it was a much more useful craft than the larger Garnier. The Iron Boat, painted a dull red, was already putting, having been cranked into life by Brother Manseau, captain, engineer and navigator. Henry Tenniscoe was at the tiller.

"Ready?" Brother Grubb inquired.

"Anytime."

"Okay, boys. Get liddle cows on scow. Nice an' easy. No make it scared. No make run . . . just walk."

By this time heifers and steers had slaked their thirsts and, while wading in the river, had lost some of their fear of water and were ready for more grazing. Even though the drovers conducted their roundup in a calm manner, with such reassuring comments as, "Come on, Ursula! It's okay, Wiltrud!", the heifers' eyes opened wide in fright as they mounted the dock, heard their hooves clatter on the boards and felt the framework shudder; their eyes bulged and they tossed their heads in worry as they boarded the scow; they mooed as if remembering another voyage made by their ancestors in another age. La Marr and Angus, who were both as strong as oxen, pushed a reluctant heifer on board. When all the heifers had been shepherded onto the deck, Brother Grubb bound the makeshift gate.

All the boys were at their stations.

"Okay, Brother!"

Brother Manseau eased the throttle forward from slow to full speed until the Iron Boat was fishtailing, roaring and throwing up a rooster tail of foam. Nothing happened.

"The scow, she's stuck there somewheres," Brother Manseau informed his fellow Jesuit after he had put the Iron Boat into neutral.

"You, Ankus, and Shaggy! Get these push poles and when boat starts, push hard." Brother Grubb himself laid his hands on a third push pole, part of the scow's emergency equipment. He nodded to Brother Manseau.

Eugene and La Marr were perched like koala bears on top of their stakes, their legs wrapped around the shafts. They called out cheerfully, "Okay, Brother!"

When the Iron Boat surged forward and her bow was uplifted in strain, Angus, Shaggy and Brother Grubb leaned into the poles. The scow creaked while the liddle cows mooed.

Perhaps the "polers" pushed too hard or perhaps a heifer broke ranks. Whatever the cause, the scow's stern lifted, throwing all the heifers and steers forward and pitching both them and the crew into the current. But even before the first heifer slid into the water, Eugene and Cigar Butt abandoned ship by diving into the water away from the herd; La Marr, too, escaped by leaping onto the dock. But Angus, Shaggy and Brother Grubb slithered down the deck of the scow and vanished in four feet of Spanish River murk amid a welter of heifers and steers.

Brother Manseau brought the Iron Boat to a full stop and was instantly on his feet, cursing: "Maudit! Zhoopitaire! G--d d----d," and other expletives designed to restore order at once. In between curses he shouted instructions to the writhing tangle of swimmers, animals and humans — "Get to shore, you danged fools! Swim! Swim! Get out of the danged water! Don' stay there! Don' drowns!" — and rendered what other aid and encouragement he could provide to the shipwrecked.

Fifteen of the heifers made straight for the river bank and, on gaining dry land, fled in all directions, with most of them stampeding up the road toward the village of Spanish pursued by three water-logged but laughing and shouting cowboys, Angus, Shaggy and Eugene. Three heifers, swept by the current away from the disaster, floated downriver, all the while valiantly trying to change course for shore and safety. Immediately behind one of the heifers was Brother Grubb shouting "Help! Help!" but unwilling to let go of Trixie's tail long enough to wave for fear he would sink and drown.

La Marr, who had been watching the spectacle from the dock, espied Brother Grubb. "Haw! Haw! Haw! Hey, Beedj," he managed to blurt out. "There's Brother Grubb goin' with the cows." He pointed to four swimmers all drifting at the same nautical pace and bearing for the open waters of the North Channel and, beyond that, Lake Huron. "Haw! Haw! Haw!"

Brother Manseau sped off to the rescue.

Directly across the channel, five hundred metres away, were two truant heifers standing chest deep on a sandbar calmly feeding on reeds. How they had got there by swimming at right angles against a port current was the subject of much speculation at the school for some years after the incident. Not even Father Dufresne, whose platform perch afforded him a bird's-eye view of the disaster unfolding below him, could give a rational account of the passage of Ursula and Erna. All he could recall with any clarity were the outrageous blasphemies uttered by Brother Manseau.

Meanwhile, Angus, Shaggy and Eugene, all three bald-headed according to summer tonsorial style, and weighted down with baggy overalls and coveralls and heavy work boots, did their best to overtake and head off the escaping heifers. At Kelly's Bakery on top of the hill some of the heifers went left toward Brennan Harbour, while the rest turned right toward the main part of the village. Old Mrs. Kelly, seeing only the inmates running from the school, but not the cows, believed the boys to be making their escape and promptly phoned the school and the police. Finally, between McLeod's and Muncaster's, the cowboys headed off the runaways and escorted them back.

Archie Pancake had not abandoned ship; he and Boozo continued to bail the scow for the better part of the day, until someone remembered them.

It took the entire day to round up the truant heifers, including the three who had taken themselves to Brennan Harbour and the two who had been stranded on the sandbar. The picnic lunch was almost forgotten.

It was nearly a week before Stella and Marie and their sisters and brothers recovered their composure sufficiently to undertake the journey to Aird Island — under a different escort.

At the end of the school year we watched in envy as Eddie Coocoo, John Latour, Joe Lazore, Leon Abraham, Wilfred Trudeau and Snowball (Mitchell Loft) walked up the road in the evening to catch the train and leave Spanish, never more to return.

The Best-Laid Plans . . .

Things did not always go according to plan or with the solemnity that priests and nuns wished of life. Like boys and girls, priests and nuns were subject to the laws and passions, the rules and emotions that govern the religious and the secular; they were no more exempt, by virtue of their vocations, from accidents or misadventures or mishaps than anyone else, although their discipline may have ensured that they suffered fewer accidents than ordinary mortals.

Neither sanctity nor grace prevented Father Richard or Father Dufresne from hastening to the tabernacle at communion time, vying with one another to be first to take possession of a particularly handsome ciborium enclosed therein. The struggle for possession of the beautiful ciborium, with one priest pulling from the front of the altar tabernacle and the other tugging from the back, was spirited but brief, and never violent enough to do damage to the sacred vessel or to delay the service.

Miss Leutsch was not only a fine musician but, as well, an accomplished brewer of root beer; and so was called upon to brew root beer for the bazaars held in the missions along the north shore all summer. Many were the barrels that might have been found brewing in the cellars of St. Joseph's.

As a visiting missionary pastor to the needy parish of Mississauga, Father Hawkins, in order to sustain his little church and congregation, had as much need of a barrel of root beer now and again as of the liberal donations of old clothes from the generous souls in Toronto.

"Of course! Of course," Sister Leutsch gushed when Father Hawkins asked for root beer.

The only event that could spoil a bazaar was rain. If the good Lord would stay His hand for just twelve hours, it would be a fine bazaar on Saturday, commencing with mass, followed by an outdoor breakfast. Only after they had filled their bellies would the parishioners be willing to spend their money in the sales booths, play the games of chance and sit down for bingo. In the afternoon a baseball game was scheduled between the St. Peter Claver's boys' team from Spanish. During the game a hat would be passed around to help defray the expenses of the visiting team. And if everyone who was invited from Iron Bridge, Blind River, Algoma Mills, Cutler and Spanish came to the bazaar, the parish could realize a tidy profit and dispense with the need to bother the Bishop for grants or to beg for further donations. "Better make that two barrels, sister."

"Two barrels?"

"Yes, two barrels, sister. Double the profits, don't you see?"

Miss Leutsch brewed two barrels of root beer, which Father Hawkins took delivery of on the night before the bazaar and transported to Mississauga by means of a wagon hitched to the back of the Model-T. On his arrival Father Hawkins conscripted some husky Indians to help store the barrels in the cellar of the church. By way of thanks Father offered each a drink of root beer.

One of the movers remarked "Gawaetaunih mino-waugummih maundah zhowmin-aubo," which was to say, "Mighty damn good stuff, this wine."

Before returning to Spanish for the night, Father Hawkins consulted the Ladies' Auxiliary to make sure that everything was in order, then went to Mike Chiblow's to ask what the weather prospects were for the morrow.

As Mike had predicted, Saturday began gloriously and went along gloriously. All Father Hawkins had to do was to circulate and pay visits to booth managers and games attendants, making sure that everything was running smoothly. So brisk was the trade in old clothes that Father Hawkins frequently had to return to the manse with the Ladies' Auxiliary to release more old clothes; he scarcely had time to chat with his parishioners.

"When you gonna start selling the root beer, Father?"

"Not till this afternoon," Father Hawkins laughed. "Why? You getting thirsty already? Ha! Ha! Ha! Why don't you make a sacrifice for another couple of hours? Ha! Ha! Ha!"

"Well, we're getting kinda thirsty."

By 11:30, though, Father Hawkins was getting anxious. The men were just a little too happy, laughing and giggling and carrying on as if they had been drinking; nothing serious, mind you, but a situation that called for investigation before it got worse. He didn't want a scandal connected with his bazaar. Both the Bishop and the Father Provincial would make inquiries and want answers.

To confirm his suspicion Father Hawkins deliberately engaged one of the giggling men in a brief conversation. Yes, there was an unmistakable sweetish odour of wine on the man's breath, faint but present.

The priest broke away from the giggler in order to enlist two or three boys to keep an eye on the men and to report their movements. Each clutching a shiny new quarter, the boys raced off and applied themselves to the games without having seen anything unusual.

From that moment on Father Hawkins turned his attention from the bazaar to the detection of the source of wine that was already, at just 1:30, sending the starting pitcher, the catcher and the shortstop into transports of uncontrollable laughter and impairing their ability to play. A few more swigs of the stuff and none of them would be able to find the bases. The game would have to be forfeited and cancelled. If the Indians from Cutler came along, a pickup team could be organized, but something had to be done fast. Father Hawkins now kept an eagle eye on all the men, trying to perceive a suspicious bulge in anyone's pocket or to espy some furtive movement. He kept an equally sharp eye out for white men, especially the bootleggers from Blind River or Iron Bridge.

Several times during the next half hour the ladies from the auxiliary interrupted Father Hawkins in his preoccupation with inebriates to request fresh supplies of old clothes, interruptions that ought to have cheered him greatly. From the proceeds of the sale of old clothes the coffers were growing. But the news raised his spirit only moderately.

In the manse, Father Hawkins opened another crate of old hats and corsets. At the rate they were going they'd sell the entire shipment by mid-afternoon, a tremendous success, except . . .

As he stepped outside, Father Hawkins received a slurred but hearty greeting. "Good mornin', Father, real nice day for bazaar."

He looked into the happy visage of Nigunaub, a carefree parishioner. At that moment Father Hawkins would have liked nothing better than to grab Nigunaub by the throat and shake hell out of him, except that there was a major impediment to his carrying out this idea: Nigunaub was six foot three and weighed about 230 pounds, whereas Father Hawkins hovered at around the five-foot-seven mark and tipped the scales at 150 pounds. Besides, it was most un-Christian to harbour such thoughts. Whatever his feelings regarding Nigunaub, it was better to extend the hand of brotherhood and open the forgiving heart. Especially since this was the first time Nigunaub had condescended to speak to him or even to come near the church. It certainly did not reflect well on Nigunaub's training in Spanish. As long as there was a chance of enticing Nigunaub back into the fold from the realm of the lost — a real prodigal-son case if there ever was one on the north shore — the priest wanted to be as friendly as possible.

"Good morning, Nigunaub! Good to see you here. I'm glad you could make it."

"S-s-sorry. I'm not c-c-come to church in long t-t-times. [Hic.] Too b-b-busy all times. But [hic] one th-these days I'm goin' to come," Nigunaub declared with conviction.

"Glad to hear that. I'll be looking for you . . . and praying for you," Father Hawkins added with difficulty. He hurried away; he had never had an easy time dealing with inebriates.

For some while afterwards Father was uneasy in conscience. He could not forget Nigunaub. Putting off the big Indian could well mean damnation for the man for non-attendance at Sunday mass, for intoxication, for swearing. The Lord only knew what other evil the man had done, but Father Hawkins could imagine. It could mean damnation for himself for passing up the opportunity to save Nigunaub's soul. Even if Nigunaub's penitence had been inspired by Four Aces or Slingers, particularly insidious wines, and would all be forgotten on the morrow, still the man deserved a chance. Providence operated in mysterious ways: it might even operate through wine.

Father was slightly depressed. Why could the drunks not have waited for another occasion? Why at his bazaar?

One of the members of the Ladies' Auxiliary touched his arm shyly. "Father, the men is goin' to church."

Father Hawkins bent his eyes in the direction of the church door. It was true. The word "miracle" came to his mind directly . . . and Nigunaub was forgotten.

At the bottom of the church steps were three brown parishioners; two more were perched precariously on the railing of the deck. Truly it was a miracle, such as he had never before witnessed or heard about. Two men emerged from the church and two went in, and the three at the bottom of the steps moved up. Forty Hours' Devotion came to mind, in which the faithful entered and left the church in relays.

Father looked and looked. At first there was cause for rejoicing, but he soon found equal cause for consternation. Those emerging from the church were laughing and talking and waving their arms; those next scheduled to enter pushed and shoved as they went in, most impious conduct quite unbecoming in visitors to the church.

Father Hawkins strode toward the church. The worshippers waiting on the deck and on the stairs made way for him to hurry up the stairs unimpeded. As he opened the door to enter, the priest was almost knocked back and down to the deck by two blithe parishioners who came barging out. Father grabbed his hand in pain while the two parishioners tried to stifle their mirth.

"What are you doing in the cellar?" Father Hawkins demanded sternly.

"D-drinking r-r-root beer, Father."

"Liars," Father Hawkins grumbled as he pushed his way in and opened the cellar door. Loud talk and raucous laughter assailed his ears, while the sweet odour of wine assaulted his nose. He was enraged.

"Out, all of you," he roared.

At his command seven or eight shapes got up and skulked out as silently as phantoms.

Alone in the dark, dank and dismal cellar Father Hawkins peered about and groped around for the offending bottles. He could find none. Still, the odour lingered, sweetish and light, just out of reach. On the floor rested two massive kegs, casting darker shadows.

As his eyes grew accustomed to the gloom Father Hawkins made out the shapes of two tomato cans sitting quite smugly on the lid of a barrel. He snatched one of the tins and in doing so splashed some liquid on his hand. He sniffed the can, tasted the liquid on his hand carefully with his tongue and smelled the contents of the root-beer barrel. Wine, wine, wine.

Father's anger dissipated and he forgave the drunken members of his flock. Fortunately, the other barrel of root beer was quite harmless. The bazaar was saved and the ball game was played with the help of some men from Cutler.

When the barrel of good root beer was trundled outside for sale at five cents a cup, the line-up was extensive. Many of those in line were men.

One of the patrons complained: "This stuff's not very good, Father."

On his return to St. Peter Claver's Father Hawkins telephoned Miss Leutsch. "Sister! This is Father Hawkins. I have a complaint. Do you know that you nearly ruined my bazaar by getting most of my male parishioners drunk? I asked you to make root beer, not wine. And don't tell me that the root beer must have been transformed into wine by a miracle. You could have caused a scandal. Can you imagine, sister, the uproar in chancery at a headline in the Sault *Star*: 'Indians Drunk on Nun Brew.' " Then he hung up. Only after a very distressed Miss Leutsch phoned a day later did Father Hawkins explain.

You can't live the way your ancestors did; you have to organize your time, your work, if you're going to get anywhere. You can no longer just move in together and live as husband and wife; you can no longer get names for your children from the first thing that you see or hear after the birth of a child; you can no longer . . . you can no longer . . . you can no longer. . . . From now on you must do things the civilized way, the lawful way, the moral, Christian way.

Stingy (Harvey Ermitinger) fell in love, madly in love, so madly in love that in due course he asked the love of his life to be his woman. An alumnus of Spanish, he then went out and bought an engagement ring as the first step in doing things right.

Right after mass the very next Sunday, Stingy asked Father Barker, the visiting missionary pastor of Mississauga, for a private appointment. This Father Barker readily granted.

In the manse Stingy was afflicted by a sudden shyness that interfered with his train of thought and speech. "Me an' my girl, here, we're in love an' . . . we gotta get married," he blurted out. His girl hung her head and blushed.

Father Barker was properly scandalized. "You gotta get married," he repeated.

"Yeah," Stingy confirmed, brightening up considerably after he had got the matter off his chest.

"Gotta get married," Father Barker intoned sarcastically. "You get a girl in trouble and then come running to the church to bail you out. You're all the same. Why can't you wait until you are married like decent people. You! Stingy! You should know better; you were brought up in a Catholic school. I'm surprised and disappointed."

Stingy was surprised; surprised by the priest's onslaught on his upbringing and on his girl's virtue. "We're in love ... that's why we gotta get married. My girl here she's not in no trouble. I'm not get her in trouble."

"Oh. I'm sorry. I didn't understand," Father Barker apologized. "It's just that I never thought ... that is to say ... I'm glad. ..." His voice trailed off in dismay. "Sit down and we'll straighten this out."

Stingy and his girl sat down while Father Barker finished taking off his vestments and putting them away.

"Now," he said, bringing out an ancient journal, "when do you want to get married?"

"Guess, last Sa'rday in, in July or maybe first Sa'rday in August."

Father Barker consulted his appointment book, over which he ran a pencil, then said, "Last Saturday in July appears fine. ... How's ten o'clock sound to you?"

"Sounds fine to me, Father ... that okay with you, Hon?"

Hon nodded.

Father Barker, who knew the couple and their families through his parish work and ministry, did not have to ask too many questions. "We'll have to publish banns; you know all about that already anyway. ... Have you any questions?"

"Yeah. How about totems, Father? Me and my girl here we belong to the same totem. Like brother and sister supposed to be, us." Stingy was bothered by this relationship not a little.

"Oh, that. Don't worry about it. Just part of old pagan primitive beliefs and practices. Come on, Stingy, you should know better than to believe in or worry about superstitious practices," and with a wave of his hand the priest dismissed several thousand years of Anishinaubae history. Father Barker continued: "There really is no need to do so in detail, but I do have to mention them," and he outlined the laws of the church governing the marriage act, the duties connected with raising children and the penalties imposed for any infraction of the aforesaid laws. "And you'll need birth and baptismal certificates and a marriage licence. Understand?"

"Yeah," said Stingy, glad that it was over.

"Well! Good luck to both of you." Turning to the young woman, Father Barker teased: "Ten o'clock, now. Don't be late. Heh, heh, heh! Like all the other women. Heh, heh, heh! And you, Stingy, make sure you show up. No stags the night before."

In the shade of a pine tree afterward, Stingy and his woman made plans. More precisely, Stingy outlined the wedding plans.

"Yeah! We'll have a good wedding. I'll wear a suit — navy blue — an' you'll wear a white dress. Your brother can be best man; your sister can stand up for you. After church we'll have a banquet in the Council Hall and git some wine." Stingy paused to reflect a moment before continuing, pleased with the arrangements. He waited for his girl to make some comment, but she said nothing. "Just like the white men," Stingy went on, eager to impress his girl. "Nobody ever done anything like that around here . . . and we'll have a honeymoon, too . . . in the Algonquin in Sudbury."

"What's a honeymoon?"

"That's going home after the wedding dance all alone and being alone together for the first time and sleeping in the same room . . . maybe in the same bed."

"Why don't we stay home, at my house? My dad said that when I got married I could stay at home."

"I know," Stingy admitted, "but you know what it's like around here when anyone gets married. Guys sometimes kidnap the groom or a bunch o' guys runs around outside the house yelling all night an' not knowing what they're going to do next. I want to sleep. We're going to be tired. In a hotel, nice and quiet. Nobody'd bother us."

"Yeah, but dad can stand watch."

"Hmph," Stingy snorted. "Hell, he's one o' the worst. Gets the guys together, you know, an' if he's alone, does it by himself."

"But I never been to Sudbury. I don't wanna go."

"Then you're going to have to listen to them guys all night saying an' yelling out, 'Did you fin' it yet? You know how? Need any help? Get started yet? Hey! The house is on fire!' Sometimes they even break into the house and. . . ." Stingy paused to let these terrible things sink in.

The girl relented. "Maybe it's better to go to Sudbury."

During the next few weeks Stingy was busy making preparations, renting a hall and hiring an orchestra, getting the Ladies' Auxiliary as caterers and arranging delivery of the finest wine the Blind River bootlegger could deliver. In addition, Stingy and his girl secured all the necessary papers.

The last Saturday of July arrived damply. By nine o'clock Stingy was standing, with his soon-to-be-brother-in-law, Abraham, along with several of their friends, on the landing at the back of the church.

A few minutes later Stingy's wife-to-be and her retinue arrived in a well-dusted Ford affectionately known for its roar as B19. They stopped in front, where they awaited the arrival of Father Barker.

At the back of the church, Stingy and his companions stood leaning against the walls beneath the eaves, which sheltered them from the drizzle. Stingy rolled a cigarette and fidgeted. His companions chatted and joked. As 10:00 A.M. drew nearer, Stingy looked at his pocket watch more and more frequently.

"Priest should be here by now," he observed.

But Father Barker was far away, conducting a bazaar at Whitefish Lake Indian Reserve near Naughton.

"Don't worry, he'll be here," Stingy's friends reassured him.

Ten o'clock came, ticked away. Everyone looked expectantly down the road in the general direction of Highway 17. Stingy rolled another cigarette.

"Wonder where that priest is?" he said to no one in particular.

It continued to drizzle, but no one made a move to join the wedding guests huddled beneath the trees in the pine grove.

Eleven o'clock came, but Father Barker did not.

"Priest is late," Stingy observed.

Some minutes passed, during which more makings were rolled and the watch often consulted. Then Abraham suggested that somebody phone the priest.

"Let's wait a few more minutes," Stingy urged half-heartedly.

At that moment a little boy ran up with a message from the hall. "The cooks say dinner is goin' to be ready right at noon. They wanna know what you gonna do."

This news meant that Stingy had to make some decisions, fast and hard. He instructed Abraham to go phone and find out what was holding the priest up. "About time," Abraham grumbled on his way out. But the matter of the meal was not so decisively resolved.

"Let's wait till Abraham comes back," Stingy pleaded wearily. "See what he has to say."

Brrrrrng! Brrrrng! Brrrrrng! The phone rang and rang and rang at St. Peter Claver's until finally Brother Laflamme answered. "Hello!"

"I'd like to speak to Father Barker."

"He's not here."

"Okay, thanks."

Abraham duly reported on his return that there was no answer.

"May as well eat; meal's going to get cold."

Stingy assented reluctantly.

The moment the word was given, the guests trooped to the council hall, where they sat down to a sumptuous meal of beaver, pickerel, bannock, pies, cakes and blueberries set out on tables that had been artfully arranged in a U-shape. Under pressure from the congregation Stingy and his woman reluctantly went to the head table and sat down.

Though they sat at table and were enormously hungry, they resisted all exhortations to eat. "Can't. Gotta go to communion." Both Stingy and his love were staunch Catholics. Not a crumb, not even a drop of water must pass their lips. But as he sat there, Stingy was beginning to doubt the sense of civilized marriage customs and rituals.

"How about drinks? A toast? Yeah!" shouted several enthusiastic voices.

Abraham seconded the motion heartily. "Best idea I heard yet. Let's have a few drinks. Priest may not show up; no use saving it."

Stingy gave in to the demands, lest his guests and his best man grow weary of the wait and go home. Promptly two cases of Four Aces were brought out and the wine bottles passed around. Several members took healthy pulls at the bottles of "poverty champagne."

At one o'clock Stingy dispatched Abraham to make another phone call.

Brrrrng! Brrrrng! Brrrrng! the St. Peter Claver's phone rang.

An annoyed Brother Laflamme answered. "St. Peter Claver's!"

"I'd like to talk to Father Barker."

"I told you he's not here."

"Okay."

"No answer," Abraham laconically reported on his return.

"Hell, we're gonna miss our bus," Stingy complained.

"More wine! Bring on the wine! Damned good stuff."

Abraham, as well as being the best man, was the steward in charge of the spirits; cheerfully he broke open the fourth and fifth cases of Four Aces and passed out the bottles, which went from hand to mouth, hand to mouth. The mood and the disposition of the wedding guests improved considerably. From time to time Abraham rewarded himself with a mighty guzzle before depositing the bottle, his very own, on the floor behind the leg of the table.

"How about a toast," someone blurted out. The proposal was soundly seconded and carried by the majority.

Stingy objected. "It ain't right. We ain't married yet. After. . . ."

Abraham rose to his feet, bottle in hand. He took a healthy swallow and held the bottle above his head. "Hey, everybody!" he said in his native Anishinaubae language. "Listen! Stingy here is about to marry my little sister, here. A real good woman, my sister. Stingy here is my friend and now my brother-in-law, a good man. Them two's going to make a fine couple. Come on! A toast to the Mister and Missus," and Abraham tilted his head backwards. Everyone did likewise, some with wine, some with water.

"Speech! Speech! Speech!"

"No! Ain't right . . . we ain't married yet."

"Come on, brother-in-law," Abraham half growled, half pleaded. "Be a sport. Say something. 'Twas your idea in the first place. Come on!" He went to Stingy's chair, pulled it out and lifted his future brother-in-law by the armpits.

"Like Abraham said, I got me a good woman," Stingy blurted out, then sat back down quickly, patting one of his girl's shoulders.

The party went on, lively and friendly. More cases of Four Aces were opened, followed by Slingers, which was regarded as a more potent beverage and was therefore kept till later.

Two o'clock.

"Can you phone again?"

"Sh-sh-sh-shore." Abraham staggered out. When his courier did not return fifteen minutes later, Stingy began to entertain all sorts of doubts, to relieve which he smoked numerous makings and even asked his future wife if he could have a little drink. She refused.

Brrrrng! Brrrrng! Brrrrng! The telephone echoed in the cloister at St. Peter Claver's. Brrrrng! Brrrrng!

"Yes!" Brother Laflamme answered.

"I-i-i-ish F-f-father Barker there? I g-g-gotta talk to h-h-him 'bout s-s-s-something imp-p-portant."

"He's not here and I don't know where he is. He left this morning without leaving a message. Is something wrong, like an accident or a death?"

"Hell no. It's w-w-worse."

Brother Laflamme hung up; he didn't want to talk to drunks.

Abraham eventually returned with an explanation or explanations that hardly made sense, but added to Stingy's growing anxiety.

"Th-th-there's no answer there. I c-called the priest in Blind River, b-but he said h-h-he c-c-can't come. Gave some k-k-kind of excuse. I even c-called the minister b-b-but he s-s-said you're the wrong church or s-s-something like that," Abraham reported.

Three o'clock.

No longer able to trust any of the men to act as his courier, Stingy had to look after his own affairs. He borrowed the B19 to go to make his phone call.

Brrrrng! Brrrrng! Brrrrng! the telephone wailed, demanding attention in the cloister. "Now who this time?" Brother Laflamme complained as he went downstairs.

"Yes. Who is it?"

"It's me. Stingy."

"Oh, it's you, Stingy. This is Brother Laflamme. What can I do for you?"

"I'm supposed to get married today . . . this morning at ten o'clock. Father Barker was supposed to have married us."

"This is awful. Father left this morning. I don't know where he's gone; he didn't say anything to anybody. He just left like he always does. This is awful! Where are you? Would you stay there? I'll call you back. What's the number there?"

Stingy smoked one cigarette after another as he waited for twenty minutes or so.

Brrrrng! Stingy grabbed the phone. It was Brother Laflamme. "I found him, Stingy, with a little detective work. He's at the Whitefish Lake Indian Reserve holding a bazaar. He'd completely forgotten about the wedding, but he'll be with you as soon as he can get there. He's leaving right away."

It was with some difficulty that Stingy announced in the hall that the priest was on his way and that he would not likely arrive earlier than five o'clock. In the meantime the guests were free to go home or to stay until then.

Shortly after five Father Barker roared up to the church in his Studebaker. He walked briskly up to the hall to summon Stingy and his future bride to church for the wedding. Stingy checked to see if Abraham could navigate on his own. Since this appeared doubtful Stingy asked Mike to escort the best man to church. What remained of the crowd followed, though many had grown impatient and taken themselves elsewhere.

In church Mike had to sit by Abraham in order to prevent him from collapsing completely.

In looking over the congregation Father Barker noticed that the bride's father was missing. "Where's your father?" he whispered. "He's supposed to give you away."

The young woman shrugged her shoulders as if she no longer cared.

When word of this fresh disaster spread throughout the congregation several men went out as a search party to look for the old man. They returned with him a few minutes later, still drowsy from a deep sleep that he'd been having under a table in the hall. He yawned as he took his place.

Now the ceremony went smoothly. Bride and groom repeated the terrifying "I do."

"The ring," Father Barker requested.

"Abraham! The ring!" Stingy whispered aloud. "The ring!" Mike repeated, shaking Abraham at the same time.

Abraham twitched his neck and tried unsuccessfully to open his eyes. His head sagged.

"Get the ring from his pocket," Stingy instructed Mike, who dug a hand into Abraham's coat pockets. The best man flinched and stiffened, and his glazed eyes opened.

"K-k-keep your d-damn hands out o' m-m-my pockets," Abraham protested.

"The ring," intoned Father Barker.

"The ring, we need the ring," Stingy repeated.

"K-k-keep your d-damn hands out o' m-m-my pockets," Abraham demanded in surly pride, "an' k-keep your h-h-hands off me. I can stand up alone without your help."

Taking him at his word, Mike let him go. Abraham's knees buckled; just before he fell in a heap on the floor, Mike and Stingy caught him and held him erect, though with difficulty.

Abraham fished in his pocket.

"There," he said. "Got it." But he could remove neither fist nor ring. He struggled briefly with his coat pocket. With a grunt Abraham yanked. There was a sound of tearing cloth as Abraham extracted his fist and a flash of gold as the ring flew upward, spinning over the heads of the wedding party. Priest, Stingy and Mike clutched vainly at the flying ring, which fell to the floor with a "cling" of bouncing metal and then tinkled down the grate.

Father Barker, servers, groom, bridal attendant and Mike got down on their knees to study the interior of the grate.

Abraham sank into the pew and promptly fell asleep. He snored noisily. Unable to rouse him, the woman beside him used her own unfailing remedy, a kick in the shins. At once Abraham's snores subsided, and the good woman nodded with satisfaction.

"You must get the ring," Father Barker insisted. "You can't get married without a ring. Mike! Get some men together and go downstairs. See if you can open the flues."

As requested, Mike recruited a small search party from the congregation and led them down to the cellar of the church.

While the search party was busy bashing and hammering whatever it was they were dismantling, Father Barker asked Stingy if there was any way that he could to make amends for all the inconveniences that he had caused the young couple.

"Yeah! Me and the missus were going down to Sudbury for our honeymoon, but we already missed our bus ... even bought the tickets. Can you take us?" Stingy whispered.

"Oh! My hat! Drive another hundred and twenty miles today!" Father Barker complained weakly. "But I guess that's the least I can do."

The clanking and clanging in the cellar stopped suddenly. Soon after, Mike reappeared, his hair and coat covered with soot. "No use, Father. Can't find it. Better borrow a ring from somebody."

"Will somebody lend us a ring?" asked Father Barker.

A lady kindly offered her own gold band. With the borrowed ring the ceremony was concluded without further mishap.

In the hotel room that night Stingy remarked: "Never knew it was so hard to get married."

Neither Felons nor Angels: And One Beast

Food was the one abiding complaint because the abiding condition was hunger, physical and emotional. Food, or the lack of it, was something that the boys could point to as a cause of their suffering; the other was far too abstract and therefore much too elusive to grasp. But food was a reality that the boys could understand; it was a substance that could not only allay hunger but also bring some comfort to a desolate spirit and soul.

However, it was more than a full stomach that the boys craved when they complained about the mush that was sometimes lumpy, sometimes watery. To grumble that the school served nothing but barley or pea broth, both like consommé soup, and lard, while it offered staff and faculty roasts of beef and pork and poultry was actually a protest against abuse and maltreatment. "Hey, Father, why dontcha eat our food if it's so good?" was really a roundabout way of saying, "Come on, Father, knock it off; get off our backs." In the words, "I hope a plague of locusts eat all the barley . . . then maybe they got more sense, them bugs," there was an implied wish for the concurrent destruction of the entire institution.

To say "This mush is too salty," or "Why'd we have to have raw carrots? Why can't we have a sandwich once in a while?" was quite acceptable; it was a complaint that the prefects could tolerate. Saying that so-and-so prefects had no feelings would have been regarded as a statement tantamount to biting the hand that fed and nurtured and instructed, making us a wild band of ingrates. So the boys took out on peas, barley, mush and onions what they could not take out on the prefects. And yet they would not have dared, as Oliver Twist had once dared, to ask for more.

Perhaps more than anything else the boys resented the never-ending surveillance that began in the morning and ended only late at night, after they had all fallen asleep; a surveillance that went on day after day, week after week, month after month, year after year, as if the boys, singly or in concert, were about to steal the Model-T, torch the building or commit some mutinous or rebellious act. From the number of charges reported to the Minister and the punishments handed out monthly and annually, it appeared that the warden prefects were less scrupulous about the surveillance and prevention of major crimes and felonies than of such minor infractions as stepping out of bounds, not moving quickly enough to suit the pleasure of a prefect, talking in line or continuing to do so after having been ordered to "*Shut up*," whispering in chapel, slouching in line, swearing (though little of this was done), smoking and chewing tobacco, talking back, making a bed improperly, being absent during roll call, talking Indian and a hundred and one other little transgressions. Our treatment implied that we were little better than felons or potential felons.

The eyes began their surveillance in the morning, watching the washing of hands and faces. The eyes followed all movements in the dressing of the beds; the eyes were transfixed on the backs of worshippers during mass. Throughout the day the eyes traced the motions of hands at table; the eyes glared at the figures bent and coiled in work; the eyes tracked the flight of ball and puck and the movement of feet during play; the eyes were trained on the prints of pencil on paper; the eyes censored letters received and letters written. The eyes, like those of the wolf, peered in the dark in watch over still, sleeping forms. The eyes were never at rest.

For many offences punishment was swift and arbitrary, administered by means of various weapons at hand — a ruler, a rod, a bell, a pointer, the open hand, the closed fist, a leather riding boot. We were brought up by hand and boot, just like Pip was, as Julius observed when we were studying *Great Expectations*. And if the weapons at hand did not bring the malefactor about or would never bring him about, there was always, "Just wait and Father Hawkins fix you." From the frequency with which his name was invoked, and from the accounts of such malefactors as Donald Fox, Benedict Shigwadja and many others who had been fixed through a thrashing, Father Hawkins became in our minds the arch-Executioner and Flogger who "just waited" for evildoers to be sent to him. Father Hawkins may have been unfairly used as the "thrasher" by prefects, and thus undeserving of our fear and resentment, but an object of fear and resentment he undoubtedly was.

If a good rabbit punch on the head or a good thrashing failed to straighten out the wayward or the "bullheaded" (or to produce what is today euphemistically called "behaviour modification"), the threatening image of the reform school could be invoked; Burwash and Guelph were often mentioned as the most infamous of such institutions; even worse than Spanish, for instead of thrashings, the wardens delivered lashings on a regular weekly basis, we had heard, "and not on the han's, either, but on the bare ass." Hence it didn't do one's cause any good to be sent to Father Hawkins for a thrashing on too many occasions; once or twice, maybe, but not three or four times . . . or so we had heard. Donald Fox and all those guys could be going any time. As to whether any of our predecessors had actually been sent on to this form of higher education, no one could say for certain; though there was the story of a boy who, after serving his sentence in a reform school, was no longer able to sit down. Poor guy! How does he go to the toilet? The very thought of such a horrible fate was enough to inspire heroic resolve and heroic effort to toe the line as much as possible without surrendering one's dignity, freedom and integrity.

Grumbling about food was a daily exercise performed with varying degrees of bitterness and ingenuity. Such expressions of discontent would today be regarded as healthy, good for whatever ails you, a psychological release and cure-all, despite the fact that they changed nothing.

But the situation could scarcely be considered volatile, considering the size and ages of the malcontents, who were unhappy and disgruntled, but quite incapable of insurrection or riot. Still, some prefects were nervous.

Four women whose background is still a mystery unexpectedly came to the school one day, arriving just at dinner time. To make way for these strangers the seating in the refectory was rearranged, with two Grade 8 boys and two Grade 6 boys shifted from their regular places to sit with the little shots at other tables.

The entry of the strangers caused considerable consternation and speculation. Even though these women may have been only in their thirties, they looked ancient — as antiquated as anyone over the age of twenty appears to thirteen-year-old eyes. Women! Old women! What were they doing in a boys' institution? Weren't they out of place here? Didn't they belong in the other institution, far from the society of men and boys? Why were these Eves and Jezebels allowed into an institution from which women were usually excluded? Moral considerations aside, quite a few boys, inspired and moved by male vanity, swept their hair back from their eyes with their hands, buttoned up their shirts, and even tied up their shoelaces. And though the boys did their best to make themselves more presentable for the admiration of female company, modesty and unfamiliarity with girls and women prompted them to cast their eyes down and to put a brake on their speech.

There was almost as much suspicion as there was speculation. As a result, the refectory was quieter than usual. "Pass the tea" was uttered in muted tones, the clash of spoons was less like the clash of swords between gladiators on this occasion. All the boys were discomfited by the female presence, some a little more and some a little less, depending on the distance from the opposite sex. Those sharing the same table kept their eyes fixed on their plates and their speech in check, kicking a fellow diner in the leg to get his attention and then pointing to the jug with the lips, in the traditional tribal manner, instead of saying "Pass the tea." Boys who had stored lard under the table for noon use could only think of that chunk while they swallowed dry tasteless bread. Somehow their sense of what was proper prevented them from retrieving the lard from its storage with their fingers; they could only hope "someone doesn't thief it 'fore supper." Boys at other tables cast furtive glances at the intruders — suspicious, curious glances.

During the meal all the boys, the little wee ones included, were bedevilled by the same thoughts, from which they framed the same questions. What were these women doing here? Who had invited them? Who had sent them? Who were they? Where did they come from? What were they writing in those books? They weren't here for nothing! Strangers never came for nothing. How come they were eating that swill? It must be important, though, otherwise they wouldn't be here. I wonder what it is?

After dinner and for the entire afternoon the questions were directed at the boys who had shared the same table with the strangers.

"Hey, Boozo! Who are those women? Where'd they come from? What they doing here? What they write in those books, anyway? They coming back?"

But Boozo, whose eyes had been downcast during the entire meal and whose tongue had been tied, was unable to give any kind of explanation regarding the presence of the women. He could not even tell what the women were writing. Boozo was as bewildered as the other 135 boys.

Speculation continued. "Hey, Father! What them women want?"

Back came the women at supper, just as unexpectedly as they had come at dinner time. They occupied the same places as at noon. Just as unexpectedly, instead of lard, there were pats of butter on a tin plate, and the soup was thicker than usual, with more meat and vegetables — almost like stew. A few of the boys searched their memories to discover therein the cause of this good fortune. The women ate heartily, frequently observing how good and wholesome the bread was, how full of body and vigour the stew, and how smooth and mellow the butter ... and writing notes in their journals and making entries on graphs.

"What's your name?" one of the old women asked Frank Commanda.

"F-F-F-rank ... C-Comm-Commanda."

"Where are you from?"

"T-T-Timagami."

"How old are you, Frank ... eh?"

"F-F-Fourteen, Miss."

"We call him Bunny, Miss," Dominic abruptly volunteered. Bunny blushed, as he nearly always did, before giving Dominic a dirty look.

"Yooou're cute! My, what a cute name," the old woman gushed. "What a handsome young man you're going to be in four or five years. If only I were a little younger," she said wistfully.

Dominic found this hugely amusing and volunteered more information. "Miss! You should see him play hockey. Only thing he loves."

Frankie's mouth turned down at the corners in a shy smile, and he wriggled and fidgeted as he was suddenly afflicted in the arms, legs, neck and back by hordes and waves of crawling goose bumps at the reference to his good looks and his hockey skills.

After supper there were good-natured calls of, "Ha, ha! Bunny likes old women." It would have been worse for Frankie if we hadn't been so busy trying to guess what was going on.

"Hey, Boozo! Why dintcha ask them women what they were doing here when you had a chance? What's the matter with you, anyway? Them women coming back?"

Boozo didn't know, but the women were there the following morning with their notebooks, waiting by the door as the boys lined up.

"Hey, Boozo! Ask them women what they're doing here this time, okay?" someone whispered.

"Cut out the talking!"

Mush day it was. Mush, hot steaming mush on platters. Next to the mush was a bowl with eggs, boiled . . . and there was butter again, instead of lard. Some boys rubbed their eyes. They couldn't believe what they beheld. Was it an illusion? Or was the cook finally coming to his senses? To what did they owe this good fortune? Was it a new beginning?

As direct as always, Boozo came to the point. "Miss, we wanna know what youse is doing here."

"That's a fair enough question, young man. We're here to inspect the food and to make reports on the quality of your meals. By the way, what's your name?"

"Harold! But people at home — Garden River — çall me Boozo."

Dominic broke in. "Miss! Harold here is the bes' goal keeper this school ever had. Him an' Bunny, they're the stars."

"Isn't that interesting."

Boozo carried on. "How long you going to stay?"

"A week, perhaps . . . just long enough to get an idea of your diet . . . how well you're fed."   ˒

"Oh," Boozo muttered, as understanding dawned. The women went on eating and making notations.

When Boozo broke the astounding news of the inspection of food, the boys discussed how best they might assist the investigation and provide testimony. The prospects were enormous.

"About time," the boys said. "At last someone must've tol' on them priests . . . at last someone listened. Boozo! Tell them women the truth about the mush, and the soup . . . an' the raw cabbages an' the raw carrots and raw turnips. Tell them the truth, Boozo, tell them everything. Tell them that Skinny and his brother, little Skinny, is skinny an' about to get sick because they ain't got enough to eat . . . an' that's why there's no fat boys aroun' here. Tell them everything, Boozo; you and Bunny and McComber."

"Yeah! But how about that John Caneau; he's kinda fat, him."

"Well, you tell them that John Caneau's not fat, jus' chubby; you tell them that when he came here from Caughnawaga he was bigger, an' that he'll be skinny jus' like everybody else pretty soon. Tell them all that, Boozo."

"I don't know. I don't trus' them women."

"Aw, come on, now, Boozo! Tell them anyways. It's the only chance we got; never have another one."

Three more days passed before Boozo screwed up enough courage and trust to confide in the women, whom the boys assumed to be inspectors. Boozo told a tale of woe and misery, of hunger and neglect, but it was hard to give the lie to the meals that had inexplicably improved while the women were there.

"Yes! Yes!" the women assured the boys, they would "tell the world"; and they left with their notebooks.

If the meals fell to their former standards the day after the women went up the hill and back to wherever they had come from, and the boys grumbled, they didn't much care because as soon as the world heard the story, "Then them priests would get it." In the days that followed the boys almost smirked whenever they looked at a prefect. The prefects smirked back.

A month passed; two months went by, during which nothing happened. No police came to the school to investigate, as the boys fully anticipated and expected.

In early spring someone saw a mimeographed letter posted on the bulletin board next to the weekly work schedule. As he read the letter, other boys crowded around.

Most Reverend Father Superior:

We beg to submit this interim report upon our recent investigation of the nutrition provided by your institution for the boys under your care.

Up to this point we can only report in generalities, but we do have enough information to state that it is our impression that the Indian boys are receiving as balanced a diet of proteins and carbohydrates as is necessary for their growth and health. In fact, Reverend Father Superior, you will be pleased to know, we were surprised by how well the boys were nourished and cared for. They are indeed lucky to be under your care.

While we were in your school we heard many complaints about the food, but that is to be expected from any group of boys who know nothing or care little about the nutritional value of food and who would prefer to subsist on candies, cookies, chocolate bars, hot dogs and soda pop. . . .

Your devoted and humble servants.

The reader didn't finish reading the letter; he ripped it from the thumbtack and tore it to shreds. But the boys who had had a chance to see it had read enough to circulate its contents to the others.

Throughout the school there was a sense of betrayal and helpless bitterness directed at the new cook, at the women, at the prefects and at the priests. "They was working for the priests, them! An' that cook did that jis so's he wouldn't get in trouble . . . serving us butter an' eggs . . . an' if those women ever come back here we . . . we'll string them up from the rafters of the barn."

But life went on, dully, painfully, its routine unchanging. Awaken to bells, move to bells, be still to the sound of bells. Eat mush, soup, soup; Boston baked beans, soup, soup; mush, soup, soup. Work, work, change work once a week. Check the schedule Monday morning. Sweep the recreation hall; one week, sweep the corridors; one week, sweep a classroom; one week, sweep the dormitory; one week, sweep the refectory; sweep, sweep, sweep. For a change, work in the toilets, in the kitchen, then back to sweeping. Choir practice. "Sing it again! Louder! Once more!" Go for walks. Rangers' Camp, Canadiens' Camp, Maple Leafs' camp, walk, walk, walk. Play; play hockey, baseball, softball, basketball; always the same team winning, Frank Commanda's team. Always the same thing.

It was boring. Everybody was bored; but Alvin Nashkewe was the most bored of all. If he didn't do something new and different soon he would stagnate and petrify. What he wanted more than anything else was to go riding, horseback riding, bareback as he used to do when he was at home in Cape Croker. But riding alone is not much fun, and riding with Lloyd, his brother, who would surely come without hesitation, would not be much more fun. What Alvin needed was a kindred spirit. Of all the boys, Chauncey Benedict was the most likely kindred soul.

"Chauncey! Ever go riding horses?"

"No! Why?"

"A lot of fun, Chauncey! Don't know what you're missing. Would you like to try? Easy."

Willing to try anything once or several times, Chauncey agreed. "Shore, so long as it's not Pitou."

"Hell, no; not that crazy thing; but he'd be a natural 'cause he's built for racing. Maybe we'll try him after. We'll start with them ol' nags."

"How you gonna work this, Alvin?"

But Alvin had already worked out the details of the horseback-riding venture. The way Alvin had it figured out, it was quite simple; he would stay awake until the prefect, Father Brown, was snoring; then he'd wake Chauncey up, sneak down the fire escape and sneak back in afterwards. There was nothing complicated; no risks involved, so far as Alvin was concerned.

As Alvin unfolded the plans and described the delights of horseback riding, especially on borrowed mounts, back on the reserve, Chauncey's excitement and generosity escalated, so that he wanted others to share in the joys of the forthcoming venture.

"Six horses in the barn. Let's get three more guys . . . more fun that way."

At first Alvin demurred, but he relented when Chauncey pointed out that the risk of being tattled on was reduced in proportion to the number of friends taking part. Three more accomplices were recruited without trouble.

It was hard for Alvin to believe that Chauncey's experience in life was so limited. "Don't they have no horses in St. Regis? Don't anybody ride there? What youse guys do anyways?"

"We run," Chauncey explained. "That's why all the Mohawks good runners like Tom Longboat. You Adirondacks ("bark eaters," a Mohawk name for the Anishinaubae tribe) got anybody like Tom Longboat?"

Unable to think of a fleet member of the tribe, Alvin sniffed: "Why run when you can ride? After you ride a few times, Chaunce, you won't wanna run again."

That night Alvin kept watch until 12:30 or so. He woke his confederates with a nudge and whispered "Come on! Time to go . . . shshshsh" only after he was pretty sure that Father Brown was asleep.

After some initial difficulties in mounting the sleek-sided work horses, Alvin's band of Indians finally got themselves horsed, bareback, just like the Crow Indians. Even after they had got underway, the riders had difficulty staying mounted. As the only experienced horseman, Alvin had to instruct and remind his confederates, "You gotta go with the motion of the horse, the way the Plains Indians do it. Jis' takes a little practice; you'll get used to it. In a week should be able to ride a galloping horse."

Under Alvin's leadership and coaching the night riders went as far as Brennan Harbour, returning to the barn and slipping into the school around 3:30. Though it had been a marvelous experience that all the boys agreed was worth repeating the next night, the riders paid the price the next day with aching crotches and burning eyes.

Night after night the boys went out riding, just as Blackfoot and Crow Indian boys had done as part of their training, and within a week the confidence in their horsemanship had grown to the point where they were urging their steeds to canter and to trot. Within a few more days the horsemen were speculating which of the six resident steeds was the fastest, a question that could only be settled by a race. "I'd like to try that Pitou," Chauncey chortled. A race would be a test of their horsemanship.

The boys unanimously and enthusiastically agreed to put the horses and themselves to the test. The course set was the road running behind the chicken coop and up the hill toward the Grenier–Trudeau residences, with the starting line paralleling the chicken coop and the finish line some 400 metres up the hill, marked by a lone maple standing to one side of the road.

During the next hour — or maybe longer — the road behind the chicken coop rumbled and trembled under the pounding hooves of work horses as they raced heat after heat to settle which was the fastest; each heat slower than the last. But the jockeys aboard the losing steeds would not admit that their chargers were slow of foot and made all kinds of excuses — for example, that their steeds had worked harder during the day than the winners. Nothing was resolved, and the boys agreed to rerun the races the very next night.

In the morning Brother Van der Moor could not figure out why the horses were wet with perspiration. Fearing that the perspiration might have been brought on by a fever preceding hoof-and-mouth disease or some other pestilence, he promptly checked the temperatures of the horses and inquired of Brother Grubb how the cattle were. Their temperature readings were normal. He checked Pitou, but Pitou was also his normal self.

By mid-morning the ploughboys were complaining to Brother Van der Moor that there was something wrong with the teams. "Go maybe forty, fifty yards, then stop like they was tired or lazy." It was hard to figure out, but whatever was afflicting the horses had to be solved fast, otherwise they'd not get the ploughing done. To spare the horses and to keep an eye on them, Brother Van der Moor had them turned in to their stalls for the balance of the day.

Well after midnight, Chauncey, who was keeping watch, awakened his fellow riders and led them to the barn. By this time the horses were fully restored, ready for more racing. As they had the night before, the boys competed with diligence, racing heats as they had on the previous evening. Heat after heat they ran until the horses were panting, their ribs heaving. While the riders were giving the horses a rest, they agreed that Dan was the fastest horse in the barn next to Pitou. The agreement was a means of discontinuing the races, which were losing their novelty. When the horses had recovered their wind, the night riders urged the animals on toward Brennan Harbour. There they circled Ed Folz's house twice, a-whoopin' and a-hollerin', to scare the paganism out of Ed and his family before heading on to Cutler.

Finding his horses bedraggled, their hair matted with perspiration, Brother Van der Moor reported their condition to the Father Superior, who convened a staff meeting and ordered an investigation. In consultation with Father Minister, a special night watch was posted to keep an eye and ear on the barns and main building during the night. Father Brown, a prefect, was appointed to carry out this duty.

As they had for many nights past, the boys assembled by the fire escape to sneak out and down the stairs, quietly. "Shshshsh."

From the dark a voice whispered "All right, boys! Where do you think you're going?!"

It was Father Brown.

"Well, we were thinking of going horseback riding," Alvin admitted resignedly.

"Okay, boys, the jig's up. This is the last night that you ride, is that clear? And I'm coming with you on this last trip. I've never ridden a horse, and it's something that I've always wanted to try. After this, you will ride no more. Promise? And I won't say anything."

The boys promised, then took Father Brown on a leisurely ride to Cutler and back. The rides ended that night.

As they discussed Father Brown's warning and advice, the boys expressed their admiration for the new prefect. "He's a good guy, him," they said. What Chauncey regretted most was that he'd never had a chance to ride Pitou.

Pitou ought not to have been in Spanish; he ought not to have been in a common barn; he ought not to have been used as an ordinary draft animal pulling a democrat sometimes filled with straw, often with manure, frequently with hog carcasses, and occasionally with the corpse of a priest, a brother or a nun. Not only was he misplaced, he was, as well, miscast.

Pitou really belonged in Lexington, Kentucky; he ought to have been quartered, if not in a royal stable, certainly in nothing less than a baronial one; he ought, at age thirty-three, to have been retired in his declining years to stud, a service he would have performed with finesse and delight; he ought to have been in the company of his peers, horses of breeding and nobility, bearing and grace.

But he was in Spanish and, like the boys, an exile performing services for which he was ill-suited. Being proud, though not vain or conceited, Pitou resented being locked up in a common barn with common horses and fed common hay; and he resented the bit, bridle and reins, which he regarded as instruments of slavery, punishment and ill-will meant only for the low-born.

With the right people, who knew of his moods and of his aversion for rein and whip, Pitou could tolerate bit, bridle, harness and common labour with some dignity, as a slave under yoke could still preserve his integrity. Father Vandriessch and Brother Manseau were among the few in the institution who rendered Pitou the respect proper to his intelligence, love of liberty and breeding.

Never did they command or talk down to Pitou; instead they addressed him in terms befitting his intelligence and status. They made no attempt to steer Pitou; he did not need the reins, and Brother Manseau and Father Vandriessch let them hang free.

Pitou was then in charge, leading rather than being led, setting the pace rather than being urged to walk or run. Once in harness, Pitou would strut out from the barn, head held high. When hitched to a democrat, buggy or cutter, Pitou would start only after *he* had turned about to see that *his* passenger was ready; then he would snort contemptuously, arch his neck and prance with princely step up the road. In command, Pitou would run or walk and stop when it pleased him, not so much to rest as to demonstrate his independence, his right to stand sniffing the air and surveying the fields and the groves of pines as if they belonged to him. For that trip, Pitou was master, leader, captain.

Not all trips were as pleasant for Pitou, and not all teamsters were as considerate. The daily delivery and pickup of mail at 1:00 P.M. ought to have been a joyful occasion; more often than not, however, depending on the teamster, it was a battle from beginning to end between the driver and Pitou. Sometimes Pitou won.

To the boys and most of the staff, Pitou was just a horse, no different from any other breed, be it Belgian, Percheron or Clydesdale; they were all the same; strong maybe, but dull and stupid, meant only for work. A horse would not move until commanded to "giddap," nor stop until told to "whoa," with a tug of the reins; unless directed by "gee" or "haw," and a corresponding pull on the reins to left or right, a horse would crash into a wall or walk over a cliff. According to this line of reasoning, Pitou — a horse with no more than horse sense — should be treated like any other horse.

Well, not quite. He was not like Jack and Dan, or Bill and Prince, or some of the others who were dumb as well as docile; Pitou, dark brown with a strip of white from forehead to muzzle tip, was skinny and sleek like a race horse, and moody and sullen, given to temper tantrums that needed a firm hand at the driver's end of the reins. Was not a horse to be driven? Led? Were not teamsters to drive? Lead? Did not logic, reason and practice so decree?

But Pitou defied reason and the traditions humans had established for their own convenience. Pitou rebelled against the principle that man was ordained by God to have dominion over animals, and against the practice as well. In his battles Pitou made no distinction between laity and clergy; in his eyes or at his rear anyone with too tight a grip on the reins was an enemy.

From experience the boys knew that they had to beware of Pitou and his moods. For his part, Pitou looked on the boys with contempt and made no secret of it.

It was wise and common practice for the teamsters to sound out Pitou on entry into the barn. This was done by addressing him courteously: "Pitou! Pitou!" If Pitou acted deaf, it was relatively safe to harness him. However, if he snorted and bucked and danced and kicked in his stall, he was hostile, and the chief objective became not so much to subdue him as to harness him without injury to oneself.

From a tactical standpoint Pitou was initially at a serious disadvantage; he was tethered and enclosed in a narrow stall. In this situation Pitou could not defend himself with his hooves in rearguard action; he could only bite. For teamsters to harness Pitou without injury to themselves, it was best to approach him from the front and from the flanks.

Even when harnessed and hitched, Pitou did not give up the battle; for him it was only the beginning. The boys knew that Pitou was just biding his time, and that he would strike eventually. To prevent any sneak or surprise attack — a bolt over a fence with the buggy, for example — the teamsters drew firmly on the reins, which they pulled one way or the other to steer Pitou. But to Pitou there was no treatment more humiliating than to be treated as a stupid and servile animal. Any trip from school to the village was an uneasy truce, and a safe return was regarded as a minor victory.

There was no guarantee that any journey would be without incident, even when Pitou was in a good mood on setting out. He could be instantly provoked into outrage by anything that rattled his composure and held him up to ridicule . . . flying stones, for example.

One day Adam Commanda and Julius, two of our more sensible colleagues, were elected to deliver mail. On that day Pitou was in such good spirits that he docilely lowered his neck for the halter and accepted the bit without biting. As the vehicle, its occupants perched atop a movable seat, clattered across the yard with Pitou stepping high, Alvin, motivated by envy or mischief or both, extracted a sling from his back pocket and loaded the leather holder with a flat stone. "Watch this," said Alvin, and let fly.

His aim was true. The stone whistled over Pitou's head almost between his ears. Startled out of his wits, Pitou bolted left, nearly leaping out of his traces. In so doing, he dislodged Adam and Julius from their seats, hurling them to the ground. Ballplayers scattered to give way to Pitou, who galloped in terror not back to the barn but toward the chicken coop and beyond, in the direction of Brennan Harbour, trailing a cloud of dust.

A search-and-rescue team under the supervision of Brother Manseau was sent out to find Pitou and bring him back. Boozo and Ti Phonse reported that Pitou was stuck fast in a muskeg bog, his favourite refuge, and in an unbelievable fix: wedged between the shafts of the democrat and immediately behind Pitou's rump was a poplar sapling fifteen feet high. For Pitou to come to rest in that position he would have had to leap forward and then descend straight down. Unless the sapling had grown while Pitou was there?

Flying objects that buzzed near his ears were not the only things that disturbed Pitou; unmoving and strange vehicles also offended him. And when Pitou felt slighted or ridiculed, he took revenge with a vengeance.

Brother Laflamme, the short, roundish, bald-headed, cheerful launderer and infirmarian, fearing that the democrat was about to collapse from neglect and decay, decided one day to mend and repaint the vehicle. After repairing the chassis and frame, he painted the wheels and shafts a cardinal red and the seat, crib and undercarriage a macabre black. Sitting in the barnyard the democrat looked positively new.

As the restorer of the democrat, it was, I suppose, only fitting that Brother Laflamme should take the vehicle on its maiden voyage. He harnessed Pitou and led him to the refinished democrat. Pitou followed willingly enough, but when he saw the contraption, he whinnied in horror and shied in disgust as if the democrat were a coiled rattler. He immediately went into reverse, towing and jerking Brother Laflamme, who was desperately holding a rein. But going backwards with his rump lower than his forequarters, in order to keep the enemy in front in full view, added to Pitou's terror; he could not see who or what was behind.

While Pitou was leaning backwards and back-pedalling, Brother Laflamme, a rein's length in front, was also leaning backwards and back-pedalling — but to no avail, since he was actually being pulled forward by jerk and lurch. During this tug-of-war, Brother Laflamme pleaded with Pitou: "Whoa! Whoa! It's your democrat, just freshly painted; there's nothing to be afraid of; settle down now, boy." Brother Laflamme's quavering pleas did nothing to compose Pitou.

At last, after much circling around, Pitou backed into the wall of the barn and came to a trembling stop. Brother Laflamme, beads of perspiration sparkling on his bald head, patted Pitou's neck and head. When Pitou stopped shaking, Brother Laflamme guided him backwards between the shafts of the democrat and, with the help of two boys, succeeded in hitching Pitou to the vehicle.

It may have been the odour of fresh paint, or perhaps it was plain ordinary suspicion that prompted Pitou to take an anxious glance rearward; but when he saw the red arms of the black apparition clutching his flanks, he sprang forward and raced for the barn. Behind him was Brother Laflamme, yelling "Whoa! Whoa! Whoa!" Pitou did not hear; or if he heard, he chose not to listen; he ran headlong in through the barn door — or at least he tried to. There was a resounding crash as the democrat's front wheels struck either side of the barn door. With the cart's sudden stop, Pitou was thrown forward, heels over head, clear of the traces and the shafts. When he regained his feet, he came out, cast a vengeful eye upon the wreck and, as if to complete its destruction, turned around and delivered a double-hoofed kick to the offending vehicle.

Damage to the democrat was extensive: the two front wheels mangled, the shafts fractured, the frame warped and the woodwork splintered. That day Pitou snorted and whinnied frequently, in derisive and triumphant tones.

The cargo could also unsettle Pitou. Three or four crates of eggs and the mail he did not mind; manure and hog or cattle carcasses, perhaps because of the naked flesh, he detested. As for corpses . . .

Father Belanger passed away during a visit to a mission somewhere along the North Shore. His body was shipped via the Canadian Pacific Railway to Spanish for veneration and interment. When his body arrived, the station agent duly notified the Father Superior.

Boozo and Rudy Rice were selected, without being told the nature of their errand, "to pick up Father Belanger at the station." Both boys fairly shot out of the study hall into the bitter January night.

On this night Pitou was in a good mood. He neighed and snorted in eagerness, sending clouds of steam from his nostrils into the crisp air. So cold was it that the runners of the cutter squeaked on the hard-packed snow, and the clip-clop of Pitou's hooves echoed across the fields and re-echoed in the woods.

Below McGrath's at the bottom of the graveyard hill Pitou cast an anxious eye, as he always did, in the direction of the crosses and tombstones that impressed spectral shadows upon the snow. As always, he leaned as far to the right as possible without dumping the cutter into the ditch, in an attempt to give the graveyard as wide a berth as the road allowed. Not until he turned right at Kelly's Bakery did Pitou take his eyes off the cemetery, and as he did so, he quickened his pace to a trot to put as much distance in as short a time as possible between him and the inhabitants of the graveyard.

At the railway station Boozo went to the waiting room to fetch Father Belanger, while Rudy kept Pitou company outside. On inquiring about Father Belanger, the station agent told Boozo that the priest was on the baggage wagon . . . in a coffin . . . outside . . . dead.

Rudy backed the cutter against the platform, and Boozo, the station agent and two local residents who had been conscripted to help transferred the casket from the baggage wagon to the crib of the cutter . . . clunk, clunk.

Pitou stiffened and sniffed the air.

From the station to Kelly's Bakery Pitou looked behind him repeatedly, as if checking to see if Boozo and Rudy were still aboard; but not only that, he cantered at a very uneven pace, sometimes trotting, at other times high-stepping without moving forward. And he shook and shivered. "Somethin' funny with that horse," Rudy remarked.

As teamsters, horse and cargo drew near Kelly's Bakery, Pitou's course and manner became positively erratic. He was almost squatting, and his hooves beat a staccato as he moved forward and yet sideways in a series of fits and starts; Pitou would not take his eyes off the graveyard.

Boozo tried to settle Pitou. "It's okay, Pitou, there's nothin' to be afraid of . . . they can't hurt you, them . . . they're dead." At the word "dead," Pitou sprang violently sideways and then forward, sending the cutter sliding from one side of the road to the other and then into the ditch, almost toppling over. The cargo shifted, and with a rip-saw crackle the left panel of the crib broke and the casket slithered into a snowbank. Boozo and Rudy were flung into the same bank. Pitou fled to the barn, where he waited with injured pride to be unhitched.

Boozo and Rudy ran in terror back to the school, where they unfolded the details of the disaster. Another party of boys and a team consisting of Jack and Dan were sent to retrieve the casket and to accord Father Belanger the reverence and solemn respect owing to his state.

To shy from graveyards, to be frightened by corpses or to scurry from missiles represented an act of cowardice unbecoming to Pitou's pride and dignity. He could hardly look anyone, human or equine, in the eye. But with the proper encouragement Pitou could face danger bravely. There was nothing to it, no formula. All that was needed was for the teamster to talk to . . . no . . . carry on a *discussion* with Pitou.

Father McKey had experience of Pitou's courage under the most trying circumstances.

In the days before Father McKey had a car, when the road between Spanish and Walford was no more than a wagon trail, he had to drive to Walford both to check on the growth of the school's potato crop and to rekindle the flagging piety of the Walfordians. Pitou was seconded to draw the buggy.

A mile or so beyond the outskirts of Spanish, Pitou shuddered to a halt, his ears twitching nervously as he heard the distinct chatter of some unknown instrument, and the occasional boom. To Father McKey, the rat-a-tat of jackhammers and the rumble of dynamite were welcome sounds that signified the construction of a new highway, an important link between Spanish and Walford.

Father leaped off the buggy, not sure whether "discussion" with Pitou would persuade the horse to continue on to Walford. It was worth a try.

"All right, Pitou! There's nothing to be afraid of. Just men working, making a road. By fall there'll be a new highway. What you hear are jackhammers ripping up rock, and the explosions are blasts of dynamite." Pitou trembled from muzzle to stern, and his ears slanted backwards as if he were about to dash into the woods. But, like an overgrown puppy, he followed Father McKey, nestling his head against the priest's shoulder. Father McKey walked on slowly, talking steadily and softly, afraid even to pause for breath. Even when there was a distant shout of "Fire!" followed a few moments later by an explosion, which the priest carefully explained to the horse, Pitou did not bolt, though he flinched and trembled and leaned more heavily and urgently against Father McKey.

As they got closer to the construction site, which rang with the clank of shovels against rocks and was rank with the smell of burned cordite, Pitou unashamedly burrowed his head under Father McKey's left armpit. While holding Pitou pressed against him in close embrace, Father McKey found it difficult to walk upright; he too leaned against Pitou. Somehow, the priest managed to conduct Pitou across the construction zone with Pitou's head curled around his waist.

"Mornin', Father! . . . Nice day, Father!" the workmen reverently greeted Father McKey. He merely waved his free hand and continued talking steadily to Pitou. The men stared. "Holy Moses! He's talking to that damned horse!" commented one worker in disbelief.

Not until they were well beyond the work site did Pitou take his eyes off the men and their strange equipment and remove his head from underneath Father's protective and comforting arm. Then he trotted, head held high, into Walford and back again to Spanish.

Pitou was a proud horse, haughty almost, from years of triumphs.

Pitou had been old for a long time, had lived longer than most horses manage to do; he had resisted clergy and laity for a horse's age, and he fought off decrepitude with the same passion. But by degrees age took its toll and, like all mankind and animalkind, Pitou eventually had to yield.

He still looked the same; the fire in his eye gleamed as brightly as ever, and the pride of his spirit glowed as it had always done. It was his strength that ebbed away. To be sure, there were occasions when he would kick and bite, but these were infrequent, frail and half-hearted efforts. It was in his pace that infirmity was most noticeable. Like an old man or woman he plodded, drawing the democrat behind, his neck bent as if bearing great weight and sorrow, and stopping frequently to rest. Finally, out of pity, Brother Van der Moor withdrew him from mail-delivery service, setting him free, whenever it occurred to him, in the field behind the barn. Otherwise, Pitou was tethered in his stall.

Pitou was sad, I suppose, because there was now no one to talk to him. Father Vandriessch and Brother Manseau had gone on to their eternal rewards; Father McKey had acquired a Ford and no longer had need of Pitou; moreover, he had been assigned to more northern missionary work. There remained only Brother Van der Moor to feed him and to let him run free once in a while, but the brother was only a keeper and preferred Belgians, Clydesdales and Percherons, working horses.

One May morning Brother Van der Moor went into the barn to feed the horses. Pitou whinnied and bucked.

"What's the matter, Pitou?"

Pitou whinnied again.

"Ah! Just like the old Pitou. I'll look after you first this morning." But Pitou would not eat the oats that Brother poured into a box; he continued to whinny and snort and stamp his hooves.

"Wanna go out, old fellow?" Pitou neighed. "Well! I'll let you out then."

When Brother Van der Moor opened the gate at the back of the barn, Pitou rose high on his haunches, neighed once more, and galloped with tail raised and mane flying down to the end of the field and, like a two-year-old, raced back. Then, at Brother Van der Moor's feet, Pitou lay down and died.

Farewell, Spanish Justice, and Farewell

One winter evening after supper, which may have been in January, February or March — it makes little difference, because it was a winter evening like any other — there was a commotion in the recreation hall in the vicinity of the stairway doors. Standing by the doors were Charlie, Eugene and Johnny Migwans, dressed up — really dressed up — in black trousers and black coats, and grinning like carefree minks. Around them boys pressed in close, then closer, asking, "Where are you going?"

"We're leaving, we're getting out of here," the three almost chirped in chorus, so happy were they. They had been sprung, released earlier than their scheduled date. La Marr, Angus, Ben, Gilbert, Tony, Shaggy, Cheeby and even Mike Taylor crowded in, envious of their friends' good fortune. They laughed and made jokes like, "Better not make the prefec' mad, might change their minds . . . or maybe it's jis' a trick an' you're not really going nowheres." The ones staying behind tried to make light of the parting, but it was not an easy thing to say goodbye to friends who had shared a brotherhood and sustained one another through periods of dejection over the two, three, four, five and six years past. For those leaving and saying farewell it was easily the happiest occasion, and "Farewell" was uttered without regret. But it was not an easy thing for the boys left behind to see this bond, formed out of the dissolution of families, broken. For them, saying goodbye was a re-enactment of the day the bond with mothers and fathers and grandparents, brothers and sisters and homes was sundered with "Goodbye."

Eugene and Charlie said goodbye to Kitchi-Meeshi Hec and me.

"Tell my mother when you get home to get us out of here, too," Kitchi-meeshi Hec pleaded.

"We're not going home though," Eugene confessed. "We're going to Toronto; we're going to work for the Primeau Cement Block Company just north of Toronto."

"Why didn't you tell us that you're leaving?" we remonstrated with our lucky friends.

"Because we didn't know until today, this morning," Charlie explained.

"Hey, Charlie, Eugene," someone whispered on our behalf. "Tell everybody what it's like here."

And that was the way it was. Charlie, Eugene and Johnny boarded the train at 7:30; they had served their time and now they were gone for good.

There were now just Kitchi-meeshi Hec and myself; old-timers from Cape Croker. Although Alvin and Lloyd Nashkewe, Joe King, and Stewart Johnston had joined us in the institution, I was not very close to them, not as close as to Kitchi-meeshi Hec.

Every Saturday night during hockey season we were allowed special entertainment. A radio, usually sequestered in the senior prefect's room, was unsequestered and installed in the club room on the third floor for the listening pleasure of the senior boys in Grades 6, 7 and 8. The Grade 5 boys were given a special dispensation to stay up a little later, not only to inspire them to greater efforts in their studies to attain seniorhood, but also to acclimate them to the privileges of higher rank. All the boys sat around the radio to listen to Foster Hewitt's evangelical hockey broadcasts: "Again from coast to coast, it's hockey night in Canada. . . ." Foster's tone and delivery were dramatic and electric. Never was there a more attentive group of Grade 5, 6, 7 and 8 boys; nor a more submissive one. I think that Foster could have taught them arithmetic, geography and even grammar. No supervision was needed, except for the odd spot-check by the senior prefect in the form of a discreet opening of the door and a quick glance about for forbidden doings. It was during the hockey broadcasts that smokers used to take illicit puffs, their heads stuck out the windows and their rumps stuck inside.

At the other end of the club room was a large table piled high with month-old newspapers and religious magazines.

On this occasion, Kitchi-meeshi Hec and I were hunched over a newspaper, either reviewing the war or reading the comic strips; utterly indifferent to the hockey game and to anything else taking place in the club room.

"That's yours?" the senior prefect asked, unsettling us by his unexpected tapping of our shoulders.

Naturally we looked under the table where he was pointing to check which article of property had got lost.

Lo! There at our feet was a cigarette, lit and burning. How it had got there neither Kitchi-meeshi Hec nor I had any way of knowing or explaining. We could not even think that some third party might have tossed the burning cigarette at our feet to get rid of incriminating evidence. And there it lay like a gunshot victim, blood oozing from the wound, stretched prostrate on the ground.

No evidence could be more prima facie.

Yet Kitchi-meeshi Hec and I, every other consideration aside, answered the question "Is this yours?" directly as to ownership. "Not mine! Not mine." So far as we were concerned property in the burning cigarette was the only issue, the only question.

"Then how did it get there?"

Kitchi-meeshi Hec and I were no more able to account for a burning cigarette lying on the floor than we were able to explain ownership of the object.

"I don' know, Father!"

"Me neither."

"Go and see Father Hawkins."

Outside the club room Kitchi-meeshi Hec and I looked at one another for a few moments before consulting about how best to establish that property in the burning cigarette was vested in someone else and that its presence under the table at our feet was the work of an enemy. The consultation was brief and direct.

"What we gonna do?"

"I dunno."

"What we gonna say?"

"I dunno."

"You go first."

"No, you!"

"No! Not me!"

"Come on. You're bigger."

"No! You first. Go on," and Kitchi-meeshi Hec pushed me downstairs. He was bigger.

I sneaked downstairs. Why I tiptoed down I don't know, but I nevertheless pussyfooted down the steps. My knees knocked as I stood at Father Hawkins's office door on the second floor. Why should my knees knock? I didn't own the cigarette. I didn't know how it had got to be where it was, and I had not touched it. I didn't smoke. I was innocent. Yet I was afraid to knock, reluctant to face "Thin Beak."

Father looked not at all surprised when I walked in, in response to his "Come in"; the fact was, he appeared to be delighted to see an evildoer to relieve the monotony of his evening.

"What are you doing down here?"

"I d-d-d-dunno, Father."

"You don't know? Come now! Father didn't send you down for fun or because you were being good. Come now. Tell me!"

"I d-d-dunno, Father. Me and Hector, we didn' do nothin'; we were jis' standin' there doin' nothin'."

"Oh-ho! There were two of you, then. Oh-ho!" Father took a strap out of his desk, caressed it and bent it back and forth, as a fencer tests his weapon for flexibility. Father whipped the strap through the air. I winced. "Now then. What were you and Hector Lavalley doing? And you had better tell the truth, otherwise Heaven help you."

It is a good thing to have truth on your side when you are falsely accused of some misdeed. It lends a confidence that you will prevail over lies, false testimony and evil and ultimately earn reward. But that faith and trust in the eventual triumph of truth can be badly shaken when the Heavenly Host is invoked with the words, "Heaven help you if you aren't telling the truth." And my belief in the justness of truth and in my cause was shaken by those awful words. It wasn't quite fully restored when I blurted out the truth.

"We didn' do nothin'. Me and Hector, we were jis' standin' there when Father showed us that cigarette under the table. He thought that it was ours, but me an' Kitchi-meeshi Hec, we don' smoke, us. Somebody must o' throwed that cigarette there to blame us. We tried to tell Father that, but he didn' believe us. He tol' us to come down here to see you. We didn' do nothin', honest."

Father looked astounded as I gave my testimony and then, like a lawyer who has caught a witness in a lie during cross-examination, frowned in triumphant indignation, "Oh-ho! So you were smoking, were you?"

"No, Father."

"How many puffs?"

"I wasn' smoking."

"*Two.* How many puffs?"

"But I wasn' smoking."

"*Four.* How many puffs?"

"I didn' take none."

"*Eight.* How many puffs?"

"I don' smoke."

"*Sixteen.* How many puffs?"

"None, Father. Not even one."

"*Thirty-two.* How many?"

Thirty-two. At last what Father Hawkins was doing seeped into my skull. He didn't believe me, and he was doubling the number of lashes that he was going to deliver on my hands for each untruth that I uttered. I was to be punished for truth instead of being rewarded. Not wanting sixty-four lashes, I blurted out, "I took a puff."

"Just as I thought," Father almost crooned, as he rolled up his sleeves. "When are you going to learn to tell the truth? It's one of the lessons that we try to teach you, but if you cannot learn the easy way, then I guess you'll have to learn it the hard way. You've made your choice. Hold out your hand."

Wham! "Oowowow." I squirmed and writhed.

"The other hand." Wham! "Ooooo, oooo, oooo." I danced and tangoed.

Wham! "Eeeeewooooow, ooo, ooo, oooo." I jitterbugged. I wasn't going to tough it out; I howled.

"Oh! Get out," I was told after receiving six lashes. "Tell that Hector Lavalley to come down here, and tell him that he'd better tell the truth."

On the way upstairs I tried hard not to cry, but it is difficult to hold back bitterness and resentment when your account is discredited and you know that a lie would not have obtained the slightest remission of a thrashing by a single stroke. It was better to tell a lie than the truth when our teachers preferred to believe their own biases.

I saw Hector upstairs in the lavatory awaiting sentence. He was worried and scared; his eyes were already glazed and furtive, searching for some way out.

"Your turn." I tried to sound tough and indifferent.

"How many'd you get?"

"Thirty-two," I lied.

Hector's eyes stretched wide. "Thirty-two! Holy smokes! What'll I say?"

"Better you tell him we smoked the whole thing. May as well tell a lie, Hec, he might believe you. He didn't believe me anyways when I tol' him the truth. Not going to make no difference."

Hector came back after half an hour. He was weeping and shaking as he washed his swollen hands in cold water in the lavatory.

"How many, Hector?"

"Thirty-two."

Neither truth nor lie had obtained the slightest remission of sentence. Poor ol' Kitchi-meeshi Hec need not have endured all the thirty-two lashes if he had known that howling and screaming and bawling and dancing at the very outset of a thrashing was the method contrived by the boys to earn a reduction in the number of lashes. But he had toughed it out, whether he had wanted to or not.

Later that winter I was plucked from the classroom one afternoon and told to report to Brother Laflamme at once. On the way upstairs to the dark room I tried guessing what special assignment Brother Laflamme had for me.

"Well, my little doodlebug," he greeted me as I knocked at the open door. "Hope we can find something decent for you to wear for your trip home."

"Home!" I was staggered. It was just too good to be true, like a dream. "Home!" I couldn't believe the word; it had been written so many times that it had lost its meaning and become hollow, irrelevant and mocking in sound. Going home for me was still three years from becoming a reality. Yet Brother Laflamme had said "home" or a word that sounded very much like it. I scarcely dared to repeat what I thought I had heard: "Home?"

"Yes! Home! Don't you know? Didn't they tell you?"

"No."

Shaking his head, Brother Laflamme expressed his disbelief. "I can't for the life of me figure out some of these priests and the way they do things."

"When, Brother?"

"Tonight."

"Tonight! Today! Home!" By some miracle, today, tonight and going home, so distant in time and in meaning, merged. No longer was it three years removed, but in the present, immediate, full of meaning and reality.

I tried on coat after coat until one was found to fit — or nearly so — a black coat with a red lining whose pockets were inhabited by mothballs. Home! I was leaving! During the next little while I must have put on and cast off dozens of pairs of trousers before a pair was found to fit — or nearly so. Whether they fit well or not didn't matter much. I was going home. Both garments needed some adjustments and, because I had served an apprenticeship as a tailor, I took them down to the tailor shop for alterations, which I undertook for myself — with difficulty owing to the quiver and tremble of my hands and legs, caused by the excitement of anticipation. Soon I'd be on my way . . . if what Brother Laflamme had told me was true.

The tailors were dumbfounded and envious. They asked a lot of questions: "When? Why? How'd you know? Who tol' you? Geeeee, you're lucky. Ah, you're jis' kidding."

At 5:00 P.M. I was called to the Minister's office and told officially, "You're going home tonight on the train. While the others are in study, go upstairs, undo your bed, shower, clean up, get dressed and clean out your box downstairs. Be ready to leave by six forty-five. We'll take you to the station. That's all."

It was true. I was getting out, I was going home.

At supper, though I was hungry, I couldn't eat, I didn't want to eat, I didn't have to eat. Tomorrow I would eat properly. A bargain being a bargain I bartered my barley soup for a slice of bread and a chunk of lard, which, together with my own rations, would make a fine lunch later. My fellow diners were just as stunned as the tailors by the suddenness of my departure, which had, unknown to me, been engineered by my father in order for me to complete Grade 8 fully and properly so I could try the high-school "entrance examinations." The questions were the same as the tailors': "Where? Why? Who tol' you?" Geeeee, you're lucky." And though they laughed and joked, they were very sad, not so much to see me go, but because they were not going home, because no one had remembered them.

Between 6:30 and 6:45 I stood where Charlie and Eugene and Johnny Migwans had stood the year before, staying goodbye to the boys who crowded around. I said goodbye to Kitchi-meeshi Hec. It was the easiest thing to say, and I said it often, even to Leonard Cross and Ivan Kaboni, whom I could not stand and who in turn could not stand me. I said it often, without sorrow, without regret, but with gladness and immense relief. I would go home. Never would I return, not in person, not in memory. I would shut out all memories of Spanish . . . forever.

Just before I left, someone whispered, "Basil! When you get home tell everybody what it's like here. Tell the other boys never to come here."

At 7:30 I boarded the train. No one ever thought of saying "Farewell." It was forgotten in the excitement brought on by the anticipation of leaving the school and being restored to one's family and home; the one taking leave dared not say it lest "them" priests revoke the discharge. Not even the boys who had still to serve their sentence and were now looking on could bring themselves to say it; they were too filled with the sense of neglect.

Return to Spanish

Father R.J. Oliver, S.J., appointed as Father Superior in 1945, had considerable hindsight and a greater amount of foresight than most of his peers. In looking back to the establishing of the residential school in Wikwemikong on Manitoulin Island in 1825 and to its relocation to Spanish in 1913, he found no record or recollection of a graduate who had established himself anywhere in a business related to his interest or training, be it shoemaking, tailoring, swineherding, shepherding, milling, blacksmithing, chicken-raising, dairy farming, cattle ranching, canning, barbering, carpentry, plumbing or janitoring. Nor had any graduate, to anyone's knowledge, taken up art, sculpture, music or literature, let alone gone to an art gallery, seen the "Pietà," listened to an opera or attended a performance of *Hamlet*. Most, if they remained in school through to Grade 8, had returned to their communities embittered by memories of thrashings and blows with fists and quite unprepared by training for any occupation in the outside world except lumbering.

With machines in factories taking over more and more chores previously done by human labour, the new Father Superior could not envisage "Mishibinishima and Niganigijig Tailors" in competition with Tip Top Tailors any more than he could foresee "Gistigly Shoes" of St. Regis in rivalry with Maher Shoes. As he looked ahead and considered "whither the school" and "whither the boys," he could not imagine, though it would have represented a triumph for the institution, billboards proclaiming the Bisto Chick Hatchery, Custom Shirts by Kanasawe or Keeshig Hair Styles.

The world outside Spanish was moving much too fast. In its motion forward it was making obsolete the trades for which the boys were being trained. In looking ahead Father Oliver saw no tailors or shoemakers or chicken farmers; instead he saw bookkeepers, station agents, teachers, merchants, Indian agents, postmasters, conductors and train engineers. These were positions of substance and standing within the community, performed by men with some breeding who read Milton and Shakespeare and attended concerts.

Father Oliver favoured office careers for the students not out of any scorn for the manual or physical labour required by the KVP in Espanola or Ontario Pulp and Paper on the North Shore, but because a clerical or professional career offered security. Bush work was dignified; it satisfied a man's vanity in being "a man's work," and it fostered the Indian's sense of personal independence and resourcefulness. But such labour was always seasonal, and it seldom challenged the intellectual or artistic abilities.

As Father Oliver saw it, the boys deserved a better and a broader training than they had hitherto received. Perhaps because he too was from a broken home, he had a better understanding of the boys than his colleagues did. He also believed that the institution had an obligation to its wards to provide an education more in keeping with the modern world's changes.

From the very first day of his appointment as Superior of the school, Father Oliver dreamed of establishing a high-school program within the institution. Easier dreamed of than done.

Of all the obstacles that could undo his plans, the boys presented the most formidable one. Merely by their refusal to remain in school beyond Grade 8 in the coming year, the boys would force Father Oliver to abandon his project. But he had faith in their ability and common sense, and trusted that, in their good judgment, they would agree to further education. They had nothing to lose. Only they could scuttle his plans.

Despite his confidence in the boys' ultimate acquiescence, Father Oliver still had much convincing to do. Right from the start he conducted personal interviews with the boys, which he continued throughout the year.

He called Boozo into his office and came directly to the point.

"Harold! If you were to quit school right now, what would you do?"

Never having given the matter any thought, Harold was speechless.

Father Oliver pressed on. "Come on, don't be shy. Surely, with your graduation just ten months away you must have made some plans for your future?"

Harold had no such idea in his mind; he had nothing to say.

"Suppose, just suppose, that this school were to burn down today, and let us suppose you had a home to go to, what would you do? This is not a trick question intended to trap you, so you need not be afraid. I'm looking for information. I want to know what you intend to do when you graduate. Take a wild guess!"

"Lumber camp, I suppose," Boozo wild-guessed.

"How old are you?"

"Fifteen."

"Think they'd hire you at your size?"

"No."

"What have you been trained to do here?"

"Well, I worked in the tailor shop an' I'm working in the chicken coop right now."

"Would you like to be a chicken farmer?"

"No."

"Would you like to be a tailor?"

"No."

"Then what would you like to do?"

"I don't know."

"Precisely. You don't know what to do, any of you." Father Oliver let this observation sink in before he continued. "It is because you don't know what to do and because you'll never be a tailor or a chicken farmer that something must be done about your further education. It is to give you boys a chance for a better future that we are considering a high-school program in the school next year.

"But that's up to you boys. It's not up to me or the faculty; it's not up to the government; it's not up to anybody but you boys whether this school institutes a high-school program. We would like you to think about it . . . and let us know soon.

"Should you decide to remain for Grade 9 through to Grade 12 or 13, we will at once proceed with the plans . . . and there would, of course be changes, many changes in the entire program to make it appropriate to your education and your maturity.

"You will have to go school all day; no more of this half-day school, half-day work business, though you will still be expected to do some chores before and after classes.

"You will study Latin, French, English, algebra, history, geography, science, art, physical health and industrial arts. They are difficult subjects; your days are going to be full, but you boys should be able to handle these subjects.

"I want to emphasize, so that you clearly understand, that no one can make you stay in school as of next year. No one can force you to go to high school. But if you give your word that you'll go to high school and then renege, we'll all look like a bunch of magpies.

"Think about it, Harold, and let me know soon. We haven't much time."

Father Oliver addressed the other boys in similar terms. The only one who had any idea of what he wanted to do in life was David Jocko; he wanted to be an artist. The others were as uncertain about their future as Boozo.

But it was the first time the boys had been challenged to think about their futures and their careers. Each one asked himself the same question. After Grade 8, what? Quit or go on? One by one Harold, Alfie, Julius, Dominic, Frankie, David, Alvin, Alphonse and Chauncey considered the question and gave their replies: Yes, they would remain if a high-school program were offered.

With the boys' agreement to remain in Spanish, the way was now clear for Father Oliver to seek the permission of the Reverend Father Swain, the Father Provincial of the Jesuit Order of Upper Canada. Permission was readily granted.

It was therefore with some assurance that Father Oliver wrote a letter to the Department of Indian Affairs seeking an increase in the daily allowance for each student from forty to ninety cents to make up for the increased cost of living caused by inflation; he also asked for an additional $1,200, representing the combined salaries of two certified teachers to be added to the staff in the proposed high-school program in the next academic year.

The department neither denied nor approved the request. It didn't even consider an adjustment in the amount requested. It made no reference to the merits of the case presented by Father Oliver.

Indian Affairs wanted information; Indian Affairs wanted more information. Indian Affairs then wanted information about information. Father Oliver supplied information, more information and then information about information.

What most disturbed the department was the matter of precedent, precedent for instituting a high-school program in an Indian residential school. There was no record that such a thing had ever been done. If there was no precedent, there was no format to follow; if there was no precedent, there was no authority, and therefore it could not be done. How could this priest know what to do without some previous experience to guide him?

Equally vexatious to Indian Affairs was the amount of money requested for teachers. Only for two? Why not seven or eight for each grade, as with other high schools? Was the man short-sighted or was it his *modus operandi?* In a period when teachers were in short supply, where were two additional ones to be found? They'd have to keep an eye on this priest, otherwise he'd put one over on the department.

And space: classrooms. Was not the building barely large enough to accommodate 140 boys? How did the Reverend Father Superior propose to create additional classroom space? By expansion? By adjusting admissions? Keep a brake on this man. This may be only the start. There'll be more requests for more funds.

Equipment, books, apparatus, maps, globes and such! What was the projected annual cost for these items? Did the school expect the department to bear the entire cost? Were the school and the Jesuit Order prepared to assume some of the burden? Watch this man! Stall! Put him off until he trips over his own feet. Eventually, he'll give in.

But the key to the entire program was the Indian students themselves, and the academic record. How could the Reverend Father Superior be so certain that he could retain Indian boys through high school, when the national and tribal predilection was for dropping out? On what did the Reverend Father Superior base his optimism that the Indian students in Spanish could be dissuaded from quitting school at Grade 8, just like their kind across the land? And what about the policy and program of integration? It was difficult enough to persuade Indians to enfranchise and take their places alongside the rest of Canadians. Wouldn't this proposal further entrench them in tribal isolation? Wasn't the Reverend Father Superior delaying and even obstructing the process of integration by proposing a high school only for Indians? How were Indians under this system of education going to learn to adjust to the outside world — the real world?

On what did the Reverend Father Superior base his confidence that he could maintain control and discipline over a group of Indian boys whose disparate ages, growth and maturity required different rules and regulations? How was morale to be maintained among the younger students under differing standards?

And how did the Reverend Father Superior expect the department to continue furnishing the wherewithal for the purchase of bolts of denim, flannel and corduroy or making donations of same to clothe the boys?

Furthermore, what possible benefit would Latin, algebra and chemistry be to the boys if they did not have a corresponding familiarity with the basic etiquette and social graces of the civilized world? Why, all of them would as soon drink the water from a finger bowl and devour the lemons as rinse their fingers, and wear moccasins or even running shoes with suits or other fine clothing. Did the Reverend Father Superior have a program in mind for the social development of these Indians whereby at least some of their coarser manners might be expurgated? Ask questions. Keep him on the defensive. Keep asking for more information, until he flags. Don't let up.

At first Father Oliver obliged the Department with the information that it wanted in the belief that cooperation would speed up the grant of the additional moneys requested.

The request for moneys representing the salaries for two certified teachers, Father Oliver pointed out, was occasioned by provincial educational standards which decreed the presence of at least two certified teachers on staff if the high school were to receive sanction and recognition. No more than two such teachers were required. Other teachers would be conscripted from the ordained faculty, all of whom had thirteen years of post-secondary school education. Even the scholastics on staff possessed the equivalent of a B.A.; and in the event of a pinch, the lay brothers could be seconded to teach. The institution was asking for no more than a nominal sum to hire two certified teachers. The other instructors would provide instruction without stipend.

With the school offering a high-school program, enrolment was naturally expected to increase. For years school registration had fluctuated between 125 and 140 boys, but the institution was large enough to accommodate up to 172 boys if a few adjustments were made, such as converting the club room and the tailor shop into classrooms and the infirmary into a small dormitory. Moreover, there were wide-open spaces in the school's cellar that had not yet seen use. Space was merely a question of making adjustments in the school's design.

In planning to do away with the tailor shop to create classroom space, Father Oliver was doing more than just creating space; he was taking the first step in phasing out the industrial trades program and replacing it with an academic one. In the years to come the boys would be acquiring new and different knowledge, and they would be expected to assume ever more responsibility in providing for their own needs. The old tailor shop would no longer roar with the whine of Singer sewing machines; instead it would buzz with the recitation of declensions, conjugations and readings from Shakespeare.

And just as the institution had always made do with the space available, so it would make do with used equipment, used books, used chemistry apparatus; hand-me-downs the staff would borrow or beg.

Anyway, as Father Oliver indicated to the department, the boys could learn as well with old books and old test tubes as with new ones. For those who seldom had anything new, used books and equipment would make little difference.

On the basis of their ability the boys deserved a chance to further their education, Father Oliver argued. They ought not to be penalized by the past performance and experience of Spanish or other residential schools; they ought to be judged on their character and general merit alone. Father Oliver wagered his cassock that the boys would, with training and preparation, compare favourably with the top 20 percent of other students of corresponding age and grade level.

"There's Harold Belleau of Garden River, for instance. As keen an observer as you would ever meet. With such a faculty this youth has done well in the industrial arts, and will do well in the sciences. It is this same trait that has made him an outstanding athlete, a self-taught goaltender. Despite his parents' estrangement, Harold has an abundance of good humour, combined with a lot of common sense. He is not afraid to speak his mind.

"Since his arrival from Whitefish Falls in 1938, Julius Niganigijig, from a broken home like Harold, has maintained above-average grades, especially in English. From reports it seems that he has the same flair for description and expression as his sister, Stella, whose story "The Other Wise Man" was published in the *Catholic Register* three years ago. Brother O'Keeffe reports that this young lad has a fine mind and a capacity for the abstract.

"Alfred Cooper, a waif also, has the best temperament, disposition and discipline of all the boys, combined with the talent necessary for scholarly studies. Had he a vocation, the young lad would be an outstanding candidate for the priesthood. Good in all subjects. On determination and drive alone Alfred Cooper has made himself if not an exceptional athlete, at least a valuable member in intramural sports. It is this kind of resolution that will earn this lad success.

"For level-headedness there is hardly a youngster that can match Alphonse Trudeau of Wikwemikong. He too, like the rest, is a waif. In the classroom and on the ball field Alphonse is always imperturbable. Nothing seems to bother him. A little too easy-going, but he can do the work.

"Few youngsters have as quick a mind and wit as Alvin Nashkewe of Cape Croker. Along with his brother, Lloyd, Alvin came to this school following the death of their father in an automobile accident. He grasps data and facts quickly without effort. All he needs is a little discipline to harness the potential.

"Dominic McComber of Caughnawaga, Quebec, is one of our two resident Mohawks. The fact that Dominic is likewise a waif does not seem to have affected his academic work or his disposition. He works and produces best when he is in competition or believes that he is in competition. A bit impulsive now, but he should outgrow it within the next two or three years.

"The other Mohawk is Chauncey Benedict from St. Regis. In the three years that he has been here, Chauncey has shown flashes of above-average ability. That this lad has not been more consistent in his academic work may be attributed to his youth. But what is encouraging is that he has the essential ability to do more advanced work.

"If Frank Commanda of Timagami expended as much effort and drive on his studies as on sport, he would achieve above-average grades. As it is, he is getting average grades. He may not be a scholar, but he is an outstanding athlete; if he grows beyond average size, he could well be a professional hockey player. He inspires the other boys with his leadership in sports, and the other boys inspire him with their work in the classroom.

"The above-named boys are nimbler in mind and body than David Jocko of Golden Lake, but none is as original or imaginative. He may not recall facts instantly or sort out details as quickly as others, but David, if given time, will come up with a sensible answer or a reasonable explanation. Through his art and compositions David exemplifies the principle that the difference between the quick and slow-witted is time."

Despite all the information and explanations that Father Oliver supplied on request, the Department of Indian Affairs undertook no commitment. Eventually, in exasperation over these stalling tactics and lack of cooperation, Father Oliver notified the department that he was proceeding with plans to institute a high-school program in Spanish come hell, high water or Indian Affairs, and that he was going to go to the press with full particulars of the department's opposition to Indian residential-school students' further education.

Just what happened in the department's headquarters in Ottawa may be inferred from the rapid growth in the number of civil servants in the offices and a corresponding proliferation of forms during that year and succeeding ones. It was not until later, much later, that the Department of Indian Affairs came through with the funding in the amount requested.

From the moment he resolved on a high-school program for the school, through all the protracted negotiations with the Department of Indian Affairs, Father Oliver proceeded with his plans and arrangements as if funding by Indian Affairs were a *fait accompli*. He didn't have much time. The boys for whom he was making plans and arrangements would be entering Grade 8 in the fall. Within the next twelve months Father Oliver and his staff would have to prepare the students to write the tough provincial examinations in the spring and then to admit them into the high-school curriculum come September.

Certified teachers were scarce, and the way Indian Affairs was reacting to Father Oliver's request, money was even scarcer. Father Oliver recruited teachers from within the institution.

"I want to see you in my office this afternoon at 1:30," he told Brother Manseau after lunch one day.

During the next half hour Brother Manseau must have scoured his conscience for lapses in the continent usage of the English language in the recent past, and wondered whether he were about to be sent on retreat again . . . and for how long.

"Sit down, Brother," Father Oliver said affably in French when Brother Manseau entered the Father Superior's office promptly at 1:30.

"Between now and September, Brother, I want you to learn all that you need to know about English grammar. You will teach Grade 8 this coming year and Grade 9 the following year. If you need books or any kind of help, come and see me. Is that clear? Do you think that the chicken coop and tailor shop can manage without you for a couple of hours each day while you learn and teach?"

"Hell, yes . . ." Brother Manseau checked himself. "I'm sorry, me, Father," he apologized. "I mean . . . of course, the dang chicken, they can look after themself an' lie by themself for a whiles."

"Very good! You may start your studies today. And by the way, you'll be amazed at how much your own usage will improve," Father Oliver added, with a wink and a smile.

Brother Manseau set out to learn English with the same devotion and resolution with which Brother McLaren had mastered the dictionary when told to do so.

Next, Brother Laflamme.

"During the next year, Brother, I want you to read; study more about anatomy and health. I also want you to learn the theory and practical aspects of electricity. Because as of next year you are going to teach the two subjects in high school. Think you can manage along with your other duties?"

"With some adjustments in my schedule, I'll manage," Brother Laflamme assured Father Oliver.

Later the same day Brother Van der Moor was summoned.

"Next year this school is going to have a high-school program. We are enlisting staff. Because you're the only one who knows enough about motors and repairs, you are our designate to teach auto mechanics. In the meantime you are to read everything about the subject in preparation for your teaching duties. Any questions?"

"No, Father; not right now. Perhaps later on."

"Very good."

The willingness of brothers Manseau, Laflamme and Van der Moor exemplified the general eagerness of the brothers to undertake any tasks they were assigned, of whatever character. Up to this time candidates who aspired to enter the Society of Jesus as brothers were not required to possess any particular qualification other than a genuine vocation for the religious life; nor during their two-year novitiate in Guelph did they receive special training in philosophy, theology, scripture, Bible history or Latin, as candidates for the priesthood did. What knowledge and skills the brothers needed to serve God through the Society of Jesus were acquired in the course of fulfilling their vow of obedience and accepting whatever challenges their superiors provided. Hence, with the same passion and zeal with which they had learned their trades and everything else, the brothers set out to acquire the new knowledge that would qualify them to teach.

When later Brother Manseau entered the classroom as a teacher, he announced to Harold, Alfie, Julius and their colleagues, "I'm going to teach you the English. You're going to learn the gerunds and the participles . . . and you're going to parse the sentence, otherwise I'm going to kick you in the ass."

No asses were kicked, but an awful lot of chalk and blackboard brushes, along with Jupitaires and maudites and G--d---s flew in the direction of "the jackass" who confused a gerund with "the participle" or wrote a sentence with "the dang hanging participle."

In September 1946, a high-school program was inaugurated. For the first Grade 9 class, Harold, Alfie, Julius, Frankie, David, Dominic, Alvin, Chauncey and Alphonse returned to the school.

At the end of March 1945, three months short of completing Grade 9, I dropped out of Regiopolis College in Kingston to return to the sanctuary and comfort of Cape Croker.

In the fall of the same year, when my father left the reserve to seek his fortune in the lumber camps, I was left in sole possession and proprietorship of the family estate, which consisted of a log house, a log barn and a log privy situated on a parcel of land of twenty-five acres, more or less. Formerly my grandmother, Rosa, had owned it.

Upon my father's departure, survival — mine — became my first and only object in the sixteenth year of my life. With trout near extinction in Georgian Bay and pulp depleted, opportunities for survival were scarce for everyone but farmers. To go on "relief," as welfare was known in those days, was unthinkable. No man worthy of the name would ever think of asking for relief, and people at the Cape proudly boasted that only two people got relief during the Depression.

I would make the people of the Cape proud of me. In the waning days of August I began to assess the community's business needs, its resources and my expertise. In training I had Grade 8 and half of Grade 9, which was of no value to anyone. According to my analysis there was one constant need in winter: fuel. And as far as my keen eye could see, the resources were limitless. All that was required in the way of capital expenditures was an axe. I already had an axe.

Before launching my timbering operation, I conducted a mental market-research survey, in accordance with the finest business and economic principles. There were Pulch (Mrs. Isadore Pitawaniquot), Meeks (Stanley McLeod, my uncle), Shabow (Mr. Francis Nadjiwon), Bee Dee (Peter Nadjiwon), Kitchi-Flossie (Mrs. William Akiwenzie), Chick (Walter Johnston, my uncle), Kitchi-Susan (Mrs. Susan Taylor), Shawnee (Charles Jones), Kitchi-Low See (Mrs. Lucy Nawash), Christine Keeshig (my grandmother's sister), Maggie (Mrs. Desjardins), Eezup (Andrew Akiwenzie), Pollock (Mrs. E. Akiwenzie), and many, many more.

Revenue! More than I had realized. I calculated that I could cut a load of poles every day. At three dollars a load, less a dollar to the teamster for delivery, that was sixty dollars a month — a handsome profit. I'd survive. More than survive! Except that there were Sundays and Saturdays, and that my potential customers would not burn a load of fuel each day. I reduced my estimates accordingly. Then I realized that many of my potential customers cut their own wood, and that I would be in direct competition with my uncle Stanley. There wasn't as much revenue in cutting wood as I had originally thought.

I needed advice. I went to my Uncle Stanley, who was an expert in survival. He suggested that I go into the fur industry, at the primary level, trapping or harvesting raccoons. And he showed me a price list issued by one of the fur buyers on Spadina Avenue in Toronto to illustrate how profitable the raccoon industry was: up to twenty-four dollars for a prime pelt. I panted and drooled. Uncle was willing to share both his expertise and his resources. There were more raccoons than my uncle and I together could harvest. All I needed was to kill one fat raccoon every day and I'd be in business.

Uncle was generous. He conceded to me as my own hunting territory the ridge, a part of the Niagara Escarpment formation that extended from the Lighthouse to Cove of Cork, bending inward as it followed the contour of Little North Bay, outward to Benjamin's Point and then south-west until it sloped into the flat sedimentary rocks at Pine Tree Point. In addition, all the territory between was mine to hunt.

One of the advantages of this kind of enterprise is that little capital investment is required. My total capital equipment consisted of two enthusiastic but inexperienced dogs and an axe. But that was all that was needed for this kind of business.

After the trawling season was over it was my daily routine to set out with a lunch in an old army haversack, axe in hand and preceded by two exuberant dogs who raced ahead and ranged the bushes in search of any beast worth barking at: squirrels, rabbits, chipmunks, groundhogs, skunks, porcupines, foxes, partridge — anything, so long as it was alive. I had to investigate every round of barking, otherwise the dogs would not leave the quarry; or worse, they would mutiny and go home. Instead of walking ten to twelve miles, which would have constituted the whole round-trip distance of my beat, I frequently walked anywhere between twenty and twenty-five miles, often for nothing.

On returning home in the evening I had to cut wood, make a fire, cook a meal, and, if I had got a raccoon, skin and clean the beast and stretch the pelt on the roof or side of the barn. By the time I had completed these operations, I was ready for sleep.

My hunting technique was primitive and simple, but effective. If the dogs treed a raccoon, I'd chop the tree down and, if need be, two or three other trees. As soon as tree and quarry fell to earth my assistants would be instantly upon the raccoon, holding the victim for the coup de grâce, which I delivered with the flat of my axe. If the dogs ran the raccoon into a cave or burrow, a torch made from a mixture of leaves and pine gum stuck at the end of a pole would flush it out. Once the raccoon emerged, my assistants would seize it and hold it fast in their jaws for execution. Once, as I delivered the fatal blow, my dog Chalk sprang at my victim for one extra bite. I hit Chalk instead of the raccoon. From the way my dog quivered and convulsed, I thought I had killed him.

Despite their numbers, I didn't kill as many raccoons as I expected. Nevertheless, I killed enough to cover the roof and sides of the barn with raccoon hides.

Only once did I kill more than two in a day; on that occasion I killed six in one cave. Killing an enormous moose or catching a net full of fish may be the dream of most hunters or fishermen, but the dream may turn into a bad dream. I killed the six raccoons at Benjamin's Point on my return patrol. I looked at my victims with the practised eye of a fur appraiser; at least fifty dollars. My energies were instantly restored. And even though my energies and strength could have borne the total weight of the six raccoons, I could no more carry six flopping raccoon corpses than I could carry two greased monkeys, no matter how I tried. I resorted to the simple expedient of carrying forward three at a time for some distance, leaving them on the ground, and then returning for the other three. By this means I eventually arrived at the old Bert Ashkewe homestead and corner. It was already dark and I still had a mile to walk. Only the vision of fifty dollars sustained me. While I mentally caressed the bills I heard the snort of horses and the rumble of wagon wheels. It was Charles Jones, Jr., known as Shawnee in the village. I hitched a ride.

After I was done skinning the raccoons, I reviewed my production and estimates of revenue for the coming winter — a market forecast of sorts. Up to this point the raccoon division of my fur operations was not yielding as much profit as I had originally anticipated, and it would yield even less during the winter, that was clear. I would have to diversify.

Once more I studied the price list. The only fur bearer on the list that inhabited our reserve in sufficient numbers to justify hunting was the squirrel: black, red, grey and flying. In fact, there was an over-population of black squirrels, especially in Peter Nadjiwon's sugar bush. At $1.25 for a prime black-squirrel pelt, there was a tidy profit to be realized.

I diversified the very next morning. With only a slingshot I blasted fifteen fat squirrels from the trees before half the afternoon was over. Besides a handsome profit, there was meat.

At home I studied the deskinning manuals that my Uncle Stanley had given to me. According to the instructions, squirrels were to be unskinned from the ankles, then over the head, inside out, in much the same way women remove their nightgowns. After the squirrel is unskinned, the pelt should be sheathed inside-out tightly over a pointed arched wooden frame, much as a dress is slipped over a mannequin. Not only would I have to deskin the squirrels, I would have to make the frames. Fortunately, across the road, there was a cedar-rail fence; ample raw material for frames.

I couldn't wait to perform surgery; the manual, with its diagrams, made the operation look simple. All one had to do was to follow instructions. Because I did not have the proper instruments, I could not begin immediately. Again the manitous provided me with inspiration.

Guided by manitous, I went across the road to my neighbour, Francis Nadjiwon, to borrow the proper surgical instrument.

With proper instruments and as directed by the diagrams, I cut an incision from ankle to ankle, following, as it were, an invisible inseam. Just as the manual had promised, it was easy. Step two was to peel off said squirrel's hide down and over its arms and head. I peeled, but the hide did not peel off as easily as promised in the diagram. As I undressed my patient, tissue, sinew and fat clung to the hide and would not let go. I consulted my manual, but it offered no guidance on a method of removing skin from tough tissue, or of pinning down a limp squirrel long enough to divest it of its skin. I resolved this difficulty by tying the squirrel's hindpaws to a nail. At least I had some control over the beast, and I peeled its pelt off as far as the head where, in my haste, I peeled too indelicately; I tore the skin. Discouraging as was the wasted work and the loss of profit, I consoled myself with the thought that at least I had the meat. I could not indulge in self-pity too long. I had to go on.

I operated on the second squirrel without accident. By sawing, chopping, splitting, carving, whittling and shaving I eventually constructed a stretching frame. As gently as I could, I slipped the pelt over the frame, pulled and stretched downward. Either I pulled too hard, or the pelt was too thin; my squirrel pelt split.

Two gone and wasted; thirteen to go. It was now 9:30 P.M. As yet I had not eaten. At this rate of deskinning, I would not be done until noon the next day.

On I worked, resolved to deskin every little beast, even if I had to work through the night. I had to recover some of my invested time and effort. As a surgeon must take care not to skewer a patient during surgery, so did I operate on squirrel number three.

Afterward I mounted my patient on a frame. I felt proud as I earned $1.25, which had taken an hour and a half. By 3:00 A.M. I had deskinned two more.

Hungry, sleepy, cold and stiff-fingered, I decided there and then to close down my squirrel diversification program. To hell with squirrels; raccoons were easier.

Maybe it would be better to go back to school. I had heard vague rumours that Spanish was offering a high-school program. If it were true, I would return. It was my only chance to escape a life of cutting wood.

Though raccoons were easier to harvest, they did not generate enough income to support even a marginal existence. To keep from starving and to uphold the image of being a man, capable of self-support, I undertook whatever work was available: trawling the waters of the Cape the entire summer, fishing with nets in the fall with Casimir Taylor, drawing water for Resime Akiwenzie and Herman Taylor during their hog-slaughtering sessions and, finally, working for Frank Nadjiwon as farm-hand. For Frank I made a crooked ladder and dismantled a bicycle I was unable to reassemble. I felled trees with style, dug post-holes with grace and spread manure with finesse. I also told Frank about the high-school program being offered at Spanish, and spoke of my intention to return to an institution to which I had not given a single thought since I left it.

Frank said, "Yes! You ought to go back, it's your only chance." I guess he knew better than I suspected that I was never going to be a carpenter, plumber, farmer, blacksmith, mechanic or any kind of tradesman. He knew from his experience in the army that no one ever got very far with only Grade 8, not even soldiers. Spanish, no matter how tough, could never be as bad as the army.

I had been cutting poles all day. It was a day like any other during the past winter when I had cut poles. It would be no different tomorrow, the next day, the month after; I would be cutting poles.

The only respite was sleep. On this particular night, getting on toward morning, I dreamed of the bush, of maple, oak, ash, ironwood, birch and hemlock. As I stood next to a birch, sizing up where best to sink the blade of the axe, the nearby trees began to whisper, "He's going to kill the birch! He's going to kill the birch!" and their whispers beat upon my ears like hail. I planted the blade deep into the flesh of the birch, which shuddered and gasped in pain. The other trees hissed, "He's killing the birch! He's killing the birch!" Again and again I drove the blade deeper into the core of the birch; with each stroke the tree moaned and trembled anew. At last the birch toppled to the ground, where it convulsed for a few moments before lying still. As I cleared the limbs from the birch, the trees shrilled, "He's killed the birch! He's killed the birch!"

Appalled by what I had done and mortified by the accusations of the trees, I coiled and then uncoiled to cast my axe far from me, but the axe clung to my hands: it was bonded to my being. Try as I might, I could not get rid of that accursed implement.

It was during this struggle that I woke up with a start, drenched in cold sweat. I put my hands together. There was no axe. I almost leaped out of bed, so great was the sense of relief. Never had I got up from bed more readily, more freely, more gladly.

Unsettled by the dream, I thought of the future for the first time.

So it was a dream that finally persuaded me to request admission to the high school at Spanish. Later in the spring I received word that my request for admission had been granted.

New Learning and Cultural Conflict

On my return to Spanish in the fall of 1947, I was summoned into Father Oliver's office for an interview. The gist of his remarks was that I was being admitted into the Grade 10 class on condition that I complete the Grade 9 program by Christmas and pass the examinations; otherwise I would have to repeat the entire course with the current class of Grade 9 boys three to four years my junior. To allow me to complete Grade 9 by Christmas, the administration was excusing me from all chores so that I could devote the extra time to the Grade 9 subjects I had missed by dropping out two and half years earlier.

Every day from 8:00 to 9:00 A.M. and from 3:30 to 5:00 P.M.; from 8:00 A.M. till noon on Thursdays; and for an unspecified period on Sundays I was to review and read Grade 9 work.

It was not difficult to readjust to life in the residential school in Spanish, for some things had not changed. The daily and weekly schedule and the routine of rising, praying, eating, working, studying and sleeping were much the same as they had been when I left three years before. Brothers Manseau, Laflamme, Van der Moor, O'Keeffe and McLaren were still there performing the same duties. Father Richard, now in his early nineties, was still purging sinners and translating the Bible with the aid of a magnifying glass and a set of blocks, assisted by boys who, he complained, didn't know their own language. All the boys who were my contemporaries in age and grade when I left — Henry Webkamigad, Herbie Beaudry, Pius Roy, Norbert Debossige, Martin Assiniwe, Benjamin Buzwa, Joe Migwanabe — had graduated and gone; but there were now Harold Belleau, Alfie Cooper, Frank Commanda, Dominic McComber, Julius Niganigijig, David Jocko, Chauncey Benedict, Alvin Nashkewe, and Alphonse Trudeau. All were between one and three years younger than I, but I had known them before I left. Then there were the chores — milking, sweeping, cleaning out the barns; they had not changed ... they never would. On the surface, little had changed.

There were changes, however, minor ones perhaps, but changes nevertheless. The Garnier — which had sunk at her moorings during a violent storm in the autumn of 1942 and been refloated and refitted through the combined talents and efforts of Brother Van der Moor and Gerry Labelle — was now gone. So were the Iron Boat, the Red Bug and the punts. Even the wharf was tumbling down before the unremitting current of the Spanish River and the ravages of the breakers driven by the west winds across Lake Huron. But there was no longer a need for these vessels or their docks. For the past two years the Greyhound bus and the Canadian Pacific Railway had transported arriving and departing students and would continue to do so indefinitely; trucks and transports would deliver produce that was not cultivated on the farm. The mill was now no more than a decaying warehouse used for the storage of odds and ends, junk and anything that Brother Van der Moor was too attached to to cast out.

Except for brothers Manseau, Laflamme, McLaren and O'Keeffe and Father Richard, the staff was new. Brother Voisin, who had replaced Brother Grubb in the management of the dairy operations, was asked his nationality by the boys shortly after his arrival. "Choiman," he replied; and "Choiman" he was thereafter to all the boys. Brother Westaway was installed as governor of the kitchen domain. Assisting Father Oliver as Minister administrators of the institution at various times and terms were fathers Rushman, Hannin and Barry. From 1947 to 1950 the prefects were fathers Schretlin, Farrel, Cornett, Belyea, McKenna and Johnson. Lay teachers were Mr. J. Sammon, B.A., Mr. Wheeler, B.A., an itinerant Irishman, Mr. William McGrath, Mr. Marrin, Mr. (now Father) Bazinet, Mr. Grisdale and Mr. E. McCart. These men were not just new to the school; they also represented new attitudes, a fresh outlook more in tune with the modern world.

Under Father Oliver's administration the meals improved — at least, the noon and evening meals did. Instead of dining on thin onion, pea or barley soup ad nauseam every noon and evening, we now ate soup with considerable body — almost stew-like — or meat, vegetables and potatoes. Although, despite the simplicity of the recipe, the art of making consistently good porridge eluded Brother Westaway, the boiled eggs that were served as *hors d'oeuvres* or extras on Mondays, Wednesdays, Fridays and Saturdays made up for the indifferent mush.

Not only were the purse strings of the school loosened up for better nourishment; rules and codes and regulations were loosened up for the high-school students. Boys were allowed to smoke in the club room and outside the school grounds.

The traditional Thursday day off underwent change too. No longer did the high-school boys march in columns along the shoulder of Highway 17 on their way toward Cutler, Walford or Smith's Lake (now known as Walford Lake), passing straight through the village of Spanish. Now, they were allowed to enter any one of the shops — Solomon's, Dugas's, Bishop's, St. Denis's, Joncas's or Gignac's — to buy such small articles as chocolate bars or packets of tobacco. The favourite place was Gignac's; it had a jukebox, and the boys could hear the latest Hank Williams, Red Foley, Eddie Arnold and Ernest Tubb hits while awaiting service. The prefect always had to enter this den of iniquity to hurry the boys along.

On occasion we were allowed to go up to Gignac's unescorted to congregate around the jukebox and to play pool. Within weeks many of the village girls began to patronize Gignac's; that is, Rhonda and Lorna Dugas, Billie McGrath, Marina Decouteau, Theresa Joncas and sometimes Faye and Arbutus Bishop. They would arrive a few minutes after we did. They must have had an efficient "village telegraph" to enable them to synchronize their movements with our own. All the girls were attractive, which provided us with a strong incentive to return to Gignac's as often as possible.

During the next three years, to the strains of "Cold, Cold Heart," "Your Cheatin' Heart," "Walkin' the Floor over You," "Foggy River," "Rockin' Alone in an Old Rockin' Chair," many romances waxed and waned between the young Indian swains and the white girls. But despite the volumes of rapture and passion, only one of the local damsels captured an Indian, an Indian from Cutler.

It is not surprising that the beauties of Spanish should have been smitten by the young men from the school. That they fell in love with "the Indians" was not entirely owing to the scarcity of eligible young men in Spanish; my colleagues could have turned heads anywhere. Gone from their speech were such quaint colloquialisms as "sad ol' shoes" or "just meaning it"; now they discussed a wide range of topics, from *H.M.S. Pinafore* and *The Pirates of Penzance*, which they had performed the year before, to the character of the tourists who annually visited Timagami. They were no longer preoccupied with leaving "the place" now that they had some control over their lives and their destinies.

Part of the fresh outlook and attitude was self-generated and part was influenced by young men such as Adam Commanda and Maurice Pelletier, residents with no previous heritage of institutionalized living and thinking, who now entered the high-school program on the basis of personal choice. They brought with them pride in dress, in manner and in their persons.

Even the name of the school was changed. It was no longer St. Peter Claver's, nor the Spanish Indian Industrial School, nor the Indian Residential School; it was now the Garnier Residential School in honour of St. Charles Garnier, one of the Canadian martyrs.

In keeping with all the little changes, Mathew Pitwaniquot, a handyman from Wikwemikong, was hired to spruce up the lawn and the grounds, to give the old school a fresh image.

For some days Mathew worked alone with a spade digging a trench where the old wire fence had formerly been situated. Right from the start of the excavations (whose purpose was a mystery to almost everyone), two very ancient and infirm but curious Daughters of Mary began to stop in their daily 4:00 P.M. promenade to the shore of the Spanish River to watch Mathew put his back to work. They stared. When the two old women halted, Mathew suspended his labours and sat down facing his spectators. He too stared. From his shirt pocket Mathew very deliberately extracted a cigar, which he lit with great solemnity and dignity, much as a business tycoon would. Mathew appeared to derive as much relish from that cigar as any cigar smoker. We could never quite understand how Matt, as we called him, could survive those cigars, let alone enjoy them. They resembled and smelled like tar-caked rope.

"What are you doing, Mr. Pitwaniquot?" the Daughters ventured to ask one afternoon.

"Nothing!" Mathew replied, spitting in finality.

The good Daughters had not anticipated such a reply and were quite unprepared to frame another question. They turned on their heels and continued on their way down to the shore. As soon as the sisters turned to go, Mathew resumed work. He did not like an audience.

"Why are you digging a hole, Mr. Pitwaniquot?" the good sisters tried again, on their return.

"Is not hole; is ditch," Mathew explained.

"I see! I see!" the sisters murmured in discomfiture.

For the next few days the sisters were content to observe Mr. Pitwaniquot as they walked by.

In the next stage of his work Mathew was splitting stones.

"What are you doing now, Mr. Pitwaniquot?" the sisters wanted to know.

"Splitting stones."

At last, when Mathew was installing a metal balustrade atop the low stone fence, which was about three feet in height, the good sisters were moved to observe: "Mr. Pitwaniquot! Don't you think that cows will jump over your fence? . . . It's a bit too low."

"Is not goin' to be pasture," was the laconic reply.

Across the road, St. Joseph's Residential School was also undergoing changes that no one would have foreseen or thought possible five years before, especially under the rigid and conservative direction of the Daughters of Mary. But change it did, because the boys' and girls' schools operated in tandem. Whatever course the boys' school set, the girls' school followed.

At first the idea of a high school was regarded as a novelty by the people at home and the younger students in the school. Some elders found the idea that sixteen- to twenty-year-old men were still attending school somewhat hard to believe and accept, and they expressed their misunderstanding and skepticism in different ways. Not a few had some doubts as to the motives inspiring youth to remain in school. "At your age, I was already at work for five years and helping my parents." Still others doubted the intelligence of the students. They could not understand why a boy or girl needed four or five extra years to learn to read, write and count. "Didn't take me that long to learn read an' write . . . three, four years, that's all. What's the matter with you young peoples these days? You goin' to grow ol' in them schools."

Then there were the "little shots" from the primary school who wanted to know what the older boys were studying.

"What's that book about, anyways?"

"That's algebra."

"What's that about?"

"It's about unknowns."

"That hard?"

"Sometimes. But it's not hard when you know how. See! If you want to figure out somethin' that you don't know, you use an X. You could use a Z or a Y or an A or a B, or any other letter, but it's easier with an X. That's why the book uses more Xs than any other letter. You ask Alfred Cooper; he's real good at algebra and mathematics."

As well as arousing curiosity, the new knowledge and learning caused at least one family schism. In all our years at school we were repeatedly assured that education would bring about personal fulfilment and development, as well as serve the public interest and general good. All of us would be the better for reading Shakespeare and Milton and attending stage plays; all of our families and communities would profit from and benefit by our training and sense of civic duty. Some of our colleagues put their newly acquired skills to immediate and practical use by writing letters for grandparents or calculating the cost of building materials for their fathers. But not all of the higher learning was useful or innocuous.

According to several unimpeachable sources from West Bay and Sheshegwaning, a young scholar on summer vacation in Wikwemikong had sought to put his scientific knowledge to good purpose, with unexpected results. During a violent thunderstorm one afternoon a bolt of lightning struck a tree near the homestead, splitting asunder the trunk. Immediately the boy's father, Isaac, kindled a fire in the stove and threw therein a handful of tobacco.

With his family gathered about him, Isaac addressed the manitous in the tribal language.

"K'mishomissinaun! K'okomissinaun! Our grandfathers! Our grandmothers! Do not be too mad at us. It's not that we forgot . . . or anything like that, but we were broke and didn't have no tobaccy. We got some now and we offer you some. It's not the kind for make offerings, plug. It's Ogden's. We hope it's all right, but that's the bes' we got. We don't want to forget youse, because you are good to us. I'll try to get some good tobaccy, plug, and keep it all the times and offer you some an' . . . an' . . . I'll smoke for you. I hope you're not too mad at us."

As if propitiated by the offering, the storm that had hung low and lingered over Wikwemikong moved on, the thunder echoing from shore to shore of the bay, while lightning speared down on the homesteads and properties of other negligent tribal members in its passage toward Killarney and beyond.

Now, the young scholar who had witnessed this ceremony on previous occasions but had never given the custom any thought, asked his father to enlighten him.

Isaac was immensely pleased and gratified by his son's new-found interest in the tribal heritage. Then and there he instructed his son, explaining that the thunders were in reality the voices of their ancestors, who, feeling neglected and forgotten, were now demanding attention and propitiation. According to Isaac, an offering of tobacco was the form in which the living were to remember and pay homage to their forebears; and the departure of the storm was a sign that they were appeased.

"Dad! That's not true," the son informed his father. "Our grandfathers and grandmothers are in heaven. They can't get angry any more. Anyways, our teacher told us that thunder and lightning is caused by a bunch of hot air and a bunch of cold air crashing in the skies, and that's what you hear and see."

To Isaac this revelation was nothing less than heresy, a denial of tribal traditions and a renunciation of the accumulated beliefs and understandings of the tribe. For a few moments he was rendered speechless by his son's audacity. When he recovered his composure, he went out of doors to check aloft. It was still hot and humid. With as much authority and finality as he could muster, Isaac told his son that the presence of cold air in the heights, in the middle of the summer, was an atmospheric and seasonal impossibility and that he had sent his son to Spanish to learn to read, write and do arithmetic, not to swallow a lot of nonsense.

But however much Isaac may have scoffed at his son's explanation, and however firm his own convictions, he was unsettled, not only disturbed by his son's disbelief, but perturbed by his own doubts. Try as he might, Isaac could not dispel the little cloud of skepticism that drifted across his faith. It was a small cloud, but it cast its small shadow here and there, now and then.

Isaac was pondering the latest Band Council resolution in the comfort of his home where he had taken refuge from the bitter February cold, when the little cloud wafted across his mind.

Without a word, Isaac put his coat on and went outside. He split many armfuls of cedar kindling and lengths of oak, brought them into the house, and added them to the pile behind the stove.

"Expect it to get colder, do you?" his wife inquired with a smile, looking up quizzically at Isaac from her fingers and a ball of yarn.

Isaac said nothing. He opened wide the dampers to the cooking and box stoves before stoking the units with kindling and finely split oak. Isaac's wife watched; it was comfortable enough for her. The wood crackled and sizzled in the silent household. Soon the interior was baking. Isaac's wife doffed her tam and removed her cardigan; still she said nothing. Isaac kept loading the stoves ardently, until the lids glowed red and the temperature grew torrid, drawing beads of sweat from Isaac's brow.

Isaac's wife seldom questioned her husband's judgment or business, but at last, her face flushed, she complained: "Tuguh! Ahneen dah ae-indayin? What's the matter with you? You sick or something? You're just wasting good wood for nothing, and you're going to ruin the stoves . . . maybe burn the house down. If you don't open the door, I'll open it."

"Don't you dare." Isaac's tone was sharp. "Leave the door alone. Just wait a couple more minutes. I'm making a experiment." His wife sat back down, wiping her face with her apron.

Ten more minutes elapsed. The house was now sweltering, and both Isaac and his wife were at the point of suffocation. Isaac got up, went to the door, and grasped the knob. "Watch out," he warned his wife: "Better cover up your ears. Never know what might happen." Only after his wife complied did Isaac throw open the door and fling himself to one side. And there he stood, rigid, with his eyes closed. Nothing happened.

"What t'hell is the matter with you anyway, you damned fool?" Isaac's wife demanded. "First you try an' roast us alive . . . an' now you want us to freeze to death. *Close the damned door!*" she demanded, shivering in the inrush of Arctic air. "What the hell you tryin' t'do anyways?"

"You don't have to get so huffy! I was just trying an experiment to see if it was true that hot air and cold air make thunder like our son said," Isaac explained as he closed the door, "an' it's not true. I don't know what them priests are teaching our kids. Maybe we should take our son out of that school. Only causes trouble, that place."

The source of this new knowledge and the remote cause of this first case of cultural conflict was Mr. Joe Sammon, who had been enlisted for the princely sum of $600 per annum to come to Spanish to teach Anishinaubae, Cree and Mohawk students. On a teaching staff that included some outstanding teachers and some indifferent ones, Mr.

Wheeler and Mr. Sammon were the only teachers in possession of teacher's certificates. Mr. Sammon was not only a gifted teacher, but a dedicated one as well. It was said by those who knew him that, with his knowledge of English literature and with his experience and scholarship, he was qualified for an inspectorship anywhere in the province. Only his sartorial style — an old green cap with the crown button missing, a twisted red tie that was invariably knotted left of centre of the inverted V of his shirt collar, a brown tweed jacket whose pockets bulged with assorted chalk and other articles, and blue unpressed trousers — militated against his promotion. But with his salary Mr. Sammon could not afford suits. In terms of dedication, when dedication was the hallmark of teachers, Mr. Sammon was among the most dedicated. For him giving extra help was not merely an option, it was mandatory. He taught English grammar, literature, French in an Anglo fashion and chemistry with an amateur cook's precision. Even though Mr. Sammon had little training in French or chemistry, and still less predisposition toward them, he taught both subjects with passion and dedication.

Mr. Sammon arrived in Spanish aboard a 1929 Ford coupé, bearing a small battered suitcase. He took up residence in a small, frame three-room bungalow in the village, half a mile from the school.

Our teacher was a stocky man, almost but not quite barrel-chested, with a small nose whose pushed-in appearance was not an accident of birth but the result, we learned, of dozens of boxing matches as an amateur lightweight fighter. For this small feature Mr. Sammon earned the nickname "Nubug-johnsh," or "flat nose," which was altered to "Plug-johnsh" within months. Three years later the name was further modified to Bucky.

Right from the first we liked Mr. Sammon and respected him, not so much because of his reputation as a former boxer, but because he was a good teacher; moreover, he was also a decent and good-natured man. Within a week the boys had him pegged. When he descended from his tin flivver, entered the building with a light gait, doffed his ancient cap and tilted forward on the balls of his feet several times, Mr. Sammon was in a good mood; but if he neglected to remove his cap when he entered the classroom and snorted as some boxers snort, Mr. Sammon was slightly out of sorts, which did not occur very often. Knowing Mr. Sammon's moods from the style of his arrival enabled us to adjust our behaviour accordingly.

While Mr. Sammon usually tolerated the boys' gratuitous remarks and frequent misconduct in class, he did lose his temper on occasion. One of the more memorable occurrences was precipitated by our colleague, Stiff Bean (David Jocko), who dozed at his desk morning and afternoon, but more heavily in the afternoon. In his comatose state, which seemed not to bother the teachers at all, Stiff would lean and lean ever further to his right until, at the moment of imminent collapse, he would recover his balance with a start and pull himself erect. For the rest of us, these were moments of suspense and anticipation.

It did happen one day ... with help. Mr. Sammon was writing science notes on the blackboard with his back to the class. He was already out of sorts, having been driven there by Alvin's shout through the open window, "Why don't you bring the whole limb," to one of our colleagues who, sent to fetch a small branch, was enthusiastically lopping off a large specimen. Stiff was listing heavily to the right at a very acute angle. One more degree and he would flounder and pitch into the aisle beside his seat.

Behind me in the next row of desks, Adam Commanda whispered, quite loudly, "Watch this." Then he let fly a rubber eraser, which struck Stiff not quite full in the head but at an angle, so that the eraser ricocheted and bounced off Mr. Sammon's temple. Stiff pitched to the floor, but was instantly on his feet, fists clenched, demanding, "Who done that?" Up front Mr. Sammon whirled to assume a boxer's stance, snorting in defiance and ready to deliver a series of counterpunches. There was a series of coughs, sneezes and grunts as we tried to stifle our laughter in the crooks of our elbows. It was during this tense moment that Scumbag (Jim Norton) blurted out, "In this corner, the heavyweight champion of the North Shore, and ..." Scumbag did not finish his announcement, if indeed he had intended to say any more, for Mr. Sammon grabbed him by the armpits, lifted all sixty pounds of him and shook until Scumbag's eyes rolled and rattled in their sockets like dice. Dropping Scumbag, Mr. Sammon glared at the rest of us and issued a challenge: "Any more big fellas?" Then he moved in on Stiff — still transfixed in a boxer's stance and still demanding, "Who done dat?" — seized him by the collar and hauled him out.

Mr. Sammon re-entered the classroom a moment or so afterward, after having kicked Stiff in the rump. "Ah! Come on now, fellas ... settle down." It was a common request, which he delivered more in the tone of a petition than a command. But that was Mr. Sammon's manner and one that was entirely consistent with his nature.

Not even this incident served to stir Stiff from his chronic soporific state, however. He continued to catnap during the day. What we, that is Dominic, Alphonse and I, didn't know, but what everyone else including Father Oliver did know was that Stiff was a nocturnal person given to nighttime wanderings in the environs of Spanish; whether in quest of romance or other rendezvous, Stiff would never say.

Dominic, Alphonse and I discovered these nocturnal expeditions in the following manner.

Alphonse shook me awake well after midnight. It must have been 3:00 or 4:00 A.M., for it was still quite dark. "Hear that?" he said. From the tone of his whisper he was not just excited, but agitated, almost frightened. I immediately sat up and froze as I heard the fire-escape pole rattle. *Earthquake!* immediately came to mind, but nothing else was trembling or rattling.

"Hey, Dominic!"

"What?"

"Hear that?"

"Yeah."

"What is it?"

"I don't know."

"Earthquake."

"No! Don't think so."

"Wanna check?"

We crawled out onto the fire escape and lay on our stomachs, much as our ancestors used to do on top of buttes and escarpments when peering over a ledge to watch the movement of wagon trains.

Someone was shinnying up the pole inchmeal, and breathing heavily. Further down was someone else. Some boys were sneaking into the building. We continued to peer down.

"It's Stiff Bean," Dominic whispered. "Let's scare hell out of him when he gets up here."

We waited in ambush.

At last, Stiff's head made its appearance through the hatchway of the landing.

"Boo! Boo! Boo!" we burst out.

Stiff dropped from sight like a stone. From below we heard an "eeeeeyow," a scuttle of feet on the second landing, the rattle of the ground fire-escape pole, then nothing.

To our astonishment and disappointment there was no mention of the night's doings by Stiff, Alfie Cooper, Julius Niganigijig, Frank Commanda or any of their other confederates the next day, or in the days that followed. For our part we too kept strict silence in order to keep Stiff and his associates a little uneasy.

In December I wrote Grade 9 examinations that had been specially drafted by Father Oliver and his staff. Just before leaving for the Christmas vacation, Father Oliver notified me that I was now a fully accredited Grade 10 student, and that I would perform regular chores like everybody else — in the tailor shop — in the New Year.

On our return to school after the Christmas vacation, the hockey season began in earnest. It was earnestly observed and followed, and dominated all aspects of life. What I had heard about the hockey team, and in particular about Harold, Frank, Adam, Maxie, Rudy and Eugene, was true. As the hockey stars of the senior team, they had fulfilled dreams and ambitions nurtured since they had come to the school seven, eight and nine years before. Good as some of their predecessors had been, by virtue of better coaching this starting line-up was better and stronger than any before it and better than any starting line-up between Sudbury and Sault Ste. Marie, men's and boys' teams included.

Harold was the school team's goaltender. Like many goaltenders, Boozo had come by the position by default; he couldn't skate as well as everyone else and so he was consigned to the goal, where he could do the least damage — out of harm's way as it were.

But Boozo had other talents. Without the natural endowments of speed and agility, he studied the game and our opponents. Over the years Harold kept a mental file on all teams and opposing players, their habits and manners on the ice, the angles of the blades of sticks and where the various players were likely to shoot from. Goaltending was largely a matter of cutting the angles, it was as simple as that. Harold was meant to be a goaltender.

When an opposing player skated in for a shot, Harold smiled as he went into a slight crouch and slowly glided from his net. He smiled an "I-dare-you-to-score" smile as often as he smiled a "You're-not-going-to-figure-out-how-you-missed" smile. For low shots Harold kicked his goalie stick to deflect the puck to a teammate. A puck shot to his gloved side or in the vicinity of his ear he plucked from the air as calmly as if it were an apple. But what was most entertaining was Harold's habit of flicking out his stick, the timing and angle such that the pucks shot to his stick side, glanced off the flat of the shank, and soared over the snowbanks into the snow some distance from the rink. To retrieve the puck there was always a crowd of "little shots" assembled on top of the snowbanks ready to run and dig in the snow.

Frankie Commanda was the captain, general, strategist, tactician and head honcho of the hockey team. He was the centre on the first line and the spark of the entire team. "See this," he'd say, showing his fist. "This is what you're going to get if you don't play your guts out."

In transit from the school to Espanola or whatever town the team happened to be going to in Vic Solomon's panel truck, Frank would conduct a lesson and a strategy review.

"What wing you playing, Clem?"

"Right wing."

"Okay! . . . What's your assignment?"

"Checking."

"Okay! Who's your man tonight?"

"Sevicky."

"Okay! What's his number?"

"Nineteen."

"Okay! What you gonna do with him?"

"Not gonna let 'im score."

"Okay! That's right . . . an' he's *not* gonna score."

"Okay, guys, remember. First period, shoot high; no low shots. High, straight for the goalie's head; high an' hard. Gotta straighten 'im up first. Shoot from any place. Scare hell out of him first. Then in the second period, everybody shoot low, no high shots except to straighten 'im out, if he gets too good an' fancy. Gotta keep 'im upright, an' honest. Understand?"

"Yeah! Yeah! Yeah!"

Only once during the course of a game did Frankie give in to amusement.

We were playing the Massey men's team in their own arena. The ice surface was not of regulation size but only 65 feet wide and 165 feet long, and the rink, which was oriented north to south, was canted to the east so that a series of stout poles had been anchored into the ground and set against the side of the building like buttresses to shore up the arena and keep it from collapsing under the prevailing west winds.

It was always risky playing in the Massey arena, but it was the only other indoor rink besides Blind River's between Sudbury and Sault Ste. Marie. For starters, there were almost as many collisions with teammates as with the opposition in the rink's constricted area. But worse than the hazard of an accidental body check was the risk of being maimed by one particular Massey player whose shot splintered boards. To protect our goaltender it was team practice to shadow this man and keep him under constant check. If he did get set to unleash a bolt, it was our individual practice to dive for cover.

To give his team a chance to change lines and defence "on the fly," Eugene Fox lofted the puck toward the Massey goal. As the puck soared up over the lights and the rafters, all heads were tilted upward, all eyes were cast aloft to track the flight of the puck. But the puck didn't come down; it seemed to have stuck somewhere in the rafters.

Yet the red light behind the Massey goal was aglow, signalling a goal. The Massey players on the ice were now behind their net, pushing and shoving and shouting at the goal judge or at someone behind the goal.

"Frankie! Go see what's going on," the coach ordered our captain. Those of us scheduled for the next shift followed our leader.

The Massey players were shaking their fists and swearing and yelling at the goal judge. At first it was hard to make out what was upsetting the Massey team from the babel of shouts and curses.

"You G-d d----d blind idiot, you can't count that as a goal."

"Any man c-c-c-can d-d-do that desherves a goal . . . a-a-and it c-c-counts [hic]."

"But where's the puck? You have to have the puck in the net! What the hell is the matter with you anyway?"

"Ish right there. C-c-c-can't you see it [hic]? Ish right th-th-th-there [hic], plain ash day. What's that m-m-man's number? I'm gonna g-g-give him [hic] a goal."

"You're a damned cheat. That's what you are . . . and against your own town! You should be strung up."

"You know the rules? The puck has to go in the net to count. Can't even find the puck; it's lost."

"Ever sh-sh-sh-sheen anything [hic] like that? F-f-f-first time I [hic] ever seen a thing l-l-l-like that an' it [hic] desherves a goal. What's that m-m-man's [hic] number? I'm gonna g-g-g-give him a goal."

"Wait till we get hold of you, you son of a bitch." Then the Massey players turned to us. "Can you believe that? He says it's a goal. Look in the net, see if you can find a puck."

We looked. There was no puck.

Even the referee was arguing with the goal judge/score-keeper. Finally he yelled at all the other players to get back to their positions and asked for another puck. But the goal judge held firm. "It's gonna count. I'm the g-g-g-goal judge [hic] an' I shay it c-c-counts [hic]. N-n-n-never see that [hic] again. . . . C-c-can't you guys see that [hic] p-p-puck . . . It'sh right there."

It was Frankie who found the puck. When he took his gloves off to adjust his suspenders, he put the gloves on top of the net. There was the puck, plain as day, lodged on top of the goal, just as the goal judge had said.

The referee signalled "no goal," but that didn't appease the Massey players. They continued to shout and growl: "Get rid of that mustard! We're not playing another minute as long as he's goal judge. Get another goal judge; get another goal judge. Beat the dish out of that old buzzard." But the old inebriated goal judge was defiant; he kept flashing the red light and shouting "It desherves a goal! It desherves to be counted." He was still yelling, "Itsh a goal [hic], itsh a g-g-g-goal," as a group of honest Massey citizens seized him, bore him out of the building to some place unknown and there carried out the wishes of the Massey team; kill or emasculate him, or both.

On right wing was Adam, Frankie's cousin, as much a natural athlete as Frankie. When Adam got set to shoot, he leaned into the shaft of his hockey stick until it was bent like a bow. Then he released the shot. With the strength of his forearms and the whip of his stick, the puck shot like a rocket. Goaltenders always flinched when Adam got set to shoot.

Playing left wing with grace and style was Maxie Simon. His every motion fluid and effortless, Maxie appeared to float and glide on the ice, the basketball court and the baseball diamond. Exasperated coaches and captains sometimes thought he was giving less than his all. But Maxie was giving his all no less than Frankie. It was just that his grace masked his speed and strength.

During one game with the juvenile Greyhounds from the Sault,

Maxie was dipsy-doodling and stick handling near the blue line to give his team an opportunity to change lines. When he was ready to come off, Maxie let the puck go with just a flick of his wrists in the general direction of the Sault goal; no big wind-up or motion, just his wrists. The Sault goalie fell to the ice, clutching his head as if poleaxed. The little shots were moved to exclaim, "Did you see that?"

"No."

"What did he do?"

"I don't know really. He was just stick handling and the puck was gone . . . just like that . . . as if it took off by itself. Holy Smokes . . . he can shoot hard as Adam."

"Nah! Harder. Almost scare a beast wit' a shot like that."

It was hard not to agree with that opinion.

Max worried that he had crippled the Sault goalie and was visibly relieved when the goaltender was led off the ice, shaken and cut but still alive. But that was Max's nature; he didn't want to hurt anyone.

In the starting line-up were defencemen Eugene Fox and Rudy Rice, both superb skaters. Eugene was strong, Rudy nifty.

The second and third lines were made up of Alfred Cooper, Alphonse and Clement Trudeau, Eli Commanda, John "Bulleeblaw" Syrette, Adam Roy and Paddy Jocko, whose chief task while on ice was to harry, hound, harass, hector and check the likes of Sevicky, Vance, Pilon, the Reinhardt brothers and Bud MacIver to keep them from scoring. As diligent checkers, they scored a good share of goals.

All that winter we heard rumours that there were scouts at the games. Frankie played even harder and drove the rest to greater efforts to impress these unseen operatives. We watched for strangers who looked like our idea of scouts — men with slouch hats, slouch coats and slouch shoulders standing inconspicuously on snowbanks — but we failed to spot one. They must have been there, though, for we heard later in the spring that Frankie and Maxie and Harold were invited to training camp in the fall; Frankie and Maxie to Windsor to try out with the Spitfires, and Harold to Barrie, with the Flyers and on to Boston.

As we bade one another *adieu* on the last day of school at the end of June, Alvin Nashkewe, Chauncey Benedict and Adam Commanda pressed hands in handshake more firmly than is customary on such occasions. "Goodbye!" they said. "Six years is long enough. I'm not coming back in the fall. Maybe we'll meet again some day."

Football, Chemistry and Tired Chickens

When school reopened in the fall there were many new students enrolled in Grades 9 and 10, just as Father Oliver had expected there would be when he was contemplating a high-school program: Cecil and Donald King from Wikwemikong; Henry Pelletier, a guitarist, and his cousin, Herman, a pianist, who promptly earned the nickname of "Bone" for the lack of flesh around his cheeks, ribs, and hips; and Emil Hughes, a fiddler from the Pas, Manitoba, who, because he could pass for a Chicano, became "Senor." There were many others — Garnet Keeshig, John Nadjiwon, Charles and Ted Johnston, Terry, Bernie and Ron Jacobs; Oshkabooses and Whiteducks; Lavalleys and Chiblows; Morningstars and Meawassiges; Kinoshamegs and Sundays; McGregors and more McCombers; Shawanas and Ominikas.

Within a week the school was humming, as if there had been no interruption by summer or holidays; and the new boys settled into the routine as if they had been there for years and were as familiar as the old boys with all the operations and mechanisms of the institution.

For some, like Harold and Alfie, there were new jobs. It was said that they were banished from chicken coop duties for victimizing Brother Manseau and Henry Deere at cards.

Some years earlier Brother Manseau had developed an infatuation for bridge that he gratified every Sunday afternoon by receiving permission to play several rubbers at the Kellys' at the top of the hill. But playing only once a week merely stoked the brother's passion for bridge.

To satisfy his craving, Brother Manseau tutored his staff, Harold, Alfie and Henry, in the intricacies of the game.

After the staff had acquired a certain proficiency in contract bridge, the game became a regular function in the daily operation of the coop, as routine as feeding the Rhode Island Reds or cleaning the roosts or

197

gathering eggs. A table was set up in the back coop where a few hands were played every morning and afternoon after chores were hastily done. On Thursdays, most of the morning till noon was spent at bridge. With Brother Manseau supplying tobacco and allowing a ration of one or two boiled eggs, chicken herding was one of the better assignments in the school.

For some months Harold and Alf, as partners, against Beedj-mauss and Henry, played according to the system they were taught. But as time went by they both grew dissatisfied with the Goren or Culbertson system of bidding, or whatever system Brother Manseau had taught them, as too unreliable. They developed their system of bidding with eyes, hands and feet, a method almost infallible. With the new method, Harold and Alfie seldom lost, while Brother Manseau and his partner, still clinging to the old system, seldom won a rubber. By spring Brother Manseau had soured on his partner and then on the game altogether.

Hardly had we settled in for the new school year when Brother Manseau died on September 11. The very next day Brother Van der Moor was appointed to superintend the chickens and the boys.

Sports, intramural and extramural, were disrupted by the absence of Frankie and Maxie, who were in Detroit for their tryouts. Harold had also been invited to go to a tryout camp of the Boston Bruins, but something was bothering our friend.

His gusty and jolly "Haw! Haw! Haw!" no longer pealed across the yard or rang in the recreation hall. And he no longer trotted at the forefront of his team to lead them to the field. There was in his eyes a distant look not of sorrow or pain, but of distress and gloom. Not even "Come on, Harold" could rouse Boozo from his lassitude. He would sit on a bench, hunched forward, elbows on his knees with his chin resting on his hands, staring in the direction of the barn. When exhorted to "Come and play," or asked, "What's wrong?" Harold would respond, "I don't feel like it. I don't feel like anything. I'm tired."

No one knew what was wrong with Harold, not Brother Laflamme; not even Doctor Hamill in Blind River. Harold's blood samples were eventually sent to Sault Ste. Marie and Sudbury for analysis.

With our best players, Frankie and Maxie, gone and not likely to return, and with Harold sick, prospects for our hockey team did not look good. But undermanned or untalented teams never discouraged

Father Hannin. Fortunately for us, Frankie was returned to school for further seasoning with an invitation to report to the Detroit camp the next fall.

By the time we had returned to school, Father Hannin had completed plans for a school football team and had assisted in the formation of a league. From now on the boys would play real football — tackle football — just like the pros on the Argonauts and the Balmy Beaches teams.

But it wasn't until Sunday that we learned what had been planned for us. After dinner "Dan," as we referred to him in his absence, assembled the Grade 9 boys in the school yard, along with several athletes from Grades 10 and 11. With a football cradled in his arm, Father Hannin explained that we were going to play rugby-football against Espanola, Massey and Blind River high schools, against Grades 11, 12 and 13 boys our own age, or nearly so.

After explaining the game, the rules and the technical aspects of offence and defence, Father Hannin selected the team. As expected, Frankie was the quarterback. Eli Commanda, Julius, Joe Fox, and Clem were the ends and rovers and halfbacks. The rest of us, mule-footed, made up the line: Alfie, Dominic, Adam Roy, Alphonse, Cecil, Morris, Donald King.

As soon as the positions were settled Father Hannin had us line up in formation, heads down, rumps up. He explained that the function of linemen was not only to protect our backfield by running at and flattening the opposition but also to try to mug the opposition's quarterback and halfbacks. We were to crouch low like panthers, spring forward like panthers and bring up our forearms to biff the opposing linemen. We could hardly wait to take on bigger opponents. Under Father Hannin's directions we practised; crouch, one, two, three, spring forward. "Come on, Cecil, spring forward! Growl! Get mad!" Father Hannin then left us linemen to practise springing forward like panthers and growling like lions, so that he could work with the backfield.

For an hour we linemen moved back and forth across the yard performing these peculiar exercises under the bemused and bewildered stares of the little shots. Though we felt silly, we nevertheless persevered until the coach recalled us for further instructions. Cecil complained that he had already sprained his back.

During the next half hour we learned how to huddle, but not only that, we were allowed to listen to the conspiracies in the backfield: Statue of Liberty, quarterback sneak, reverse, end-run, pass, and the straight run directly through a hole in the line.

Play calling was primitive, certainly not as advanced or as sophisticated as that practised by the Toronto Argonauts or the Balmy Beaches, but we didn't know this. In the huddle, Frankie whispered in order to maintain the strategically necessary confidentiality. "Okay! Julius, you run like hell downfield, as far as you can go. Eli, you run about halfway and then come back. Joe, you run straight through between Dominic and Basil as if you got the ball. Clem, you run over to the sideline an' stay there, an' holler and wave your arms as if you're going to get the ball. Okay. You got that?"

"Yeah."

"Okay! Back to line . . . Set? . . . One, two, three, hike!"

Growl. Spring forward like panthers. Forearms up. Hard. Forward. Meanwhile, Julius was running downfield as fast as his heavy work boots would allow him. Eli ran twenty yards, stopped and the ball was there. That's all there was to the game: run like the wind, catch the ball and run like the wind, for those who were endowed with the speed of the wind.

Except for uniforms, we were ready. Uniforms, according to our coach, were expected to arrive shortly, courtesy of a generous donor who had been moved to compassion by Father Hannin's plea. Who the donor was we never did find out, whether it was the Argonauts or the Balmy Beaches or some other organization. In the meantime, we wore our hockey sweaters during practices.

A couple of days later the uniforms arrived: battered old helmets, assorted shoulder pads, but no pants. With the first game scheduled to take place in ten days, the situation looked bad, even desperate. It was in this critical circumstance that Father Hannin called me into his office. The discussion proceeded something like this.

"Basil. Think you can make football pants? . . . Like these?" the coach asked, showing me a picture of a football player in uniform.

"Yeah." I was persuaded by the apparent simplicity of the design in the picture. "But we don't have any eyelets for that kind of fly."

"Well! Make regular flies then, with buttons."

"Okay . . . but what kind of material are the pants made from?"

"We'll use denim. Would you check to see how much we have on hand and let me know?"

"Okay."

"One other thing. If there's enough material, how long would it take to make twelve to fourteen uniforms?"

"Not very long. We used to be able to make four or five in one morning. If we had the tailors and the machines we could make them in one morning and there's still some good tailors around . . . Belleau and Cooper and Stiff. But there's only two machines now, and that Theresa Gignac [the school's young seamstress, hired from the village] don't know how to make pants."

"Well, show her how . . . and go do what I told you to do."

"There's not enough denim, Father," I reported later to Father Hannin.

"Well then, cut up Brother Van der Moor's old coveralls and Brother Voisin's."

"Father! They'll stink."

"Wash them. And get started right away. You and that . . . Miss Gignac, make those pants. I don't want you doing anything else until all those pants are finished. Is that clear?"

"Yes, Father!"

That evening I summoned up my teammates to the tailor shop for custom measurements for football pants — waist, outseam, inseam and hips. During the measurements there were constant dubious mutterings: "Look like a bunch of farmers."

It took Theresa and me three days to make thirteen pairs of football pants from the new denim and the remnants of Brother Van der Moor's coveralls. Father Hannin was there to witness the fittings, looking very pleased as each football player tried on his uniform. But the squad was not as pleased as the coach. According to Julius, black sweaters with "Garnier" inscribed across the chest did not exactly combine well with blue denim and assorted sneakers, camp shoes or work boots. He observed that Chief Shaking Spear must have had gaggles like us in mind when he wrote "motley was the only wear."

The complaints must have persuaded our coach that there was something incongruous in the colour scheme of the team uniforms, for he assured the players that he would "think of something." While we practised in black and blue, wool and denim, our coach thought of something. After practice he conferred with Julius, the school painter.

Next morning the pants were draped over the barbed-wire fence for painting. Under Father Hannin's supervision, Julius and his crew, wielding paint brushes and drawing from two five-gallon pails of green priming paint, applied a liberal coat of dull green to one side of the pants. The pants, now the same shade as the newly painted pigpen, were left to dry in the sun and the wind for twenty-four hours, then turned over for painting on the other side. Beneath the pants the parched grass was stained green from the dripping paint.

Inspecting the green pants with Julius, Father Hannin decided that adding a strip of yellow paint on the outer parts of the pants as piping would give a touch of class to the uniforms.

On the day of the first game in Espanola we changed into our uniforms in the dormitories. Few pads, no jockstraps — just hockey sweaters and jungle-green denim pants with blotched yellow piping. We were more disenchanted with our pants after we put them on; they were stiff, as if they had been laundered in starch. We bent our knees, stretched this way and that, but it was useless. They scratched and grated, especially around the crotch.

Father Hannin came in, looking hugely pleased, to announce that Vic Solomon, our chauffeur, had arrived. Dominic complained at once, "Father! These pants are stiff as boards and scratchy as thistles."

"Once the game starts, you'll forget about it." But we weren't very reassured.

At the Espanola High School football field we filed out of Vic Solomon's van, self-conscious in our uniforms and nervous about playing bigger and older opponents. We huddled around Father Hannin.

"Okay, boys. Run out on the field; run through some formations. Look smart . . . win for Garnier!" And Father Hannin clapped Frankie and Eli on their shoulders.

We ran out to the middle of the field, neither looking smart nor feeling confident. The only one who seemed to have no doubts was Frankie. He barked, "Team huddle." We huddled. "All right, I want everybody to play his hardest . . . or else!" and Frankie showed his fist to everyone to remind us of his own determination and of what would happen to anyone who put forth less than his very best and his very all. With this kind of inspiration, we seldom lost any contest to any team. We nodded. "We'll show them how to play football." We nodded again.

Frankie moved us smartly through several passing and running patterns.

At the other end of the field cheers and handclapping erupted. "Yea, team, yea! Red and gold . . . Drink their blood . . . Yea! . . . Make 'em fold. Yea! Yea! We wanna touchdown; we wanna touch-down. E-S-P-A-N-O-L-A! Hip! Hip! Hooray!"

We looked at our opponents as they ran smartly onto the field. Not only did they outnumber us by two to one, but they were bigger than us across the shoulders and around the hips. Except for Cecil, Dominic and Julius, the rest of us were all under 140 pounds. Compared to ours, their uniforms were positively dazzling — freshly polished gold helmets, maroon sweaters and gold pants unpacked from boxes just moments before we started.

"Awright! Never min' them guys. We'll teach 'em how to play football. Keep your min' on the game!" Frankie snarled, bringing us back to reality.

The referee blew his whistle to summon both teams to mid-field, where all shook hands. "Where'd you guys get them outfits . . . tents . . . sails. . . . You guys look funny . . . har, har, har." We were seething.

Our captain, Frankie, won the coin toss; he elected to receive. As we lined up, Frankie told us that he was going to run the ball back, which he did, back to mid-field by squirming, wriggling and tacking.

In the huddle for the first play, Frankie whispered a sly play and traced a diagram on the grass: "Julius, you run straight downfield as fast as you can go, as far as you can go, no loafin' anywhere; Eli, you cut across from your position and run behind Julius. I'll pass it to one of you guys — an' don't you drop that ball if you know what's good for you. Clem, you run on the other side an' go down about halfway and wave your arms and holler as if you're gonna git the ball. Joe, you take a buck into the line and then come back and block. Now youse guys on the line, hold them, don't let 'em git through, if you know what's good for you!" We knew what was good for us. Cunning, just like Joe Krol, Annis Stukus, Royal Copeland and Billy Meyers of the Argonauts.

"One, two, three, hike!" On "three" we sprang forward like panthers, bringing up our forearms viciously as we had been trained to do; and we strained, pushed, shoved, rammed, butted, bunted and grunted without budging our opponents, who outweighed us by twenty or thirty pounds. At least they did not push us back. What was going on downfield or in the backfield we had no way of knowing. The whistle blew.

We had scored a touchdown. We ran forward to congratulate Julius, but our joy was short-circuited by an injury. "Somebody's hurt! Somebody's hurt! Dominic!" And we ran back to the line of scrimmage at mid-field to offer whatever aid and comfort we could provide to our teammate who was lying motionless in the fetal position. We huddled around Dominic.

"Hey! You okay? What happened? Bad?"

"My pants is torn!" he whispered, shame and indignation in his voice and in his eyes. "I can't play like this!" and he clutched the tattered ends more tightly to hide his legs. We saw that his football pants were rent from knee to knee precisely along the inseam. "How'm I gonna get off the field?" Dominic groaned. "Those damned tailors."

We formed a tight cordon around Dominic before assisting him to his feet. So shielded from any eyes that might leer at our teammate, we conducted him to the sidelines.

Father Hannin was solicitous. "What happened?"

"My pants is torn. I can't play like this."

"But Dominic! You gotta play! You're the only centre we've got. You're not hurt. Football players play no matter what," Father Hannin informed Dominic and the rest of us. He poked here and there in an equipment bag for a roll of black electrician's tape, which he then wound spiral fashion around each of Dominic's legs. "Okay, boys! Another touchdown."

Back to the field and the convert; then to mid-field for the kick-off. On the "whump" of the kick, we charged, catching the little halfback near the ten-yard line, where we spread-eagled him.

Although we flattened one of the enemy, one of our men was hammered into the ground: Adam Roy. He wasn't hurt, but his pants were severely injured, neatly split along the inseam from knee to knee. We shepherded him to the sidelines for repairs.

"Ain't gonna play no more," he declared.

"All right, Adam! Football players never quit. We need you — you're not a quitter." Father bandaged Adam's pants with several twists of black tape. "Okay, get back out there." He pushed Adam back to the field.

We listened to Jack Major, the 180-pound quarterback, counting, "One, two, three, hike"; behind us Frankie was shouting instructions: "End run! End run!" We flared to the left with purpose, intent on dismembering the ball carrier, who, sensing our warlike spirit and anxious to avoid assault and battery, lateraled the ball, really throwing it away. We pummelled him anyway. Frankie picked up the loose ball and ran it into the end zone for a touchdown.

While we were congratulating Frankie, I began feeling goose bumps in the area of the crotch, the kind produced by a chill draft. At the same time I was seized by a presentiment that I had become some kind of indecent spectacle. In this moment of foreboding Dominic tittered, "Cover up! Want everybody to see your butt? Serves you right. You made them." To my utter mortification my pants were ripped in the same manner as Dominic's; and I wasn't the only victim in this play. Joe's pants were gashed diagonally across the seat, and one loose end was flapping. Within the phalanx of our teammates, Joe and I went to the sidelines, clutching our tattered pants.

Father patched us up with black tape. Dominic needed and received more patchwork; I could tell that Father was getting worried, but not as worried as we were.

"You guys be careful . . . we're running out of tape. Can't waste any more." He bound Dominic's pants with surgical gauze. His last warning had a sobering effect on the linemen — Joe, Dominic, Alphonse, Cecil and the rest of us. In the huddle, Julius and Adam were chuckling aloud; Eli, Clem and Alfie were snickering. Frankie was the only one of the backfield who did not find the linemen's distress amusing. "Awright! Knock it off! We're here to win, not fool around . . . See this?" And he showed us our motivation.

And the first quarter wasn't even half played. Our chief preoccupation now became and remained for the rest of the game the preservation of our modesty rather than the demolition of the enemy or fear of Frankie's wrath or fists. No longer did we spring forward like panthers to sack the quarterback or to harry a ball carrier or to stem the rush. Our resolution to "cut them white boys an' teach 'em how to play football" diminished, and we executed our plays with the nimbleness of porcupines. While we did not exactly let the enemy through the line, fear of splitting our pants prevented us from bracing our legs apart as linemen are expected to do; instead we kept our legs primly together. Even so, despite our handicap and his size, we kept Jack Major under block and tackle; he didn't gain many first downs or many yards.

While we could relish our win over bigger and better-dressed opponents, we were not yet prepared to forget the mishaps to our uniforms; and while we could not openly say or suggest that the original idea of painting the football pants a pigpen green was harebrained, we could blame Julius for being short-sighted. In his defence Julius referred to the seams that gave way under stress, suggesting that the tailors were at fault.

As good-natured and light-hearted as the bantering may have been in the back of Vic Solomon's truck, there was real apprehension about how well the pants would hold up in the upcoming game with Massey. We had our pride and dignity to uphold. We looked silly enough wearing homemade pants that appeared to have been fashioned out of potato bags; indecent exposure would make us look even sillier.

If we were expected to risk cuts, gashes, lacerations, bruises, welts and maybe even broken bones while clinging to Jack Major or other oversized backs, we preferred to maintain some style and respectability while doing so.

"Hey, Father!" Dominic addressed the coach. "Jeez, I'm sore. I ache from head to foot and I got bruises all over. I don't think I'll recover in time for the next game."

"Heh, heh, heh!" Father chortled without sympathy. "Part of the game. Heh, heh, heh!"

Frank's mind was on the game just played as well as on the next game to be played. "Hey, guys! I figured out how to stop that Jack Major. Listen! Next time we play Espanola, I want four guys on him. Two guys tackle him low, one on each leg; and two other guys tackle him high, each guy grab an arm. I'll watch him from my position at the back and yell when he gets the ball and tell you which way he's goin'."

"Yeah, Frankie! Yeah!"

Before the next game the tardy — and antiquated — uniform pants arrived, enabling us to play the game and the rest of the season with some degree of recklessness. We dove at Major's ankles and knees and clung to them until he tripped. For our daring it took nearly a week to recover from the lumps, abrasions and bruises he inflicted.

It was particularly satisfactory to stay undefeated and win the championship given the size and weight of our opponents. What made the difference was in our overall physical strength, the play of Frankie and the backfield and the coaching of Father Hannin.

We had scarcely put away the football uniforms or recovered from our pains than we began the basketball season. But that was the system in Spanish, the Jesuit system, always playing, always occupied in something or other, seldom permitted to lounge or relax, even after meals. "Come on, boys! Outside! Hurry along!" or "Hurry and get your uniforms on and start the game."

When the school year began there were baseball and softball; after softball there was touch football; after touch football, boxing and basketball; after basketball, hockey and boxing; after hockey, more basketball and boxing. Finally baseball again. If there had been cricket and polo and lacrosse, we would have played those as well.

This year the basketball season was not quite the same without Brother Manseau, who had often volunteered to referee.

In the years past the boys had derived as much amusement from watching Brother Manseau referee the games as from watching their colleagues dodge the pillars that supported the ceiling of the recreation hall — or, on occasion, run into them. When Beedj-mauss was referee, he not only refereed, he coached as well. After blowing sharply on the whistle, he would reprimand a player: "You dang jackass, that's the double dribble . . . don't you know that? . . . Here! I shows you how!" Not only did he forget that he was a referee and not a coach during basketball games, in his intense concentration on the match and the rules, he also forgot about the pillars until he collided with one of them. The boys watched the game in anticipation of such an accident.

Within days of the opening of the basketball season, the boxing club, which had been inactive since March, was revived, and new recruits were invited to join. The main object of the training was to prepare the Garnier Boxing Club to settle the score with the Sault Ste. Marie Boxing Club after last year's losses. The best performance had been put on by Frank, who fought a boxer whose name was either Scarfoni or Sarlo. On the same card Adam Commanda had almost scored an upset. At the bell, Adam ran across the ring from his corner and delivered a haymaking left to the jaw of Nolan, who had leisurely turned around and was not expecting to be ambushed. The Garden River boxer's knees buckled and he sagged. Twice more Adam staggered Nolan with roundhouse lefts, but Nolan's experience enabled him to hang on until his head cleared. From that point until the end of the three-round match, Nolan cuffed Adam around the ring and gave him a boxing lesson. But this year's tournament with the Sault Ste. Marie Boxing Club was not scheduled to take place until March. Meanwhile, there was hockey to be played, not in the Northern Ontario Secondary School Association (NOSSA) but in the newly formed North Shore Hockey League, which was composed of teams from Espanola, Webwood, Massey, Blind River, Thessalon and Garnier. Since the boys had been granted the Southern Division championship of the NOSSA on the basis of a protest over the use of four ringers, or ineligible players, by the Blind River Team, Father Hannin's hunger for further victories and conquests had quickened. He would no longer settle for victories over high-school opponents in the district. Too easy. From now on he would only be satisfied with competition that represented a greater challenge for his team.

Without Maxie, Adam and Harold it was difficult to imagine the team being a match for any of the opponents. But this worried Father Hannin and Frankie not at all. To replace Max, Adam and Harold, Cowboy Jack (Dominic Contin), Joe "Goat" Martin and Joe Fox, all barely fourteen years of age and weighing no more than 120 pounds with their equipment on, were brought up from the intramural intermediate teams. Normally they would have been added to the team as extras — or spares, as they were sometimes called — to learn the game first by watching the team and listening to the coach's instructions and commentary during the game, then by playing a few shifts, until, toward the end of the season, they were playing more often. This was the practice the school had followed in all sports, bringing young players along slowly. Too quickly, and there would be accidents and, worse, lost games.

They all had to be brought along slowly, even Cowboy Jack with his enormous talent. Julius became the team's goaltender, while Joe Fox was the alternate. Harold, we learned, would not return this season, if ever. His illness was diagnosed as galloping consumption or tuberculosis of the glands, and Boozo was sent to the Hamilton San for treatment.

Under the coaching of Father Hannin and the guidance of the older boys, the transition for younger boys from rookie status to that of regular was usually gradual and without incident. There was one exception. Scumbag, who had shown considerable promise as a baseball player, was sent in to play centre field in the late innings of one game. The batter hit the very first pitch high in the air toward centre field. From Scumbag's motions with feet and hands it was obvious that he had lost the ball in the sun. He just stood there gaping skyward, arms outspread, as if he were transfixed by some dreadful sight in the heavens. While Scumbag was looking upward, the wayward ball came down squarely on his forehead and bounced high in the air toward Alf, who caught it for the out. With tremendous aplomb Scumbag doffed his hat and bowed gracefully to the cheering crowd.

If there were new games to be learned in the yard, there were also new subjects to be mastered in the classroom — trigonometry, ancient and medieval history, and chemistry; novel perhaps, but not as exciting or rewarding as football or basketball. From the very first day of the new school year, trigonometry was troublesome because, as Dominic observed, "it isn't logical." If someone wanted to know the height of a tree, the simple thing for him to do was to chop the tree down and then measure it instead of fiddling around measuring the shadow of the tree and figuring out the angles with some kind of instrument. Whenever we encountered collective difficulties with trig, Father Oliver summoned us into a classroom and there cloistered us until we had collectively solved the problem, usually under Alfie's direction.

We noticed that Mr. Sammon, our English, French and chemistry teacher, was more genial than ever. He had, after a whirlwind romance and courtship the previous year, got married to Florence. We, of course, kindled our teacher's bliss and geniality by inquiring about his wife every morning as he entered the classroom. Then Mr. Sammon's eyes would twinkle ecstatically, while he tilted forward and upward lightly on the balls of his feet. We soon learned the cause of our teacher's heightened rapture: he was going to be a father. After that we were even more solicitous. It is doubtful that there were students anywhere more considerate than we were of the well-being of our teacher.

For Mr. Sammon, teaching grammar and English literature was a breeze and a joy, whereas teaching chemistry — without a scientific disposition, a university credit or adequate apparatus — must have been an ordeal. Nevertheless, he persevered.

All Mr. Sammon possessed in the way of equipment were a small beaker, a test tube, and a retort stand; he carried these items about with him as if they were more precious than sacred vessels. I guess they were. The test tube was stowed in his breast pocket, the beaker in his right-hand coat pocket and the votive candle of his bunsen burner in his left coat pocket along with stubs of coloured chalk and stumps of pencils. In his hand he carried the retort stand and a paper bag containing various chemicals.

With so many limitations, Mr. Sammon had to be thorough. Every morning before teaching the chemistry lessons, Mr. Sammon would conduct pretrial experiments in the staff lavatory, which was located on the second-floor landing of the boys' stairway. We would often stop to listen to Mr. Sammon as he mixed chemicals until something exploded or hissed or produced a volume of smoke or generated a vile odour. Shortly thereafter he would emerge with the triumphant look of a scientist who has just made some startling discovery.

But whatever success our teacher may have achieved in the lavatory, for the simplest experiments, he could seldom duplicate his results in the classroom under our expectant observation. Invited by Mr. Sammon to "Come on up here and watch this," we would crowd around to witness the mixture of chemicals, compounds and other substances in proof of some scientific principle that had already been demonstrated thousands of times previously, the repetition of which we regarded as quite unnecessary. Alas! No matter how many ways Mr. Sammon attempted to produce a successful experiment in our presence by following the formula or altering the instructions, the experiment fell flat. In exasperation he could only say, "All right, fellas, that's not how it's supposed to work. Sit down and copy this." It was by copying notes that we got to learn chemistry.

While most of the experiments conducted in the classroom were aborted by something or other, there was one notable exception. After the usual, "All right, fellas, come up here" we left our seats to observe, with some doubts, the latest experiment — to show that hydrogen will not support or tolerate combustion . . . or something of the sort.

Julius, David, Ernie, Alphonse, Dominic, Frankie, Alfie and I surrounded Mr. Sammon.

"All right now, fellas! Certain elements are very combustible, such as oxygen. Others are not, such as hydrogen. And to prove this I'm going to put some crystals in the beaker and add a little H_2O. And I'll place this vessel over the flame of this candle . . . we'll pretend that it's a bunsen burner. After the hydrogen gas has displaced the oxygen in the container . . . there's displacement, too . . . we'll thrust in a flaming splint. . . . Here, Dave, hold this. . . . Julius, you hold the matches." (We all had to make some contribution to experiments by holding something.) "Frankie, you light the match after. And when we thrust the splint into the beaker, the flame will be immediately extinguished . . . and there may be a small bang. You don't have to be afraid."

"I'm not going to stan' near that thing, me! Never know what might happen." Dominic, who was holding a brown paper of white powder as his contribution to the experiment, grinned and moved backwards against the corner.

"Aw, come on, Dominic," Mr. Sammon pleaded, looking over his right shoulder at Dominic, an arm's length behind. Dominic was grinning, his granny glasses flashing. "Aw, come on now, there's no danger at all . . . just a small 'phutt,' and the flame will go out . . . just like that," and Mr. Sammon snapped his finger in demonstration of the magnitude of the burst . . . no more than a puff.

We watched the flame of the votive candle . . . the deposition of crystals in the beaker and the admixture of a small quantity of water . . . bubbles dancing. Fascinating!

"All right, Frankie, light the match. Alfie, take the splint. . . . Dave, the splint!" The splint bore a tiny flame. Mr. Sammon took the splint from Alfie. "All right, fellas, watch this! When I thrust the burning splint into the beaker, the flame will go out." We watched.

BOOM!

Amid flying glass, candle and papers, we dove for cover under the desks, sending chairs clattering to the floor. We stayed there wide-eyed, looking at one another.

"All right, fellas," Mr. Sammon's voice quavered.

We got to our feet.

Dominic was propped rigidly against the wall, his eyes closed. A streak of white powder etched from his forehead to his belt buckle; Mr. Sammon was behind the desk, leaning against the blackboard, ashen-faced and still holding the burning splint. The right side of his face was streaked with powder. He was blinking with surprise.

"Am I bleeding?" Dominic asked through compressed lips.

By now we had recovered our composure. Ernie, laughing, said "Yeah. White blood." Dominic's knees buckled and he sagged a little.

"All right, fellas! Cut out the nonsense. You're okay, Dominic. Let's get to work."

Mr. Sammon dusted himself off while we cleaned up the class-room, picking up fragments of beaker, test tube, votive candle and papers from the floor.

There were no more experiments after that for a while. Even when Mr. Sammon collected another beaker and test tube and pleaded with us to observe another experiment at close quarters, we refused to budge from our seats.

Just before the Christmas holidays, Father Hannin called me into his office.

"Basil, we're placing you in charge of the chicken coop until we get a replacement for Brother Manseau. You're the only one who knows the operations. Think you can do that?"

"Yes, Father!"

"You understand that you will be responsible for the chickens, as well as the six boys working there?"

"Yes, Father."

"I don't want any nonsense."

"None, Father."

"Dismissed."

I went out. No problem. Had I not had about two and a half years of experience superintending chickens during my first terms at the school? It was simple: gathering eggs twice a day, once in the morning and again in the afternoon; feeding the flock once in the morning and again in the afternoon; delivering eggs to the kitchen; packing eggs for shipment to St. Joseph's Hospital in Sault Ste. Marie and shipping a crate to the Hotel Dieu Hospital in Sudbury; keeping a daily, weekly and monthly graph of egg production; ordering feed, mash, corn and oyster shells; mixing the mash in the proper proportions; keeping the feeders full — molasses in troughs, water in fountains; keeping a supply of wood and the box stoves hot for the comfort of the chickens. Cleaning was equally simple. The roosts and roofing over the nests were to be cleaned daily; the straw in the coops was to be changed twice annually. Once a month there were chickens to be culled, slaughtered, and shipped off either to St. Joseph's in Sault Ste. Marie or to the Hotel Dieu in Sudbury.

The boys were another matter. I would have six to supervise. A good thing that they were all Grade 7 and 8 boys, smaller and younger than I was. I did not expect any problems, but if there was any insubordination, a "kick in the hass" would quickly restore order. Besides, the vice-principal's strap was the final resort. I was confident.

Nothing changed; nothing could distress or interrupt the unremitting labour of the chickens in the daily production of eggs. All we had to do was feed them and keep them warm and reasonably clean, and they did the rest; the 450 or so chickens maintained an average output of 350 eggs a day; about 100 chickens abstained in order to recharge their energies or gave in to sloth. There was nothing we could do to change this daily pattern or routine.

Only the annual moulting of the birds disrupted their output. I do not know the habits of other breeds, but the chickens at Spanish, without fail, moulted in the latter stages of winter, commencing around the middle of February and continuing on to about the middle of March. During this time egg production declined, the daily average holding steady near the 250 figure, and on good days, when the chickens excelled themselves, picking up to 285. Everyone just had to be patient during this annual recession.

But not even moulting chickens altered either the daily work or routine. All the chicken-keepers had to do was to gather the eggs, enter the number collected on a chart and deliver the eggs to the cook in the kitchen.

On schedule the chickens started to moult, one by one, two by two, until nearly half were moulting; the other half deferred their make-up restoration to a later date.

And as expected, egg production went down. Within a few days it had ebbed to the projected level of 250. Not to worry. That was the way with chickens. In a little while they would return to normal.

A few days later, my crew and I collected 225 eggs, an abnormally low figure even for moulting chickens; then 215; then 205. By now I was convinced that there was something drastically wrong. Whatever it was, it had to be rectified fast; otherwise I would not have fulfilled my trust as chicken manager.

I inspected the premises from end to end and from side to side: nests, roosts, straw, feeders, water supply. As far as I could see, there was nothing that could have alienated the brood to the point of mutiny. The bed of straw could stand a change; although it had been only three months since it was last changed, it was kind of smelly. Anyway, a change would not do any harm. I convened a staff meeting.

I told my men that the straw needed changing.

"Wha' for?" Iwewe wanted to know.

"That old straw is already packed and kinda matted and soggy in spots, and it smells. I think that maybe the chickens are layin' less because the straw is not so fresh," I explained.

"Jeez, we just changed that straw a coupla months ago," Iwewe protested, knowing how hard it was to throw out the old straw and transport it to the fields where the crew would have to spread it as fertilizer. That was hard work, especially in the middle of winter. Then a new batch of fresh straw would have to be hauled from the barn and spread in the six chicken coops. Cold, hard labour, that's what it was.

"Anyway, Beedj-mauss never done that. Twice a year's enough . . . an' he knew more about chickens than youse."

"Gotta be done, Iwewe. Those chickens should be layin' more than that. I'm the boss, anyway."

"Jeez, Baz! I don' think it's gonna work very good, if we have to use that little horse, Pitou. He don' like pullin' anything heavier than a coupla mailbags. Never know what he might do in the winter, especially pullin' a load o' straw . . . then, fifteen loads. He might die, ya know. He's pretty old. I wouldn' wanna get the blame for killin' him."

Iwewe was right about the balky, temperamental Pitou; but his disposition notwithstanding, Pitou would have to be conscripted.

It took four days of hard labour to trundle the old straw from the coops to the fields and to install a new carpeting of fresh straw. How good the interior smelled! How good and encouraging to see the chickens chest-deep in new fresh straw; better still after a few pails of corn has been broadcast into the fresh bed of straw. During the change of straw, egg production had hit its all-time low of 205.

"Now, Iwewe, egg production will get back to normal," I said as I watched the chickens, rumps in the air, toss up bits and lengths of straw and other debris behind them in their quest for concealed kernels of corn, and listened to their joyful clucks.

"Don' think so, me," Iwewe exclaimed morosely. "Maybe happy, them . . . but work too damn hard for two, three grains of corn. Get pretty tired, them. Maybe lay less eggs."

Over the next few days egg production went up to a respectable 240, and remained there.

"See! I told you," I remarked to Iwewe and the crew, who did not respond.

Inexplicably, the egg collector for that day, That's the Kind, gathered only 200. We counted the eggs five times over in the belief that That's the Kind had erred in his calculations. Unfortunately, That's the Kind was correct and vindicated. How could the evidence of a happy flock, to judge by the volume of their clucking and their boundless energy in scratching for corn, be reconciled with the decline in productivity? How were greater effort and production to be encouraged?

The countdown continued: 205, 195, 201. . . .

Something had to be done. I convened another staff meeting.

"Well, whaddya think, men? I'm getting kinda worried about those chickens. You know, getting only a coupla hundred eggs a day never happened before. There must be something wrong."

"Ya know, I really don' care," Iwewe said. "Be different if the boys was gettin' eggs for breakfas' every day. Instead it's only the priests an' nuns that gets the eggs. I couldn' care less."

"Come on now, Iwewe. That's not helping me. What do you think, Jim [That's the Kind]?"

"I dunno," he said, blowing a cloud of smoke at the butt of a cigarette.

"I'm tellin' you, Baz! Them chickens're tired," Iwewe explained.

"Nuts!"

"Okay, then! Maybe they is lousy. Never saw chickens scratch so much before. Gotta be lousy. Bugs."

I hadn't thought of that. "Okay! Tomorrow we clean the roosts real good."

At the end of the next day, the roosts were cleaned and scoured until the chickens reeked of nicotine sulphate; the coops reeked of nicotine sulphate; all of us reeked of nicotine sulphate and were sickened by the odour.

Although the chickens stopped scratching, egg production did not improve. It got worse: 195, 180, 215, 175.

Another staff meeting, without much discussion. My staff was unanimous in its agreement to increase the daily issue of mash to the chickens, to increase the amount of blackstrap to be poured on the mash, to increase the heat and to serve oyster shells more frequently.

"I'm tellin' you, Baz, the chickens is tired," Iwewe insisted.

"Well, how do we make the damned chickens rest?" I asked.

Iwewe thought. "If we put the lights out at seven instead of leaving them till nine . . . and if we adjust the automatic clock to ring at seven A.M. 'stead of five A.M., then the chickens would get a good res'."

"Okay, Iwewe. It's worth a try. Can't do any harm."

As we had agreed, more mash was apportioned, with a generous admixture of blackstrap molasses, a more liberal service of corn, a more frequent distribution of oyster shells. That's the Kind was kept busy chopping wood and stoking the fires for the greater comfort of the chickens, while the birds gorged themselves on mash, corn and oyster shells; they cackled in the heat. Whether or not they got more rest is a moot point, but they seemed to be the happiest flock of moulting chickens in the world.

Instead of responding to the increase in food, the chickens produced even less. Production declined dramatically: 195, 170, 160.

It was exasperating.

"Maybe they need a rooster!" Iwewe suggested.

I would have hit him in the beak, but it would have been cowardly considering he was five feet, no more, and weighed only eighty-five pounds.

One afternoon, That's the Kind and I lugged a crate of 145 to Brother Westaway in the kitchen. He looked at me. "It's a wonder you guys aren't fat considering all the eggs you eat, three to four dozen a day."

There was little I could say, for it was true that we consumed two eggs each daily, but the insinuation that we were eating three to four dozen hurt; and my inability to explain hurt even more.

The next afternoon when I happily reported 205 eggs, Brother Westaway told me with a smirk that the vice-principal wanted to see me right away.

I went up.

"Close the door."

The vice-principal stood up; he shook his head. "I can't understand it! . . . How six boys could eat twelve dozen eggs a day. . . ." (The number had mysteriously multiplied.) "I can't understand it! We trusted you; it's obvious we were mistaken. You can't handle responsibility. I've asked Brother Van der Moor to take charge of the chicken operations again. I guess the brothers will have to do all the work for you boys. And *you* . . . you're to work with the carpenters. Dismissed."

"But we didn't eat all those eggs, Father!"

"Dismissed."

I slunk out, crushed. It was bad enough to be judged incapable of discharging responsibility; what was worse was having to work with the carpenters out in the cold, repairing the barn.

A week or so later, one of the good people of Spanish was caught stealing eggs. He confessed that he had been helping himself to the eggs during the past few weeks in order to feed his family. The Jesuits did not press charges.

I was not restored to the management of the chickens again.

In the spring the chicken coop was dismantled.

The Bean Rebellion and
Graduation

In the first week of September, we returned to Spanish from our summer jobs for our final year of school. Just ten more months of privation and deprivation, and then the residential-school experience would be a thing of the past. It was hard to wait. But even at this late date in our lives some of us still had no clear idea what career we would take up after graduation. Should we enter the civil service in the Department of Indian Affairs, as was sometimes suggested? Join the Canadian Pacific Railway or the Canadian National Railway? Apply for the Postmastership of Manitowaning or Caughnawaga? Go to normal school in order to become teachers? Or take over a village store and become merchants? Our knowledge about the world beyond our reserve communities or beyond the confines of Garnier Residential School was equally scanty; we didn't know what to expect of that world or what it expected of us. Some of what little we knew of the outside world came from hockey trips made to towns along Highway 17 between Sudbury and Sault Ste. Marie, where, after hockey games, we would be served a luncheon consisting of sandwiches and hot chocolate or hot dogs and hot chocolate; and we would listen to the conversation of our hosts and answer their questions in our most refined style.

Among those who returned to Garnier for Grade 12 was Ernest Nadjiwon, friend, partner and sometime accessory in several ventures that he and I had undertaken in our younger days. He was Robin in our imitation of Batman and Robin, a youthful undersized Robin attired in a homemade costume who needed to be pushed from the haymow of his father's barn because he did not leap into space as readily as his idol. He it was who perched near the top of a poplar, hardly more than a sapling, rocking the tree back and forth, instructing me to put the axe to the trunk each time the poplar leaned landward away from the pond waters. As instructed, I put the axe to the trunk, sinking the blade deep into the tree, which was to become a jumping pole. But the timing of my strokes was not synchronous with the motion of the tree, which I struck at the wrong time. My aspiring pole-vaulting friend clung to his perch like a porcupine as the tree arched and pitched him with gathering speed into the icy waters of the pond. He it was who, as I was passing water behind the community hall one cold and dark November night, rushed up and stood directly in front of my operation and demanded "Where's the moonshine? Where's the moonshine?" and then leaped back in shock, declaring, "You p--d on me; you p--d on me." It was good to share an education with Ernie.

Besides an education, what Ernie was in quest of was romance, or so I gathered. Almost the first information my friend asked for was on the relative merits of northern women compared to southern belles. I couldn't enlighten him, but by Christmas my friend, unaided, had discovered his sleeping beauty. Or perhaps it was Lillian who found in this young man from southern Ontario the prince of her dreams. Within two years they got married.

If Ernie sought my guidance in romance, I had need of his advice in matters relating to sports. Father J. Johnson had appointed me captain of the Canadiens, to which team he had assigned a certain Verlin Akiwenzie as a means of keeping the Cape Croker natives as closely associated as possible and to reduce Verlin's sense of alienation. It would be comforting for Verlin to be among friends in those first days of being away from family and home. "Know this Verlin I've assigned to your team?" Father Johnson asked.

"Can't say that I do," I answered, sifting my memory of the boys I knew at Cape Croker of my own age and younger. But it had been three years since I had been home. During that time any of the little guys could have changed out of all recognition in both size and facial features. Or perhaps Verlin was a son of a long-absent family whom I had never heard of or set eyes on. I had but one preference in any new boy assigned to my team: that he be big and fast and athletic to make my team competitive. "I'll ask Ernest Nadjiwon; he should know."

"Ernie! Who's Verlin?" I asked my friend.

He at once broke into a grin and regarded me with a roguish look for some moments.

"Youuuuu dirty bugger," he declared. "What you want to know about her for?" He laughed meaningfully.

"A *her!! Verlin is a girl!?* . . . Come on now, Ernie! Cut the fooling. This is serious." But my vision of a six-foot, 180-pound, mean athlete was fading.

"Yeah! Verlin's a girl. Didn't you know? Bun and Isabel's daughter. What you want to know about her for? Getting ideas?" Ernie asked, still grinning rakishly.

"Listen, Ernie. They got Verlin registered here, in this school. They put her on my team, and they even gave her the bed beside mine. . . . Holy Smokes! I better tell Father Johnson . . . and get me another player for my team."

"Hey! Hey! Hey! Wait!" Ernie broke in, grabbing my arm. "Don't . . . don't tell them. Let 'em find out for themselves that Verlin's a girl. Should be fun. Come on! Don't say anything!"

But I was too concerned about my team and the loss of a player owing to a mix-up to pay attention to Ernie's idea or to savour in imagination what might have resulted if Verlin arrived late at night and pounded on the front door of Garnier for admission. It would have set off one glorious brouhaha throughout the length and breadth of the Department of Indian Affairs.

In those first days of the new school year Ernie was one of many boys who, accustomed to better circumstances, found the custom of eating not sandwiches but raw carrots, cabbages and turnips unusual. As best we could we consoled our new colleagues with descriptions of nourishment in the old days and cheered them with reminders of the brevity of their term of detention — ten months only.

Just when our new colleagues had resigned themselves to the consumption of raw vegetables till the next summer, the school received a shipment of hardtack biscuits from the Canadian government. Four freight cars in all, sitting on a siding up in the village.

During the next few days the teamsters were busy transporting crates of unwanted war-surplus hardtack from the siding at the railway station down to the mill, where it was to be kept in storage; back and forth, from morning until late evening. It was calculated that on the basis of one biscuit per boy per day, there was a sixteen-year supply of hardtack.

All the boys eagerly awaited the issue of the biscuits. No more raw cabbage, raw carrots or raw turnips; real biscuits. We could hardly contain our hunger as each one of us received a biscuit the size of a large saucer and thick as a hand — more than enough to satisfy our perpetual and prodigious appetites.

Boys, big and small, bit eagerly into the cakes. Then they gnawed at them, nibbled along the edges; they couldn't make a dent in them. Then they tried cracking them against the sharp edges of benches in an attempt to split them, and carpenters bashed them with hammers; but the biscuits were solid and unbreakable.

In disgust some of the boys took their hardtack outside and flung it away. The cakes sailed gracefully some distance before angling on their sides and then falling to the ground. A few bounced and rolled till they lost their momentum and keeled over like thrown discuses. Before long the front yard was astir with flying and spinning objects as the boys took out their disappointment on the hardtack. The prefect was scandalized by the waste but said nothing; he was no more able than the boys to bite into his biscuit.

Even the swine to whom the hardtack was eventually distributed had trouble with it, until the brother in charge, in a moment of inspiration, marinated the biscuits in the pigs' swill.

How long was it? A week, two weeks, three? It seemed hardly a day or two after the four freight cars of hardtack were unloaded, and then removed, before four freight cars of war-surplus applesauce were left at the siding. Back to work went the teamsters, transporting cases of applesauce from the siding to the school mill, horses clopping through the village, pulverizing the road gravel to a fine powder which rose like mist behind the wagons, drifted off in the breeze and settled on the houses beside the road. People came out to watch the caravan. The entire school body was cheered by this gift; we heard that there was enough applesauce to serve every boy every day for the next sixteen years. Dessert at last with meals, just like the outside world.

Emmet McCart, an English teacher, found the hardtack affair amusing.

"Don't feel too bad. Raw carrots, cabbages and turnips are better for you anyway. I wouldn't eat those damned things either," he declared. "I thought that they'd bury that garbage someplace where humans can't get at it . . . that's what they should do with it."

"Mr. McCart! What would you know about hardtack? You have cookies and cake for your lunch. Ever try it?" Dominic asked.

"Yeah! I know more about hardtack than I can ever forget. So I know how you feel. That's all we had to eat at the front, overseas, during the war. That hardtack's got to be soaked before eating. Pig feed; that's all it's good for. We had to resort to all kinds of skulduggery to get a decent meal."

"Mr. McCart! You were in the war?"

"Yes."

"Where?"

"In Italy."

"Shoot any Germans? Any Italians? Ever see anybody get killed? Wounded? Did you get a medal?"

But McCart wouldn't satisfy our newfound interest in him. "Let's get back to English."

Dominic persisted. "Okay, Mr. McCart. If you're not going to talk about the war, then can you tell us what you did to get a decent meal?"

"Well, one of our favourite stunts was to steal wine from a padre to get hammered before going to the front. You guys don't know it, but it's frightening, terrifying to go to the front to get shot at, to be shelled, to be bombed, and . . . not knowing . . . knowing that maybe you'll never come back. Or maybe you've just come back from the front and you want to calm your nerves.

"Anyway, we'd go in search of a church, a bunch of us, and find a priest, and try to get him to understand that we were scared and wanted to go to confession. We'd kneel down, clasp our hands together, point at him and cup our ears and do all kinds of of crazy things until he understood what we wanted and went into the confessional.

"Then while the priest was hearing confessions some of our guys would ransack the cellar for wine. When they found the wine they'd come into the church to fetch us with one guy keeping watch over the wine.

"When we were done and ready to leave — and to square things with the priest — we'd stay in the church for a few minutes, buy some candles, light some, and make a donation to the church, depending on how much wine there was.

"And we'd trade out hardtack for a chicken or cheese. It was easy to do that because the paisanos were so poor, they'd trade anything. They were poor, starving most of them, because the Germans had taken everything. And they'd trade wine and cheese, a chicken even, for that damned hardtack, thinking it was a good bargain. Haw! Haw! Haw!"

We liked McCart, for we saw in him a kindred spirit. He was someone we could talk to, someone who might understand human problems.

It wasn't long into the fall before we unfolded to him a grievance arising out of our daily and weekly fare. The immediate cause of our discontent was Boston baked beans. At first we believed that the disappearance of Boston baked beans from the menu on Tuesdays was an oversight of the cook's.

To remind Brother Westaway of his forgetfulness, we cast broad hints: "Forget the beans, Brother? . . . Forget the day again, Brother? . . . We missed our beans this morning, Brother."

And on Monday evenings we prompted the kitchen workers to remind Brother Westaway to soak the beans.

Brother Westaway was surly. If he didn't snap "Mind your own business" or "Who do you think you boys are anyway?" or "Who's running this school anyway?" he would glare imperiously without reply as if the boys were beneath his rank and dignity.

McCart snorted when we lodged our grievance with him. "Beans! Beans! Can't you guys find some other issue to raise? Boston baked beans stir up boys. . . . Just think of it. Just consider how silly it sounds. Didn't get their Boston baked beans; boys in a snit. Come on now, guys, just think of it. Makes you look like a bunch of little kids whining after your candy's been taken. You got more sense than that."

McCart annoyed us, not because he was right, but because he had ridiculed our grievance.

"You know what's wrong with you guys? Too naive! You're just too damned naive for your own good. You act as if the priests can do no wrong; you act as if they are always right. You look on them as if they were tin gods. Come on guys, wake up. They deserve respect but not veneration. They are men just like the rest of us, with their share of laziness, envy and pride. They get angry like anybody else. Some of them are selfish, more selfish than ordinary laymen . . . and maybe they have a harder struggle by virtue of their vocations and vows than we have. Come on, guys, you're men just like them. Why don't you talk to them and look them in the eye while you're talking?"

Mr. McCart's little speech was one of the first of many counselling sessions that we received in preparation for our struggles in the outside world.

In one session conducted in the small chapel, Father H. Barry delivered an hour-long discourse on concupiscence. Throughout the talk Father Barry wore a vague melancholy look and delivered his remarks in a vague melancholy tone. After Father Barry's explanations we were not quite certain whether concupiscence was some loathsome social disease or an aboriginal human condition akin to original sin. Directly afterwards some of us followed Brother O'Keeffe's advice, "Whenever you are in doubt of the meaning of a word, look it up in the dictionary," and took up our dictionaries to establish the meaning of concupiscence.

"Ernie! Listen to this. Concupiscence . . . strong or abnormal desire, especially sexual desire; lust."

"Oh! So that's what was bugging Father Barry. Not a thing wrong with concupiscence. I'm all for it. But why didn't he say so instead of beating around the bush? He coulda said hot, horny, dirty, passionate. When a cow wants a bull, we say the cow's in heat. Never heard anyone say a cow's concupiscent."

We had a great philosophical discussion next day at breakfast concerning concupiscence in animals. Julius asserted that cows in heat could be regarded as concupiscent, while Ernie stoutly denied that cows or beasts could lust. We were having a great time with the subject.

"What was Father Barry trying to tell us, anyway?" David wanted to know.

"That you have an abnormal desire for sex, Dave, and that women will have to watch themselves when you get out of here." Dave blushed and joined us in laughter. "That why you sneak out at nights, Stiff?" Ernie asked.

Stiff couldn't answer while trying to stifle laughter with mush in his mouth.

"I don't think so," Alfie added with some deliberation. "I think that Father Barry was trying to tell us that it's us; we're the ones who have to beware; we got to watch women."

"Aw, come on now, Alf! You got to be kidding. You mean we gotta watch out for them old hens across the road?" There was more laughter.

"What does Father Barry know about it anyway?" Ernie asked, kindling more laughter.

"What do you boys find so amusing at this time of the morning?" the prefect asked.

"Concupiscence, Father."

"Well, leave Father Barry out of it."

"But Father, he was the one who told us about it."

"Leave him out of it."

After the prefect moved off, Ernie asked, "What's eating him?"

"Ah, he's just jealous that we're having a good laugh," Dominic explained. Then he grumbled, "Treats us as if we were a bunch of kids."

Dominic resumed his complaints at supper; he was still burning over the manner of his banishment from the recreation hall at noon. He had been sitting quietly in a corner studying French.

"Come on, boys! Outside! Outside!" the prefect commanded as he herded us outside for fresh air. Dominic continued to sit as if he hadn't heard.

The prefect strode to the corner and stood directly in front of Dominic.

"Come on! *Move! Out!* Who do you think you are? *Out* means you too, you big lug!"

Dominic jumped up. "You don't have to come and attack me so suddenly like that. I'm not a dog to be thrown outside. Why don't you ask, once in a while, instead of always ordering, shouting. Orders! Orders! Orders!"

The prefect was momentarily taken aback by McComber's defiant tone and attitude and maybe even frightened by Dominic's size, but he recovered his composure quickly enough. He was even more biting. "*Out* like the rest."

"And McCart thinks that we can talk to these priests," McComber muttered during supper. "It makes me mad. I know it's only a little thing, but they can withhold the only decent food we get all week. They can forget; they can do anything, you know, and they don't have to explain, they don't have to tell us anything. Treat us like . . . as if we were a bunch of little kids. Who can you talk to? Westaway? Not him. You can't talk to him. He acts as if he's doing you a big favour if he says a few words to you. Dan [Father Hannin]? You couldn't talk to him either. If one of us said anything about the school, about anything, he'd take it as a personal thing and get mad. He can never be wrong. If he were to listen to us, to our problem, it would be like admitting that maybe we had a point, that maybe we were part right. And if he did that, it would be almost like saying that he was a little bit wrong. He can't do that. Or else he'd say, 'Make a sacrifice! Offer it up!'"

A voice of reason advised Dominic, "Come on, Dominic. Just eight more months. Offer it up." Even McComber had to laugh.

One Saturday evening, just as the study hour was drawing to a close, Father Oliver came in and whispered something to the study supervisor, who then announced: "Father Oliver would like to see the senior boys in the recreation hall." We filed down.

Father Oliver met us at the foot of the stairs. "Come with me." We followed him into the refectory. "Sit down, boys." Our eyes opened wide in anticipation and suspicion.

Two tables covered by white tablecloths were gloriously and splendidly set with china — bowls on dishes, cups on saucers, side dishes, empty platters and bowls, napkins. An array of cutlery surrounded the dishes.

We looked at one another as we sat down. For my part, I immediately got hungry and wondered what the occasion might be.

"Boys," Father Oliver began, "in another seven months you will be leaving school. There are a few things that you need to know in order for you to get along — practical things that you have not had occasion to learn here. We want people to say of you that you are gentlemen, and that you trained at Spanish. So we are going to teach you a few 'social graces' — manners — before you leave. Tonight I will teach you table manners." We giggled.

"First, the names of the utensils, the purpose and the order of use," and he named them all.

"Now, then. When you go to table, take the chair by the back, move it away from the table gently; get in front of it slowly, sit down slowly and pull it forward gently, like this," and he demonstrated.

"Sit up straight, don't bend over or slouch, like this. Take, *don't grab*, the table napkin and place it on your lap." We did as he demonstrated.

"And you'll just have to stop this habit of the biggest and strongest boy at each table serving himself first. It isn't polite; it isn't considerate, and it isn't done in polite society. The first person to take the tureen passes it to the person to his left, and so on; each one takes a portion that is no more, no less than his neighbour's so that there is something left for the last person." Father Oliver showed us the proper manner of taking soup; after that, the proper use of each of the utensils, and their order of use, and the manner of cutting slices of bread in half and buttering them. He also cautioned us not to lick the knife blades or wipe them with our sleeves or on the seat of our trousers.

We practised with whatever grace we could on empty plates and empty stomachs.

"There is one other thing you should remember and practise, not only in dining but in other matters. Just as you must cut out tearing your bread in chunks, dunking your bread in stew, hiding lard or butter under the table, sticking a bone in your pockets, punching each other at table or throwing bread across the table, you also have to cut out saying things like: 'Gimme the bread'; 'Hurry up with that jug'; 'Me first!'; 'Don't take too much!' It isn't polite and it isn't done in society. The proper manner of cultivated people is to address one another with courtesy at all times, under all circumstances. A man is 'Sir'; a woman 'madam' or 'mademoiselle' or 'miss.' At table you say, 'May I have the bread, sir,' — or madam, as the case may be. 'Would you pass the sugar, sir, please? Thank you, sir! Thank you, madam! I'm much obliged to you, sir! Forgive me, madam! Allow me! Pardon me, sir!' I want you to practise your manners with each other. And I'll try to get you some forks and knives to practise with. Good night, boys." Dismissed, we went back upstairs.

We tried manners and good breeding. "Pass the mush, sir!" "Much obliged, sir!" "Pass the lard, madam," but one of our companions objected to being addressed as "madam" to a roar of laughter; and anyway, there was no more lard to be passed. Someone lifted his fork, looked wistfully at the liquid porridge, and asked, "What do we do with this?"

The experiment petered out inside a week; scorned out of existence by Grade 5s who sniggered, "Youse guys talk funny," "What's the matter with youse guys, anyways?," "Think you're pretty good, eh?," and by the disappearance of our knives and forks. I guess we sounded and appeared absurd.

On the Saturday following we were once again summoned to the recreation hall. Father Oliver was standing there with his soutane tucked under his cincture. He looked odd. To one side was a small table — actually a washstand — bearing a gramophone.

"You're going to learn how to dance. Properly! The way they dance in cities. You're not going to be square dancing much any more."

"Where's the girls?" Julius inquired.

"No girls."

"Line up, side by side." We lined up, close together.

"Not that way; you're too close; spread out." We spread out as instructed.

"Now then. You're going to learn to waltz. You must listen to the music." Father Oliver cranked up the gramophone and told us we would be hearing the "Blue Danube Waltz." The record squeaked and scratched and whined.

"Okay, count, one, two, three; one, two, three; one, two, three." We stood there counting and wondering why we had to repeat "One, two three; one, two, three."

"Very good." He enlightened us immediately. "You have to count to the beat of the music in order to coordinate your movements and your feet." He lifted the arm of the gramophone.

"Now then. These are the waltz steps; watch me, and count. One, two, three; one, two, three; one, two, three." We watched his feet.

"Your turn; one, two, three; one, two, three; one, two, three." We shuffled, we scuffled, we plodded, we waddled.

"Aw, come on, Julius! You're not in the barn now. Come on, Dominic, on the balls of your feet; this isn't snowshoeing," Father Oliver said in high good humour. "Now, backwards; one, two, three; one, two, three; one, two, three."

Before an hour had elapsed we were gliding and swaying forward and backward to the "Blue Danube Waltz" with as much grace as our rubber boots, running shoes and other assorted footwear permitted on a tar floor.

"Choose a partner!" Father commanded. When no one moved, Father paired us. "Dominic and Alf; Cecil and Basil; Julius and David. . . . To start with, the tall boys will be the men; and remember, the men always lead."

Cecil, at six foot three, came over wearing a sly grin. Because I was five foot eight, I had to be a girl.

"Mademoiselle."

I could have kicked him.

Just before we started waltzing with one another Father Oliver enlightened us as to the proper manner of soliciting a dance. He suggested: "Mademoiselle, may I have this dance? May I have the pleasure of dancing with you, mademoiselle?" Less courtly were: "Would you like to dance?" or "Would you care to dance?" To say "Come on" or "Let's dance!" or to seize or grab a partner as was done at square dances was boorish and demonstrated lack of class or breeding, or both.

For the next four Saturdays we learned and practised foxtrots, quadrilles, tangos, two-steps, polkas and flings.

On the fifth Saturday we were summoned by Father Oliver, who met us at the study-hall doorway. He whispered, "Get washed and put on your finest. When you're ready, come down to the recreation hall. I want you to come down all together." He went out.

During our preparations, we tried to guess what the occasion might be but couldn't imagine what Father Oliver was up to now. Dressed in our finest, we went downstairs.

"Girls!" We were dumbfounded yet excited. "Girls from St. Joseph's across the road!" Among them were my sister Gladys (who eventually came to Spanish of her own volition to get a high-school education), Angeline Copegog, Rosemary Wakegijig, Lucy Nashkewe, Lillian Pelletier, Lillian Kitchigeg, Tillie Wemigwans, Violet Shawanda, Honorine Trudeau, Rita Belleau, Minnie Smith, Josephine Webkamigad. We cast uncertain, tentative glances at them, and the girls uncertainly and tentatively glanced back from a corner of the recreation hall where they were huddled like chickens under the heavy guard of their two chaperones. We retreated to the opposite corner and regarded the girls suspiciously.

Father Oliver looked amused. "From now on we're going to have a dance every Saturday night . . . provided that you dance." He cranked the gramophone and a high-pitched Virginia reel squeaked and squalled.

"All right, boys! Come on! Ask the girls to dance!" I pushed Cecil; Cecil pushed Ernie; Alfie pushed David. No one wanted to be first. Father herded us gently across the hall, reminding us to ask the girls politely for a dance as we had been tutored.

We all made for our sisters.

"Mademoiselle, may I have this dance?" I asked, feeling silly and flushing.

"What's the matter with you?" Sis muttered. "Why don't you ask me right? Where'd you get this 'May I have this dance?' Never heard of anything so silly and stupid."

We danced the "Grand Change," eventually with partners other than our own sisters. At the end of winter we would be quite accomplished in the art of dancing and poised in the presence of girls — Indian girls.

Events were moving fast. Even before our dancing tutorials were completed, Father Oliver, who seemed to think of everything, confided that a special retreat was arranged for us. We groaned.

Friday morning at 9:00 we were ushered into church, which was already occupied by the senior girls from St. Joseph's. We took our places in the pews across the aisle from the girls. Feeling thoroughly disgruntled, Dominic, Julius, Alfie, Ernie and I sat in the last row.

Father McDonough, sixty or sixty-five, balding and tall, came out looking very nervous. We all knelt down to pray with him as he beseeched heaven for guidance — and maybe for inspiration.

Very slowly and deliberately he genuflected as if all the sins of the world were bearing down on him. He moved toward the railing painfully. First, he looked at the girls and then at us, as if in sorrow and great pity, before fishing a piece of string from his pocket. We craned our necks to watch, ears and every pore open in anticipation.

"Today . . . ahem . . . this morning . . . ahem," and, preoccupied with the string which he pulled and stretched, caressed and stroked, twisted and curled in hundreds of forms and loops as if he were going to warp and squeeze revelation from its fibres, Father McDonough held us coiled in mental knots.

"Ahem . . . I have a very difficult subject ahem . . . to discuss . . . ahem . . . with you . . . today . . . ahem . . ." More stretching and spiralling of string. And we were squirming and fidgeting in rhythm.

"I want to talk to you . . . ahem . . ." and he pulled the string in his hand so violently that it flew from his grasp and floated to the floor. He paused to pick it up, looking at it as if to see if it were injured. "I . . . ahem . . ." addressing the string, "I want to talk to you . . . ahem . . . about . . . sex . . . ahem, ahem."

"Hell!" Ernie said smugly, poking me in the ribs with his elbow, "I know all about that already. My brother told me."

"Shut up," I wheezed in anticipation of enlightenment. Julius,

Alfie and Dominic were shaking with laughter. Ernie sat back, his arms folded, a knowing grin lighting his face.

"My dear young women . . . ahem. . . . My dear future brides and helpmates . . . ahem. . . . My dear symbols of virtue. . . ." The girls sat up, and Father McDonough twisted the string in his fingers violently. "My dear vessels of virginity . . . ahem. . . ." That damned Ernie was hunched over in convulsions. Father McDonough, intent on his string, did not look up. "You . . . must help . . . boys . . . ahem. . . . Boys are . . . more . . . ahem . . . passionate than . . . ahem . . . girls . . . ahem."

"He means you, you dirty bugger," Ernie piped out, not out loud mind you, but loudly enough for those in the back to hear, poking me in the ribs with his elbow. The suddenness and forcefulness of the movement knocked me out of my trance of attentiveness and almost out of the pew. All the girls and boys in the rear pews turned around to catch a glimpse of the "dirty. . . ." Julius, Dominic and Alfie were hunched over, shaking, hardly able to stifle their mirth. I hunched over too, but not in mirth.

"All right! Knock it off back there. This is a church and this is a serious homily," our prefect reminded us from the front pew. "Turn around."

When everyone was turned around, I stomped out of church in humiliation and rage. On the way up to the classroom I decided that I would beat the crap out of Ernie. I waited in the classroom.

An hour later I heard laughter, chuckles, giggles and the clomp of army-style boots as my companions returned from chapel. "Yeah, that sermon was for him," someone said to a roar of laughter. "Would'a learned somethin', him." More laughter.

As soon as my classmates filed into the classroom and Ernie entered, I leaped and charged like a panther, delivering a haymaking roundhouse in the direction of Ernie's nose. Down he went, covering up immediately. I jumped on top of him in blind rage, flailing at his head and neck and back. But he did not fight back. He just lay there covering up as best he could, rolling about with laughter.

In rage I stood up trembling. "Come on, get up, you coward." The other boys just stood around roaring.

A blow to the back of my head knocked my glasses off and sent me sprawling against a desk, which tumbled over. I was up immediately in boxer's stance, ready for combat against one, two or the whole gang. I could just discern the blurred image of my teacher, also in boxer's stance . . . and he was snorting.

"What's going on here?"

Someone handed my glasses to me. They were broken.

I stomped out. In the principal's office I unfolded my tale of woe, which Father Oliver found amusing. Besides telling me to forget the incident, he promised to speak to my teacher and to have my glasses repaired. Not much, mind you, but it was something.

In my rage I boycotted the remainder of the retreat and sulked with my books.

The result was that I remained unenlightened in matters of sex. I was somewhat mollified to learn later from Cecil that Father McDonough had not imparted anything new or striking, so that we all still remained green and raw on the subject.

In addition to guidance sessions on social graces and concupiscence, Mr. Bulger, an inspector, came to the school on several occasions to conduct intelligence tests and career-counselling talks. It was from him that we now heard in greater detail about law, medicine, dentistry, engineering, architecture, veterinary science, electronics and accounting. In our previous lessons, Father Oliver had only touched on these professions, though during the past two years he had adverted less frequently to postmasters, railway conductors, station agents, Indian agents and merchants.

Were it not for these sessions one day would have passed like any other, according to plan and schedule, with nothing unusual to report: rise, pray, eat, work, class; eat, play, class, work, study; eat, play, study, to bed and to sleep.

Instead of taking Thursday afternoon off as a holiday by going for a walk, many of us in our final year at the school elected to cut wood in the bush with "Choiman." The incentive for surrendering our day off was an immense cold roast of either beef or pork, along with bread and butter and good black tea for lunch. Besides, it was good to work for "Choiman." No priest or brother, then or before, was as respected and as well liked by the boys as he. To them there was not a mean bone in the man's body or a mean thought in his mind. The boys who worked for "Choiman" in the barn were convinced that he would do anything in his power for them.

The woodcutters worked in pairs, making up to six two-man crews who in a race — or, more accurately, a competition — could fell, saw and pile an average of four cords per crew in a day. On the way back to the school at the end of the day there was always light-hearted banter: "Hey, Choiman! That was good roast beef. How about roast pork next week? No! Pork chops instead, and pie. Gee, Choiman, we'd cut five cords per crew if you brought steaks. Who wants steaks next week? Yeah, steaks! Okay, Choiman, we want steaks." Brother would laugh, shake his head and say, "I'll see what I can do about roast pork," as if there were some doubt. And perhaps there was.

At Christmas just before we were released for the holidays the recreation hall was converted into a theatre by means of decorations, curtains, a wooden platform and row seating for a series of dramatic performances presented by the various grades.

Just before our own performance we were standing to one side of the recreation hall watching Mr. McCart's class perform a play that he himself had written. It was both farce and parody. Its theme was hunger, mush, starvation, lard, hardtack, malcontented boys, raw carrots, emaciation, Boston baked beans and sulking boys. It embarrassed us, but lines like "Yes, they'll have applesauce and mush coming out of their ears" sent all the boys into fits of laughter.

"Look at Dan," Cecil whispered, poking me.

Father Hannin was the only spectator whose countenance showed not a trace of amusement.

On our return from the Christmas holidays there were no beans.

When the cook was asked about the beans he growled, "There aren't any beans." But such answers served only to inflame our suspicions.

We were lounging in our beds in our own small dormitory one Sunday morning in February discussing the cook and his qualifications.

"Yeah! He should be working in a barn instead of Choiman."

"Yeah!"

"And Choiman should be the cook."

"Yeah! Ha, ha, ha!"

"Know what he said the other day?"

"No . . . what he say?"

"That there's no more beans."

"Yeah? He said that? . . . You believe that?"

"No! Bet they're just saving them for themselves."

"No! Dan got mad about that play at Christmas and he's getting even."

"Maybe it's true that they run out o' beans."

"You believe that . . . you?"

"Hey! Let's go down to the cellar an' check."

"Good idea," and everybody rolled out of bed and filed out. Down the cloistered stairway we tramped, through the kitchen and then down to the cellar. The door to the special cellar was chained.

"Come on, boys," Dominic urged. We inserted our fingers, following Dominic's example, into the space between the rough door and the frame. To a command of "Heave," boards cracked and the hasps gave way. Inside were bags, bags piled on bags, tons of beans, or so we thought. After propping up the door, we filed out.

Between ten and twelve of us occupied a corner in the recreation hall, where we sat in sullen protest. Many students, big and small, suspecting that something was amiss, crowded around. The prefect on duty strode over.

"All right, boys! Move! Outside!" and he cuffed a few heads belonging to some unfortunate Grade 5 and 6 students who had not instantly betaken themselves outside on command. When the prefect had put the students to flight, he came over.

"Didn't you hear me? Move!"

"Want to try and make us?" Dominic asked in a defiant tone.

The prefect withdrew, but returned some moments later with his colleague. "These boys had the impudence . . . they won't do what I told them," he was saying. "Move! Outside!" he commanded.

"You can't make us," Dominic answered back. "We ain't movin'. We're not dogs that you can throw us outside anytime that you feel like it. We're men too, like you. We got feelings. We're going to stay right here. We're not bothering anybody; we're not doing anything to hurt anybody or break anything."

The young scholastics looked shocked; their lips quivered and they fidgeted. It was true. There was nothing that the young frail scholastics could do to enforce their commands on a dozen or so young men, three of whom were six-footers and the rest strong as little bulls. The prefects retreated.

And so we sat in our corner undisturbed, considering how we had got into the afterend of a canyon and how to get out of it unscathed and alive.

"You shouldn'a done that, Dominic!"

"Couldn't help it. I'm sick and tired of getting pushed around, ordered around, yelled at, growled at. Nine years . . . and you'd think that they'd let up just a shade in our last year."

After dinner we returned to our corner more in self-defence than continued defiance. We were uneasy.

"You shouldn'a done that, Dominic . . . just cause nothing but trouble."

"What trouble?"

"I don't know."

"What can they do? Nothing. There's nothing they can do . . . not a thing. See them over there, watching us. They're scared of us. . . . You guys with me or against me?" Dominic suddenly asked. "Are we together or are we going to give in?"

"We're with you, McComber."

"What do we do now?"

"I don't know."

And so we sat, silent for the most part, because we had no idea what the consequences of our insubordination might be or what we might do. Finally someone suggested that we go see Father Oliver just in case the prefects had reported us. "There's no telling what they might say."

We marched into the cloister, straight to the Father Superior's office. We knocked and, at the words "Come in," filed in. Father Oliver, who had visitors, looked up; his eyes showed only the briefest hint of surprise before he remarked, "A delegation?" With a wave of his hand, he dismissed us. "I'll see you later."

It was with relief that we went back out and reoccupied our corner. At last our grievances would be given a hearing. In the ensuing discussion we agreed to limit our petition to the restoration of Boston baked beans to the regimen, even though there were many other grievances that needed to be settled. Beans would be the complaint easiest to adjust and would bring the most immediate benefit. We would show our magnanimity by excluding the rest of our indictment of the system and the prefects.

Outside, our fellow students, big and small, had by now got wind of our discontent and the forthcoming hearing.

"You guys gonna get our beans back?" We nodded.

"Tell Father Oliver that the prefec' hit me for nothin' yesterday." We nodded.

"Tell them priests to give me back my hat." We nodded.

"Tell them priests that I never go home for seven years now." We nodded.

Heroes we must have seemed to the little guys, who followed us whenever we moved as once the kids of Hamelin followed the Pied Piper.

Just as the 5:00 P.M. study got underway, Father Johnson delivered a message to the study-hall master. "Father Oliver would like to see Cecil King."

At the back of the study hall, we, Cecil's colleagues and co-rebels, looked at one another. Cecil made his way out. When the doors closed after him, we whispered to one another. We all had the same doubts, questions, anxieties, apprehensions. "Why not all of us? We're all in it together. Why just him? Why him? Jeez, I hope he says the right thing. I hope he doesn't make it worse. Wonder if them prefects reported?" The atmosphere of study hour was electric after that.

We were already seated at table and passing the platters around when Cecil, our spokesman, looking flushed and uncomfortable, returned.

"What did he say?" the interrogation commenced.

"I can't tell you."

"We going to get the beans back?"

"I can't tell you."

"What's he going to do?"

"I can't tell you."

"What did you say?"

"I can't tell you."

"What do you mean, you can't tell us?" We were astounded. "Come on, Cec, we're friends . . . we're all in the same boat!"

"I can't tell you. He made me promise. He'll tell us after."

There was something ominous in the sound of "He'll tell us after" and in Cec's subdued manner. It was useless to pursue the matter any further; we ate the rest of the meal in silence.

After Benediction we stood in a knot in the recreation hall waiting for the Sunday-evening movie to begin. Father Johnson rang the bell for attention. "Father Oliver would like to see the following boys now in his office," and he called out the names.

We smiled. At last . . . we would tell our story.

We filed into Father Oliver's office, almost circling his desk. He was writing.

"All right, boys! What'll it be tonight, train or bus?" he asked, his tone sharp with menace and his grey eyes ablaze. We were thunderstruck with the finality of his question and the fire in his eyes.

"Well, train or bus?" he repeated.

"You! Train or bus?" Father aimed his voice and glare at Alfie.

"I don't wanna go," our colleague stammered.

"What do you mean, you don't want to go." Father Oliver's words were coated with ice. "You don't like it here. All fall you've been complaining about this and that; whining. If you don't like it here, you're free to leave. We won't hold you. In fact, we'll be glad to see you elsewhere, some place where you'll be happy. That's what ordinary people do when they don't like a place. They leave. But you . . . you complain and grumble and when you're given the opportunity to leave, you refuse. I don't understand. Well, train or bus?"

"I don't wanna go."

"What's the complaint?"

"We want beans, Father; we don't have enough to eat," our companion blurted out.

"Beans!" Father spat out contemptuously. "Beans. Hungry! Starving! Underfed! Undernourished! Abused! Beans, my foot." He stopped abruptly.

"How long have you been here, Alfie?" Father Oliver turned on Alfie.

"Twelve years."

"How big were you when you came here?"

"I was pretty small."

"How tall are you now?"

"Five foot seven, five foot eight."

"How much do you weigh?"

"One-fifty."

"Have you ever been sick?"

"No."

"Have you ever missed a meal?"

"No."

"Have any meals ever made you sick?"

"No."

"Then what seems to be the problem? You've all grown since you've been here. No one has ever got sick from the meals served; no one has died. You all look mighty healthy to me. And still you complain." And Father Oliver paused to let his words sink in. "Well? Train or bus, Alf?"

"I don't wanna go."

"You?" to Julius.

"No," Julius mumbled and shook his head.

"You?" to Dominic.

"No, Father."

"Anyone?"

"No."

"Get out."

We filed out . . . bent and bruised but not beaten.

The next morning — Monday — we checked the bulletin board as usual for the class and work schedules for the week. Owing to the frequent visits of priests and their occupation of guest rooms that the school had appropriated for teaching purposes, a class schedule had to be posted almost every week to inform us of any changes in venue. There was no class schedule posted.

At 9:00 we went directly to the room that was usually reserved for the math class. It was occupied by another class. In a hasty consultation we formed teams, one to scout the cellar, a second to reconnoitre the third floor, a third to check the second in search of teacher and class. The team finding a teacher was to send a courier to deliver the message to the others. On word of discovery, there was a mighty educational rush.

Every morning and afternoon of those weeks when there was an adjustment in the schedule, a group of Ojibway and one Mohawk tore around Garnier looking for teacher and instruction — a sight that would have gladdened the heart of Socrates, or any other teacher, but moved our teachers not at all.

The atmosphere was chilly; if our teachers were not friendly, they were at least teaching us. Only Mr. McCart and Mr. Sammon seemed tolerant.

Finally we agreed: "If they're not going to talk to us and not going to let us know where we're supposed to work, or where we're supposed to go to class, then we won't work. Instead of running all over trying to find out where we're supposed to work, we'll study. They're not going to break us down."

Eventually the chill between staff and the senior boys gave way, and by spring we were once more on speaking terms.

In early May Father Oliver summoned me to his office to brief me on the plans being made for the forthcoming graduation exercises, scheduled for June 7, and to tell me: "You're going to deliver the valedictory address."

"The what, Father?"

"A farewell speech."

"But I've never given a speech."

"Then you may as well start now."

"What will I say?"

"Come on, now! Use your brains! But if you need any help with your speech, ask Father McKenna; he was one of Loyola's top debaters."

I went directly to Father McKenna, who immediately wrote a speech that he duly delivered to me the next morning. It was good and seemed to contain what ought to be said on such occasions.

In that last week, while our class was suffering through examinations, Cecil King was superintending the Grade 9, 10 and 11 boys in converting the recreation hall into an auditorium fit for guests.

Even on the final day of school there was little leisure. From 9:00 A.M. on through to late afternoon, as guests, distinguished and otherwise, from far and near, arrived and looked on as spectators, all the boys leaped, ran, vaulted, relayed, shot-putted, heaved javelins and cast baseballs (a baseball throw was one of the events) in our track-and-field competition.

A quick shower and then supper. And I guess Dominic expressed our sentiments when he broke the solemn mood. "No more mush, no more lard; no more 'Hurry up, *move!*' You know, you would have thought that they would have served us beans on this special occasion . . . just for old times' sake."

Then from the table to the dormitory to put on our "best" suits, shirts, ties that we had bought with our earnings from our summer work in lumber camps. No more faded maroon sweaters.

On the way through the auditorium to the chapel, I deposited the speech in a drawer in a small table next to the lectern at the front. There it would be within easy reach when needed.

The Benediction that was celebrated for our benefit was special in two respects. It was the last time that we worshipped together at Garnier; and we didn't sing. The "little shots," who had been taught a new chant, sang like an angelic chorus for us.

In opening the ceremonies, the *Sudbury Star* for June 8, 1950, reported, Father Oliver traced the history of the introduction of the high-school course at Garnier.

"After many years of discouraging rebuffs when we proposed the introduction of a full high-school course of training for the Indian boys and girls here, we finally succeeded in securing approval four years ago," he explained. The program had been started, he said, with the firm conviction that only raising the educational level of Indian children could help them better themselves and improve their standard of living and status in Canadian society.

"The first Grade 9 classes were started four years ago," he continued. "Tonight we see the first graduates from Grade 12 in that course. There are today forty-five boys in the high-school classes and thirty-eight girls. Soon we will have our own teachers, nurses, doctors and lawyers from our own people. . . ."

Joe Peter Pangwish or Mishi-mino-auniquot (Great Good Cloud), as chief of Wikwemikong, the biggest reserve represented in the school and at the ceremonies, also spoke to the graduates.

"I hope you don' min' my English . . . I never learn . . . not like youse. Aupitchi dush igoh nauh n'kitchi-inaendum gee abi-izhauyaun [I am exceedingly glad that I came]. I wasn't goin' come; too busy on farm; can' leave an'mals jis' like. . . . Nongom dush ae-ishkawau-nauwiquaek mee gee aundaukinigaeyaun. . . . Ah nin-dowautch n'gah zhauh. [But this afternoon I changed my mind. In spite of all the work facing me] I decided to come, see what I miss.

"I went to this school apee keeyaubih pidukissingobun woodih [while it was still in] Wikwemikong, but it burn down." (Here there were tremendous cheers from the audience.) "Mee dush iwih, that's why I quit, that's why I can't talk too good in the English. Missowauh suh igoh [Nevertheless], the people wan' me chief. . . ."

"Thank you for your kind and encouraging remarks, Chief Pang-wish. We will now ask Basil Johnston to deliver the valedictory address."

My legs became spongy and my hands shaky as I walked to the podium. I smiled at the audience, grasped the knob of the drawer and pulled gently once, twice, three times. It would not give. Someone had locked up my speech.

Panic clutched at my throat, squeezed, then let go. With as much aplomb as I could manage, I placed both hands on either side of the podium, as I had seen my teachers do. My vision went out of focus, so that the audience was nothing but a mass of blurred faces. My mind went blank, but I had to go on.

"Reverend Father Superior, Reverend Fathers, Brothers, dear Sisters, honoured guests, beloved parents . . . ladies and gentlemen. . . ."

It was reported by the *Sudbury Star* that I spoke as follows: "We have been encouraged by our teachers who always had our interests at heart. . . . What our high-school certificate will mean to us is hard to express. Indians need education. They need their own teachers, lawyers, doctors and politicians.

"We have talked of our rights as the first citizens of the country, but few of us are prepared to safeguard those rights. . . . Only through having the courage to continue our studies and determination to use the talents we have for advancement can our Indian people become true citizens of Canada."

When the speech was done, I sat down, relieved that the ordeal was over. At that moment I would have preferred to run and hide, but I was bound where I was; I had no choice. The applause tendered was comforting; it made me feel that I might not have muddled the valedictory address too badly after all. But the speech was over — that was all that really mattered. (Some months later in Montreal, Alfie Cooper congratulated me on the speech. He asked me where I had got all those fancy ideas that I had expressed then. I told him that Father McKenna had written the speech, that I might have read it three times, and that I had intended to read it to the audience, but that some slimy, slobbering swineherd had locked it up.) If the speech was as good as reported, the only explanation I could offer was that Kitchi-manitou must have taken pity on the audience and me in this moment of disaster by projecting Father McKenna's text on my mind's memory screen. It was revelation, no less, that helped me remember Father McKenna's written speech word for word.

Next on the program was the introduction of the graduates to an audience swollen by a large number of parents who had come to watch the ceremonies and learn a little more about the benefits of higher education. As Father Oliver observed, "These boys may well be the first full graduating class of Indian students in Canada." Then he went on, "I'm proud to present to you Dominic McComber of Caughnawaga, Quebec. This fall Dominic will commence his studies in electronics at Ryerson Polytechnical Institute in Toronto. Alphonse Trudeau is from Wikwemikong. Jeff, as he is more commonly known, is registered in the electronics course at Ryerson. Francis Commanda of Timagami will be joining Dominic and Jeff in the electronics course at Ryerson. Also enrolled in the same course at Ryerson is Julius Niganigijig of Sheguindah. David Jocko of Golden Lake, our resident artist, will be studying art at the Ontario College of Art. Ernest Nadjiwon of Cape Croker had opted for two careers: one with the Royal Canadian Air Force and the other in marriage with Lillian Nadjiwon of Cutler. [A mighty cheer.] Alfred Cooper of Wikwemikong, who is planning a career in medicine, will be entering Loyola College in Montreal this coming September. Basil Johnston of Cape Croker will also be going to Loyola College, where he will take the pre-law course of studies. Ladies and gentlemen, these are Garnier's graduates."

After the applause had died down, Father Oliver resumed. "Ladies and gentlemen, we cordially invite you to remain for the dance afterwards, which will start just as soon as the hall is cleared by Cecil King's custodians. Lawrence Lewis and his orchestra from Cutler will provide the music."

While the recreation hall was being made ready, many guests came forward to offer their congratulations and good wishes; all of them expressed the same sentiments as those uttered by Joe Peter Pangwish earlier in the evening. "Do something for your people." We solemnly promised to do so.

At midnight the dance ended. At last we could say what we had long yearned to say from the moment of our original committal to the school: "Farewell." But despite the anticipation, "Farewell" did not come easily or freely.

"We toughed it out, didn't we? They couldn't break us down, could they?" Dominic said with pride, as we shook hands; he would not — could not — say "Farewell" or "Goodbye" or "*Au revoir.*"

Glossary

The Darkroom was a large, dark, moth-balled room on the third floor where the school's dirty laundry was prepared for transshipment to the laundresses at St. Joseph's and on its return, clean, was bundled into numbered green laundry bags for issue on Thursdays. Somewhere among mountains of socks, underwear, overalls, coveralls, trousers, shirts and pyjamas might be found Brother Laflamme sorting these articles by number for bundling in the corresponding numbered green bags.

Democrat. A light, four-wheeled wagon drawn by Pitou to transport mail, small crates, visitors and, on occasion, a corpse to and from the school.

The Garnier was a small thirty-five-foot tug, painted white with green trim, built along the lines of a luxury cruiser.

The Iron Boat, so called because of its metal-plated hull, was used as a surrogate tug to tow the Red Bug or the "scow" to shallows where the Garnier could not navigate. It was rumoured that the Iron Boat, twenty to twenty-four feet in length, was once a lifeboat on an ocean liner. Like the Red Bug, the barn, the mill and the blacksmith shop, it was red.

Prefect. A supervisor; an overseer. At the school the prefects were usually young scholastics in their regency who, in addition to their teaching duties, supervised the work, play and conduct of the boys.

The Red Bug was a large, square-sterned, round-bottomed vessel, painted red, and designed like a rowboat except that it measured about thirty feet in length and eight feet in width. It was towed by either the Garnier or the Iron Boat as a barge in transporting boys, potatoes, cordwood, apples and sometimes cattle.

Regency. The period of time spent by scholastics as part of their training in teaching and in supervision at one of the Jesuit schools or institutions throughout the country. For the Jesuits the two-year period of regency commenced only after a four-year novitiate.

Scholastic. A term used by the clergy to refer to candidates for the priesthood prior to their ordination.

245

Appendix: The Boys and Girls of Spanish

Boys at Spanish, St. Peter Claver's, 1939

NAME	NICKNAME	PRESENT SITUATION
Boniface Abel		
Paul Abel		
David Abiens	Mizeen	
Clarence Abitung		Sagamok
Russel Abitung		Sagamok, Councillor
Leon Abraham	Nigger	
Lawrence Agownie		
Charles Akiwenzie	Charlie Shoot	Cape Croker, still hunting and fishing
Martin Assiniwe		Sagamok, Councillor
Clement Atchitwans		
Herbie Beaudry	Tee deet	
Harold Belleau	Boozo	Deceased
Ben ?	Cabootch	
Amos Bisto		Saugeen
Lawrence Bisto		Deceased
Reuben Bisto		Saugeen
Benjamin Buzwa		
Dolpus Buzwa		
Francis Buzwa		
Renee Cada		West Bay, Ont. — retired transport driver
Harvey Contin	Half Chick	Byng Inlet
Irvin Contin		
Tony Contin	Tony Angus	
Eddie Coocoo		
James Coocoo		
Joe Coocoo		
Alfred Cooper, M.D.		Timmins
Joe Day		
Bruno Debossige	Calf	West Bay
Jerome Debossige	Ti Blue	West Bay
Leonard Debossige		
Norbert Debossige		West Bay

246

Louis Diabo		
Tommy Diabo		
John Enosse		
Dominic Eshkakagun	Skinny	Sagamok
Hubert Eshkakagun	Little Skinny	Sagamok
Mike Esquimault		
Donald Fox	T'ief	
Eugene Fox		Wikwemikong
Archie Francis	Archie Pancake	
Lawrence Francis		
Louis Francis	Sa-faw-saw	
Izauk ?		
Ivan Kaboni	Whitehead	
Ivan Kanasawe		Bartender, Newberry, MI
Eugene Keeshig	Captain	Cape Croker, semi-retired
Leonard Kitchigeg	Gek	South Bay, carver
Antoine Lafrance	La Marr or Bar Poot	St. Regis, oil & fuel business
John Lafrance	Ti Bar Poot	St. Regis, oil & fuel business
John Latour		
Hector Lavalley	Kitchi-meeshi Hec	Cape Croker, semi-retired
Joe Lazore		
Steve Lazore		
Mitchell Loft	Snowball	
Norman McBride	Chippie	
Wilfred McCoy	Meeshaukoot	
Alex Manitowabi		
Theodore Manitowabi		
Simon Martin		
Joe Migwanabe		Hannaville, MI
Paul Migwanabe		
John Migwans		
Joe Missabe	Shaggy	
David Mitchell		Whitefish Falls
Harry Mitchell	Nigger	Whitefish Falls
Louis Mitchell	Nigger	
Gilbert Naganosh		
Julius Niganigijig		
Raymond Niganigijig		
Paul Nowigijig		
David Ozawabine	Poodjaugun	Wikwemikong
Bernard Ozawamik	Bullhead	
Sam Paul		
Clement Pelletier		Deceased
Ernest Pelletier	White Man	
Herbie Penassie	Harpie	
Isadore Pheasant		

Jerome Pheasant		
Angus Pitwaniquot	Neeyauss or Booki-jeet	Deceased
Alphonse Recollet		
Peter Recollet		
Paul Rice		
Roy Rice		
Rudy Rice		Wawa—Algoma Ore Properties Ltd.
Adam Roy		West Bay
Pius Roy		
Ernie St. Germaine		
Tom Sarazin		
Leo Sego		
Leonard Sego	Squadaehnse	
Joe Alex Shawana		
Benedict Shigwadja		Deceased
Emeric Shigwadja		
Maxie Simon		Wawa, retired from Algoma Ore Properties Ltd.
Norman Simon	Bearskin	Deceased
Maurice Simpson		
Gordon Solomon		
Isadore Solomon		
Leo Solomon	Leo Plug	Deceased
Orion Solomon	Orion Plug	Deceased
Archie Spaniel		
Frank Syrette	Cigar or Cigar Butt	
John Syrette	John Bulleeblaw	
Henry Tenniscoe		
Theodore ?	Moustaffa	
Robert Thibault	Teapot	Deceased ?
Jake Thompson		St. Regis—fishing
Joe Thompson	Gistigly	
Alphonse Trudeau		Wikwemikong
Clement Trudeau		Wikwemikong
Orval Trudeau	Ovilla	
Wilfred Trudeau		
Jim Wabegijig		
Isadore Wabunosse		
Alfred Webkamigad	Cheeby or Ghost	Wikwemikong
Henry Webkamigad		Wikwemikong
James Wemigwans	That's the Kind	Wikwemikong
Mike White		
Tom White		

Note: Total enrolment of boys in September 1939 may have been around 135. Without records to consult, I have had to omit about 15 names. To those whose names do not appear on the above list, my apologies.

Some boys entering the school between 1940 and 1946

NAME	NICKNAME
Chauncey Benedict	
Joe Bonaparte	
Joe Cameron	Joe Camel
John Caneau	
Adam Commanda	
Eli Commanda	
Francis Commanda	Bunny
Dominic Contin	Cowboy Jack
Leonard Cross	Cheeby-autik
Henry Deere	
Peter Deere	
John de Lormier	
Harvey Ermitinger	Stingy
Laurence Ewiiwe	
Emil Hughes	Senor
David Jocko	Stiff Bean
Martin Jocko	
Paddy Jocko	
Russel Jocko	Rusty Beans
Joe ?	Joe Tight
Joe King	Slow
Bruce McComber	
Cornelius McComber	Corny
Dominic McComber	
Jarvis McComber	
Joe Martin	Joe Goat
Arnold Nadjiwon	Grease Pot
Alvin Nashkewe	
Lloyd Nashkewe	
Jim Norton	Scumbag
Gilbert Oshkaboose	
Alex Restoule	Mars
Alphonse Shawana	
Mike Taylor	
Gilbert Whiteduck	

Some of our dancing partners from St. Joseph's Residential School

Rita Belleau	Violet Shawanda	Mary Ann Jocks
Mildred Cameron	Minnie Smith	(Jacques?)
Stella Cooper	Honorine Trudeau	Berdeena Johnston
Violet Cooper	Rosemary Wakegijig	Bernice Johnston
Angeline Copegog	Josephine Webkamigad	Ernestine Johnston

Elizabeth Eshkakagun	Tillie Wemigwans	Marilyn Johnston
Gladys Johnston		Elizabeth King
Lillian Kitchigeg	Too young to dance:	Loretta King
Lucy Nashkewe	Bernice Beauvais	Evelyn Lavalley
Lillian Pelletier	Shirley Coocoo	Annette Nadjiwon
Beatrice Shawana	Violet Coocoo	Joyce Solomon
		Lillian Solomon

To those whose names do not appear on the above lists, my apologies. I had no records to work from.

The present situation of some of the boys as adults

Charlie Akiwenzie	Still hunting and fishing. Cape Croker.
Martin Assiniwe	Councillor, Sagamok Tribal Council.
Harold Belleau	To Hamilton Sanitorium, where he was the first patient to recover from galloping consumption through the use of a new drug (penicillin?). Became teacher; barred from teaching owing to his medical history. Became X-ray technician in Toronto. Returned to Garden River, his home, where he died in 1981.
Eli Commanda	Killed in slusher drift in Algoma Ore Properties Ltd., Helen Mine, Wawa.
Francis Commanda	Somewhere in Toronto after high steel construction work.
Alfred Cooper, M.D.	Practising medicine in Timmins, Ont.
Dominic Eshkakagun	Guidance Counsellor, Sagamok Education System.
Peter Johnston	Was chief of Cutler Indian Reserve for several terms.
Eugene Keeshig	Semi-retired. Cape Croker.
Cecil King, Ph.D.	Professor, Native Studies Dept., University of Saskatchewan.
Hector Lavalley	Semi-retired. Cape Croker.
Dominic McComber	?
Joe Migwanabe	Language Teacher, Hannaville Reservation, MI.
Ernie Nadjiwon	Recently retired after 35 years' service in the RCAF.
Alvin Nashkewe	Killed by stampeding horses out west.
Julius Niganigijig	Somewhere in US
Gilbert Oshkaboose	Journalist. Editor of *Indian News*; now managing native goods outlet in Cutler.
Henry Pelletier	Was chief of Wikwemikong Indian Reserve for some time.
Herman Pelletier	Musician. Proprietor of music store.
Alphonse Shawana	After a career in the RCAF and in the electronics industry, now retired.
Max Simon	Retired after 30–35 years with Algoma Ore Properties Ltd., Wawa. Played with Sudbury Wolves Juniors.
Alphonse Trudeau	Bus Operator, Manitoulin Island.
James Wemigwans	Retired.